CLICAS

LATINX: THE FUTURE IS NOW
A series edited by Lorgia García-Peña and Nicole Guidotti-Hernández

Books in the series

Regina Marie Mills, *Invisibility and Influence: A Literary History of AfroLatinidades*

Jason Ruiz, *Narcomedia: Latinidad, Popular Culture, and America's War on Drugs*

Rebeca L. Hey-Colón, *Channeling Knowledges: Water and Afro-Diasporic Spirits in Latinx and Caribbean Worlds*

Tatiana Reinoza, *Reclaiming the Americas: Latinx Art and the Politics of Territory*

Kristy L. Ulibarri, *Visible Borders, Invisible Economies: Living Death in Latinx Narratives*

Marisel C. Moreno, *Crossing Waters: Undocumented Migration in Hispanophone Caribbean and Latinx Literature and Art*

Yajaira M. Padilla, *From Threatening Guerrillas to Forever Illegals: US Central Americans and the Cultural Politics of Non-Belonging*

Francisco J. Galarte, *Brown Trans Figurations: Rethinking Race, Gender, and Sexuality in Chicanx/Latinx Studies*

CLICAS

Gender, Sexuality, and Struggle in Latina/o/x Gang Literature and Film

Frank García

University of Texas Press,
Austin

"The Toltec," "Electra Currents," "Red Wagons," "Saturdays," "The Suede Coat," "Dirty Mexican," and "Daddy with Chesterfields in a Rolled Up Sleeve," are from *My Father Was a Toltec*, copyright © 1995 by Ana Castillo. Reprinted by permission of Writers House LLC acting as agent for the author.

Javier Zamora, excerpts from "Second Attempt Crossing" and "El Salvador" from *Unaccompanied*, copyright © 2017 by Javier Zamora. Reprinted with the permission of The Permissions Company, LLC, on behalf of Copper Canyon Press, coppercanyonpress.org.

Copyright © 2024 by the University of Texas Press
All rights reserved
Printed in the United States of America
First edition, 2024

Requests for permission to reproduce material from this work should be sent to permissions@utpress.utexas.edu.

∞ The paper used in this book meets the minimum requirements of ANSI/NISO Z39.48-1992 (R1997) (Permanence of Paper).

Library of Congress Cataloging-in-Publication Data

Names: García, Frank, author.
Title: Clicas : gender, sexuality, and struggle in Latina/o/x gang literature and film / Frank García.
Description: First edition. | Austin : University of Texas Press, 2024. | Includes bibliographical references and index.
Identifiers: LCCN 2023038200 (print) | LCCN 2023038201 (ebook)
  ISBN 978-1-4773-2942-9 (hardcover)
  ISBN 978-1-4773-2943-6 (paperback)
  ISBN 978-1-4773-2944-3 (adobe pdf)
  ISBN 978-1-4773-2945-0 (epub)
Subjects: LCSH: Gangs in literature. | Gangster films. | Female gangs in motion pictures. | Hispanic American gangs—Social aspects—United States. | Gang members—United States—Social conditions. | Hispanic American gangs—Political aspects—United States. | Masculinity—Latin America. | Masculinity in motion pictures. | Sexual minorities in motion pictures. | Latin Americans in motion pictures. | Sexual minorities in literature. | Latin Americans in literature. | BISAC: SOCIAL SCIENCE / Ethnic Studies / American / Hispanic American Studies | SOCIAL SCIENCE / Gender Studies Classification: LCC HV6439.U5 G3783 2024 (print) | LCC HV6439.U5 (ebook) | DDC 364.106/6—dc23/eng/20240227
LC record available at https://lccn.loc.gov/2023038200
LC ebook record available at https://lccn.loc.gov/2023038201

doi:10.7560/329429

CONTENTS

Acknowledgments *vii*

CHAPTER 1 Gang Subcultures as (De)colonial Praxis *1*

CHAPTER 2 The Shared Experience of (De)colonial Gang Life *47*

CHAPTER 3 The Toxified Female Masculinities of (De)colonial Gang Girls *89*

CHAPTER 4 (De)colonial Gay Locos, Disidentifications, and Counterpublics *127*

CHAPTER 5 The Queer Utopian Futurity of Failed Gang Members *159*

AFTERWORD The Immigrant/Gang Member Binary in Latina/o/x Literature and Film *183*

Selected Filmography *199*
Notes *201*
References *225*
Index *241*

ACKNOWLEDGMENTS

IN 2007, I STARTED MY FORAY INTO HIGHER EDUCATION, WHERE I would earn associate's, bachelor's, and doctorate degrees and later land a tenure-track job at Rutgers University, Newark, ultimately publishing this monograph with the leading press in Latina/o/x studies. The child of immigrant parents and the first in my family to attend college, I recognize the enormity and rigor of these achievements. Sometimes, I find myself reflecting on the geographical, social, and psychological environments I grew up in, and the financial hardships my family faced, and am utterly baffled that I have been able to accomplish what I have. I am proud of what I have achieved, and I allow myself to feel that way. And yet, at the risk of sounding grossly arrogant, I never really felt that writing this book, landing a tenure-track job, or earning a doctorate degree was that difficult for me. Graduating from high school was far and away the most challenging academic obstacle I have ever encountered.

I remember walking into my guidance counselor's office during the beginning of my senior year and explaining to her that I would like to attend college and needed help learning about the process. The elderly white woman laughed in my face before saying, "You can't," because I had not taken the prerequisite science and math courses needed for admission into a UC or Cal State. Rather than taking these classes, I had spent much of my high school years either truant or enrolled in courses in "basketball," "small engine repair," "class assistant," and even in a separate English course that community colleges accepted, but that the UC or Cal State systems did not. Once I was in graduate school, I learned that this is called tracking, that my high school had set me on a path toward learning how to fix a fucking lawn mower really well but not to attend, let alone graduate from, a university. Because my parents had never been to college, they had no understanding of what courses I needed to take, or what grades I had to earn to attend a four-year college right out of high school. Instead, the expectation was that a high school diploma was "enough"—that I should immediately get a job and start contributing to the household income. Unsatisfied with that prospect and refusing to take "you can't" for an answer, I was off to my local community college, where I spent four years trying to complete two years of general education courses in order to transfer to UC Riverside. College impaction, failing grades, and *struggling* to find the motivation and willpower to study for an exam, or do every assignment, had me frequently dropping out and reconsidering whether higher education was for me. I contemplated if maybe I should just go back to the damn lawn mower.

I say all this not out of a conceited desire to construct some overcoming narrative designed to get readers to applaud me, but because my gratitude toward those who have shaped and aided me in my academic work and journey begins with the most important people in my career: my students. I am *blessed* that I work at Rutgers University, Newark. As much as I miss Califas, I turned down multiple job offers in Southern California to come east, primarily because of the students at this university. Rutgers-Newark is anomalous in that the majority of its students are historically underrepresented in higher education and, presently, a third are first-generation college students. This university has given me an opportunity to teach so many students of a demographic I was a part of, and nothing in my career has been as rewarding. I know firsthand how taxing and impressive it is to make it into and graduate from college as a first-generation, racially underrepresented student. Writing is demandingly arduous for me, but the students in the classrooms at this campus inspire me weekly, and provide me with the energy, motivation, and gratification needed to do everything I can to excel at this job. So much of what I do in my career is for my students, and I thank you all for continually teaching me and helping me to become the scholar and teacher I am today. While this list is far from exhaustive, I would especially like to thank Claudia Pérez, Veronica Torres, Edward DeBarros, Lauren Asuzano, Jessica Sison, Selorm Babator-Tettey, Dominic Henry, Anastasia Johnson, Maurice Metivier, Elmer Recinos, Pamela Snowden-Reynolds, Henry Xie, Quadeesha Harper, Aliyah Almonte, and Bridget Barragan.

Although I struggled academically early in my life, so much of my later success happened because I was just incredibly lucky. I ran into the right people, and I owe no greater thanks than to Richard T. Rodríguez and Robert Dale Parker. Ricky and Parker, you two have gone far above and beyond in providing me more guidance, mentorship, and help than I deserve, for almost a decade now. I have zero doubt that things would not have happened the way they did without you two. You both have made my life so much easier than it needs to be, and you are everything I strive to emulate in my scholarship and teaching. I am indebted to both of you. I am just as grateful that I had the pleasure of learning from Steven Gould Axelrod at UC Riverside. When I was an undergrad, I walked around intimidated by academia, never attending office hours, and I avoided speaking to professors because I felt stupid, judged, and unsure of how to talk to such highly educated people. You were the first professor I ever went to see in office hours, and I admit I only went because I had just recovered from severe pneumonia, missed almost three weeks of class, and needed to pick up my graded work. You introduced me to the idea of graduate school with your simple "So, what are your plans?" question. Thank you for urging me to apply, for all the support and letter writing, for everything I learned in your poetry classrooms, and for showing me that it is okay to talk to professors and get help. Likewise, Devra Weber was just as encouraging in fostering my education and my research interests, and in pushing me to pursue graduate work. Thank you for your mentorship, for connecting me with other professors on campus who were also first-generation students, and for placing Luis J. Rodriguez's *Always Running* in my hands after I told you my story.

Kathleen Sell, John Briggs, Rob Latham, Keith Harris, Candice Jenkins, Junaid Rana, and Ramona Curry were also unwaveringly supportive and integral to my education. I thank you all, especially Candice, Junaid, and Ramona. You three have constantly forced me to consider how my work and thinking might improve in ways that have helped me evolve as a scholar. I could not have written this book without learning from you all. Ramona, thank you for holding my hand through so much of my early professional development, helping me through the publication process, placing me on SCMS panels, and introducing me to prominent scholars in my field and film studies. (And for you and Gene talking some Iceberg Slim with me!)

My time at Rutgers-Newark has been nothing short of amazing because of my colleagues as much as my students. I started this job during the pandemic, so my introduction to campus and to many of my colleagues initially took place online. Despite these less-than-ideal circumstances, my department and the greater campus community ensured I had a seamless transition into a welcoming, supportive, and intellectually rigorous working environment, and I have looked forward to coming to work ever since. Thank you especially to Rigoberto González, Belinda Edmondson, and Laura Lomas for mentoring me during my time here; for helping me think through this book project, reader reports, my proposal, and other work; and for just getting a drink with me, welcoming me, and helping me learn where and how to live in New Jersey when I knew absolutely nothing about the Northeast. I thank Jack Lynch, Sterling Bland, Manu Chander, Rachel Hadas, Carol Heffernan, Mal Kiniry, Amir Moosavi, Akil Kumarasamy, Melanie Hill, Naomi Jackson, John Keene, Brenda Shaughnessy, Sadia Abbas, David Baker, Patricia Akhimie, Alice Dark, Jason Cortés, Kyle Riismandel, Nancy Cantor, Jacqueline Mattis, Karen Caplan, Laura Troiano, all the folks with the Honors Living Learning Community, and especially Maddy Muñoz-Bertram (!!) and Amanda Suárez (!!) for your parts in making my time here such a pleasant, stimulating, and receptive experience. It is a pleasure to work with each of you. I am not sure if the pandemic has ever really ended, and its vestiges have impeded me from having the chance to meet many other folks on my campus and in my department, but I look forward to meeting those of you whom I have not yet had the opportunity to cross paths with. I also thank the Institute for the Study of Global Racial Justice at Rutgers, whose funding and intellectual support helped make this book possible.

This statement might seem odd to some, but I want to recognize: the search committee for my position (Jack, Belinda, Sterling, and Laura); my department; and all those at my university who have attended my research talks or read my (or about my) work. Thank you for treating this project as a serious subject of academic study—for recognizing me and the writers, artists, filmmakers, people, and cultural products I study in this book as deserving of your critical attention and as valuable contributors to overarching scholarly conversations at hand. I have lost count of the number of people at conferences, interviews, and job talks who have looked at me bewildered for studying gang literature, film, culture, and membership. It seems that every question-and-answer session or interview inevitably features some perplexed person asking some version of: "Why do you want to study . . . this?" Or, just as common, leading questions that expect me to distance myself from the violence and bigotry of the gang texts and members I study, denounce them, apologize on behalf of them or Latina/o/x people and cultures, or disclose if I am or have ever been a gang member and/or committed any of the violent acts I study. Indeed, I distinctly remember a white professor at an R1 university in the South using my job talk on Ana Castillo's *My Father Was a Toltec* (a poetry collection that features no gang shootings or mass murders) to somehow rationalize connections between gangs and mass school shootings, and to ask me if I was personally sympathetic to school shooters who commit mass murder. Scads of articles and monographs on gangs fill the shelves of countless academic libraries, many of them authored by white writers, and yet I somehow do not believe that many of these white academics receive these types of questions. Too often those of us who are of an ethnic/racial minority status (especially those of us who are visibly marked) are expected to apologize for—or distance ourselves from—the crimes, troubling behavior, or problematic characteristics of the people and texts sharing the same ethnic/racial background as ourselves. But I see no white academics apologizing on behalf of Edgar Allan Poe for being a European colonizer who married and slept with his 13-year-old cousin while an adult man—and I similarly refuse to apologize on behalf of, or distance myself from, the people and subjects this book studies. I thank my department and Rutgers colleagues for never once asking or expecting me to. I wish there were more in academia who demonstrated similar behavior.

As much as these inapt questions and comments often come up, many of my experiences presenting and discussing my work with the wider academic community have been incredibly productive. While I regrettably can no longer remember the names of these persons, I thank those at the numerous conferences and research presentations who contributed comments and questions that helped me think through this project and refine its argument. An earlier version of Chapter 4 appeared in the Spring 2019 issue of *MELUS*, and I thank its editor-in-chief Gary Totten and the anonymous reviewers for their astute feedback on that essay. Their comments stayed in my mind as I later revised that essay into a book chapter. I very much appreciate the labor that T. Jackie Cuevas and Francisco J. Galarte provided in reviewing the manuscript version of this book for the University of Texas Press. Thank you for generously waiving your anonymity and for supplying insightful feedback that forced me to raise the book's standard. I owe the same thanks to the series editors Nicole Guidotti-Hernández and Lorgia García-Peña. This book is in a better place because of your observations and recommendations. Kerry Webb has been a dream to work with, especially for a first-time author who did not know much about the book publication process. Your patience, recommendations, affability, and perspicacity have made this journey a pleasure, and I am glad you were my editor. Christina Vargas was just as integral in helping me navigate this process, and I thank you for all the assistance you supplied me.

Various cultural workers and creators were immensely generous with me in enabling me to write the book, supplying me with either knowledge, personal photographs, copies of texts, or permissions to make it possible. Thank you so much, Ana Castillo, Dino Dinco, "Jinx," and Javier Zamora.

Lastly, I thank those in my personal life who have selflessly stood by me and supported me for decades, for opening your home and lives to me in my time of need, for wrapping your arms around me whenever I broke down and just could not *deal* anymore, for sacrificing so much of your own personal desires and needs so that I can pursue my own dreams. I share them with you now. I love you.

CLICAS

1 | GANG SUBCULTURES AS (DE)COLONIAL PRAXIS

CLICAS EXAMINES LATINA/O/X LITERATURE AND FILM BY AND/OR about gay and women gang members to rewrite the universalist narrative about gang membership, gang culture, gang masculinities, and gang violence that obviates gender and sexuality. Routinely considered the domains of hypermasculine, heterosexual men, gangs are often understood to marginalize women and gay persons, granting them only nominal membership, if not outright barring them from the gang and violently attacking them. While *Clicas* acknowledges the bigotry that women and gay people encounter in male-dominated, heterosexual gangs, this volume does not allow such intolerance to excuse pursuing more complex understandings of how gender and sexuality intersect with race and class in male-dominated, heterosexual street gangs. Rather, in reconceptualizing the predominant view of gang life, this project asks and reveals how women and gay persons in male-dominated, heterosexual gangs navigate trauma and alienation to transform these gangs into subcultures that allocate them material, psychological, ontological, ideological, and cultural resistance. The book discloses how Latina/o/x gang literature and film represent how women and gay gang members may alter and use gang culture, violence, criminality, and masculinity to challenge the "coloniality" that organizes contemporary life, including the racism these gang members encounter in the US nation-state, and also gendered and sexual oppression in their Latina/o/x communities, including, ironically, their own gangs.[1]

This book's theorization of gang life also re-envisions the binary permeating the discussion of gangs in academia, popular culture, and politics. On the one hand, the academy frequently romanticizes gangs as bastions of subversive agency, neglecting how this resistance often targets and harms multiply marginalized persons in working-class communities of color.[2] On the other hand, many sensationalize the violence gang members commit toward others and in their communities, portraying gang members as nightmarish boogeymen traversing the US-Mexico border to rape white women, deal drugs, and infect the United States with the virus of gang membership, violence, and crime.[3] This book refuses both these conceptions of gang members and instead operates at the center of a spectrum. My study divulges how resistance in gangs hinges on fluidity—how gay and heterosexual male and female gang members represent figures of liminality whose oppositional actions are often generative for them, but dependent on exacerbating the trauma and precarity of other multiply marginalized persons. In this view of gang life, gang resistance and the fratricidal violence gang members may partake in are not antithetical, but instead integral, to each other. In this way, the book proposes a new model for studying gang life and culture, one that reads gang members as (de)colonial.[4]

I define the (de)colonial as Latina/o/x gang members' agential struggles of survival that contest, circumvent, and/or undermine the power relations, inequalities, oppressions, and hierarchies in the United States and their Latina/o/x barrios that intersect at race, gender, sexuality, and class. The (de)colonial projects this book studies are variegated and multimodal, often manifesting in physical, psychological, ontological, ideological, and/or cultural forms. The gang members depicted in the literature and film this book analyzes, however, are not systemically revolutionary. As much as their gang lives may help them challenge how the abstract and material effects of interlocking structures of inequality are affecting *them*, their resistance rests upon the perpetuation of trauma, violence, and maltreatment of other multiply marginalized persons. For this reason, the book qualifies the decolonial. Parenthesizing the (de) of decolonial rhetorically signifies the paradox of gang life—how the gang members represented in the book's archive are not fully decolonial, even if their actions have productive consequences that enable them to circumvent the legacy and aftereffects of colonialism, or what Walter Mignolo, Aníbal Quijano, Maria Lugones, and others have called "coloniality."

This recognition of the contradictions in the (de)colonial projects of gang life resembles what Mariana Ortega calls "decolonial woes" and "practices of un-knowing." Despite many romanticizing the colonizer/colonized binary, Ortega finds decolonial/postcolonial theorists' refusal to wrestle with the contradictions and fluidity in this dichotomy "confusing, as, following Anzaldúa herself, the decolonial move is to move away from dichotomies in the first place."[5] In embracing the idea that decolonial/postcolonial theory should reject the rigidity of this binary, Ortega terms a decolonial woe "a kind of affliction that is inherent in resistant academic practices that despite their being resistant, even radical and transformative, are at the same time immersed in what Chicana feminist theorist Emma Pérez calls a 'colonial imaginary.'"[6] For Ortega, many academics purporting to engage in decolonial thought reproduce macronarratives of coloniality by erasing women of color's contributions to decolonial/postcolonial theory, while also "working in institutions doing the service of greedy and thoughtless capitalism."[7] This erasure constitutes "'practices of un-knowing' that distort and negate epistemic practices that have themselves been deployed in order to fight ignorance regarding the lives of subjects who have been marginalized in virtue of their social identities."[8]

This book's concept of the (de)colonial operates from the antibinary trajectory taken up by Ortega, Gloria Anzaldúa (with her development of a "borderlands/new Mestiza consciousness"), and other Chicana feminist theorists, such as Emma Pérez, who situates the "decolonial imaginary" at the coagulation point of "that which is colonialist and that which is colonized."[9] Acknowledging that the gang members of the literature and film this book explores are (de)colonial and contradictory is not intended to pathologize those involved in gangs. Rather, accentuating these contradictions veers toward questions that emphasize the intersectional structural impetuses to gang membership, violence, and crime. Instead of dismissing or demeaning gang members as self-defeating, this book asks and unravels how, when, and why these contradictions in gang life occur.[10] In this way, *Clicas* aims to show how Latina/o/x gang literature and film might contribute toward identifying and theorizing the reasons for gang life—reasons that implicate gender and sexuality as much as race and class, and that encompass the abstract as well as the material.

As readers will learn throughout this volume, masculinity has a crucial part in the (de)colonial projects I survey. As such, this book conversates in prior and emerging discussions on decolonial masculinity, as well as those on colonialism's role in toxifying masculinity amongst Latino men.[11] During the late 1990s and early 2000s, Lionel Cantú Jr. and Alfredo Mirandé began examining how the material and psychic legacy of colonialism toxifies masculinity in many Latino men.[12] Since then, many Latina/o/x studies scholars, such as Arturo J. Aldama, Pancho McFarland, and Wayne Freeman, have considered how this toxified masculinity may indicate a sense of subaltern power for some Latino men. These later scholars have also pondered how to "decolonize" such toxified masculinities from, to use Frederick Luis Aldama and Arturo J. Aldama's words, the "legacies of colonization and capitalist exploitation and oppression [that] continue to twist tightly around our souls and rope-burn them—at once within our *familias*, our communities, and society at large."[13] Building from Cantú Jr., Mirandé, and these growing conversations about the need to decolonize toxified masculinity in our Latina/o/x communities, *Clicas* intimates how masculinity, like gang members, may occupy the center of a spectrum amongst subaltern populations—a center where these toxified masculinities might offer subaltern people a sense of resistance and power that depends on the abuse of other multiply marginalized persons. While this book does not *necessarily* follow the nascent trend of identifying a decolonized masculinity, the project shows how the usual victims of toxified masculinity, namely women and gay people, might respond to its perniciousness—how these persons appropriate and transform toxified masculinity into a (de)colonial performance that may afford them psychic and material resistance.

In reading masculinity on a spectrum and as a cultural performance that any gender may adopt, *Clicas* advances the burgeoning study of Latina female masculinity that scholars like T. Jackie Cuevas and Ellie D. Hernández have propelled with their writing on machas, mariconas, and butchas. Complicating the predilection for primarily identifying power and subversion in female masculinity, however, this volume unravels the uncomfortable but necessary question of how, when, and why women and gay persons in gangs may replicate the toxified masculinity of heterosexual, male gang members in ways that harm innocent people. In doing so, the book extends and complicates Lugones's observation about "the indifference that men"—including men "who have been racialized as inferior"—"exhibit to the systematic violences inflicted upon women of color."[14] Because this book interprets masculinity as a fluid performance not endemic to heterosexual men, *Clicas* recognizes and considers how, when, and why women and gay persons, as much as heterosexual men, may perform racialized gang masculinities in ways that reproduce indifference to "the systematic violences inflicted upon women of color." Attending to this matter should *not* act as a homophobic misogyny that sensationalizes and condemns women and gay persons of color. Rather, by asking how, when, and why women and gay gang members might perform masculinities that harm other multiply marginalized people, this book defies the pathologization of Latina/o/x persons and spaces. *Clicas* explicitly and frequently accents the past and ongoing colonization of Latina/o/xs—transpiring at the intersection of race, gender, sexuality, and class—that toxifies masculinities in our communities. In this way, the book implicitly points toward the avenues leading to a decolonized masculinity for gay and heterosexual gang members—men and women alike—underscoring the interlocking colonial forces that the State and Latina/o/x communities must address for certain gang members to decolonize their toxified masculinities.

Studying the convergence of masculinity, gender, sexuality, race, and class in gangs through this book's modified understanding of the (de)colonial has multiple consequences.

(1) The book's archive and interpretations of the literature and film by and/or about gay and women gang members expand the canon of gang narratives beyond its heterocentric, male tradition, as well as reshape the arguments about gangs that "normative" gang narratives facilitate. In doing so, *Clicas* showcases how gang narratives, which remain under-studied across several disciplines, can develop new—and complicate current—ideas in queer and feminist studies, and unearth neglected voices in and about gang life that display the agential strategies of women and gay persons. These voices contest the universalist portrayal of gangs as heterosexual male subcultures that refuse citizenship to anyone not embodying a heterosexual male identity.[15] In this way, the project urges critical gang studies to reconsider prior findings and beliefs about gangs, demanding that—and showing how—scholars should now consider new questions and develop evolved lines of inquiry about gender and sexuality in gangs.

(2) *Clicas*'s analyses of (de)colonial gang life extend beyond these crime-based subcultures and into overarching decolonial projects. Its revelations of how gender and sexuality always implicate the decolonial illuminate how to revisit past—and study future—decolonial projects, locating the ways that women and gay persons negotiate, refashion, and contribute to social, political, and national revolutions that heterosexual men supposedly dominate. The book's concept of the (de)colonial and the contradictions the term signifies also push scholars to depart from a rigid colonizer/colonized dichotomy. They should therefore complicate their understandings of past, present, and future "decolonial"

projects inundated in contradictions that might more closely approximate the (de)colonial rather than the decolonial. As many women of color feminists have shown, for instance, the 1960s US civil rights movements were steeped in homophobia and misogyny, even as these "decolonial" movements engaged in invaluable antiracist work.

(3) Finally, by recognizing that gang life grants psychological, cultural, ontological, ideological, and material resistance for many gang members in a way that may depend on the harm of other persons in working-class communities of color, *Clicas* inevitably reveals how the literature and film it explicates visualize the potential gendered and sexual—as much as classed and racial—impetuses for gang membership, violence, and crime. These revelations about the possible causes of gang membership, violence, and crime provide a better understanding of gang life that may inform more productive gang policies that combat violence, crime, and inequality in the barrio. The result could hopefully therefore help not only those participating in gangs, but also working-class Latina/o/x persons who become gangs' targets.

Terminology has a precise and purposeful role in this project, as readers will see that this book uses both the words "gay" and "queer," and refuses the mainstream adoption of Latinx as an all-inclusive, conglomerate, and imposed term on the field and on persons of the Latin American diaspora. The reclamation of "queer" emerged in response to the disparate sexual identities that gay and lesbian could not account for. The word has since come to function as a shorthand, umbrella term to, as Cuevas elucidates, "try to be all-inclusive of a range of specific identities based on desire, sexual preference, identity, orientation, or specific practices."[16] Increasingly, queer's umbrella extends beyond sexuality; queer signifies non-normative gender expression as well, but its usage as an all-inclusive gender and sexual identity term remains controversial. As Tim Dean and Christopher Lane explain, "No small part of the controversy surrounding the term queer stems from the sense that a single term cannot describe everyone's sexual identity."[17] Unless honoring other scholars' preferences as a shorthand umbrella when discussing their work, I do not use queer in this book to signal gay and lesbian sexual identity. Instead, when I invoke queer, I do so from the theoretical tradition that interprets it as the disruption of heterocentrism as well as gender and sexual normativity—as a term that signifies an "ability to create a space in opposition to dominant norms" and "understanding sexuality [and gender expression] in primarily political terms."[18]

Latinx as an identity term has many similarities to queer. Cuevas explains Latinx as an attempt "to move beyond the [Latina/o] binary"—one that "offers a trans, genderqueer, gender nonconforming, and gender variant intervention that opens up the possibilities of ascribing any gender, or none at all, to the term."[19] Like Richard T. Rodríguez, I see Latinx as "a term that holds deep meaning for those excluded from the seemingly fixed, gendered terms Latina and Latino," but I do not subscribe to the mainstreaming of Latinx as an imposed, transtemporal, all-inclusive term.[20] I understand Latinx as denoting a specific, temporal, affective experience, not as a conglomerate, all-inclusive category that encapsulates and speaks for the range of gender identities amongst past, present, and future persons of the Latin American diaspora. As Rodríguez notes, Latinx "cannot be assumed to apply in all situations or for every attempt to account for those who refuse or annul gender inflexibility."[21] Many of the figures in the literature and film this book studies are real people who are alive and do not identify with the term Latinx, even as some adopt gender non-conforming expressions. For this reason, I maintain the use of Latina/o to respect their self-naming preferences, while incorporating the "x" as a supplementary term (Latina/o/x) to signify the potentiality of others in the field and in gang subcultures who may find Latinx a more appropriate identity.

The Value of the Humanities in Critical Gang Studies

Since the academic study of gangs erupted during the 1980s and early 1990s, the social sciences have reigned over the field. As one would expect, an overreliance on participant observation and quantitative data drawn from questionnaires and surveys has accompanied this domination. The foundational work that criminologists, anthropologists, and sociologists like Cheryl Maxson, Malcolm W. Klein, Joan W. Moore, John Hagedorn, James Diego Vigil, Felix M. Padilla, and Martín Sánchez-Jankowski began—and that later scholars like T. W. Ward, Sudhir Venkatesh, Loïc Wacquant, and Juan José Martínez D'Aubuisson have continued—substantially informs the academy's knowledge of gang membership and culture. Much of their work serves as the bedrock that *Clicas* builds from, and this book would not exist without the infrastructure they have constructed. Nevertheless, the field would benefit immensely from more contributions from humanities studies on the representation of gangs in cultural production.

To begin, many social scientists have questioned the dependability of quantitative methods that privilege statistics, questionnaires, and surveys to study gang membership and culture. As Sonja Wolf admits, "Statistics and surveys permit broad insights into gang members' characteristics and behavior, but they provide partial and sometimes misleading representations of gang realities."[22] Social scientists are skeptical of data attained through surveys and statistics for multiple reasons. One, social scientists often obtain statistics about gangs from law enforcement databases and/or depend on interviews with police for information. Many academics have disputed the objectivity and veracity of studies on gangs that hinge on police intelligence, "because reliable law enforcement figures are especially difficult to obtain, due to institutional weaknesses, deficient data collection, and the discretionary if not political use of crime data."[23] When academics predominantly base their findings about gangs on information they gain from law enforcement, they risk reproducing police biases filled with racist stereotypes and beliefs that reify sensationalist government and media accounts of gang members.

Many social scientists turn to law enforcement for information about gangs because of the difficulty and danger of accessing not just gang members but also a coterie of gang members large and diverse enough from which to generalize. Thomas Bruneau, for instance, notes that "researchers have attempted to overcome the paucity of useful data from official sources by going directly to the gangs themselves," but doing so involves "serious risks for the researcher that may in themselves skew the result."[24] Researchers' fears of gang members harming them over their findings may lead to academics unconsciously and consciously distorting information. The dangers of involving oneself in gang life for academic study and not producing material that gangs find pleasing famously materialized when the 18th Street gang shot and killed filmmaker and journalist Christian Poveda after some members were unhappy with the portrayal of the gang in his 2008 documentary *La Vida Loca*.

Notwithstanding the potentially lethal ramifications of seeking information about gang life directly from gang members, many also impugn the credibility of the data that gang members provide in questionnaires, surveys, and interviews, and during participant-observation research. Though distinct from the rigidly structured hierarchies in organized crime syndicates like cartels or mafias, many gangs feature ranking systems that require members to attain permission from gang leaders before speaking to researchers. To conceal criminalized behavior, gang leaders rarely permit interviews or meetings with academics. Even when leaders allow access to members, they usually only authorize certain ones to speak with researchers. Many social scientists have estimated that the gang members who talk with them are a particular "type"—one whom the gang can trust to withhold information, frame the gang in a way beneficial to its members, or whose gang history does not disclose excessive or compromising intelligence about the gang. This censorship may distort the sample size of social science studies, resulting in academics only learning about one "type" of gang member. For many, even the findings of these studies that may only account for a gang member "type" are uncertain. Gang leaders will often review gang members' answers on questionnaires or surveys before returning them to researchers, and many of these answers may contain lies or half-truths to minimize risks to the gang, aggrandize its reputation, and/or delude the government and law enforcement. As Bruneau says, "[T]here is every reason to assume that many respondents are lying, to make themselves look good and/or to intentionally mislead authorities."[25]

For these reasons, supplementing the social science analysis of gangs with humanities-based studies of the representation of gangs in cultural production supplies several substantial benefits.

(1) At the bare minimum, humanities methodologies avoid the hazards (both from the State and gang members) of partaking in gang life to learn about gangs, and they often evade gang leaders' censorship, since many authors of, and informants for, gang literature and film are either former gang members no longer under their leaders' direction, or are current gang members acting without their gangs' awareness.[26]

(2) Humanities studies of gangs do not dehumanize gang members by reducing them to quantitative numbers and statistics. Emma Pérez, who, in an intervention akin to this book's, turned from quantitative and toward qualitative accounts of Chicana history, remarks in *The Decolonial Imaginary* that the social historian argues that "quantification—for example, comparing numbers and tables—will cause people to become alarmed at social injustices, and to decide that everyone deserves equal treatment."[27] While many may hope that quantitative findings create sympathy to effect structural change, relying solely on quantitative methodologies may have an opposite outcome. Reducing gang members to graphs, charts, and statistics risks dehumanizing them and alienating people who might fight for reform in their favor,

addressing the systemic inequalities that drive persons to gangs. Studies of literature and film that offer fuller, more personal accounts of gang life and the people who join gangs might humanize members and help readers/viewers identify with them in a way that impels readers/viewers to push for structural change in the United States and in Latina/o/x communities. For example, after watching the film *Homeboy* (2012)—a documentary about gay Latino men in gangs and the subject of Chapter 4—Brian Addison, a white journalist for the *Long Beach Post*, said he learned that "gang membership isn't as crazy as it is human."[28]

(3) Literary and filmic gang narratives also provide a larger picture of the psychological, cultural, ideological, ontological, and material extensions of gang life and its (de)colonial projects that often hinge upon the trauma of other multiply marginalized persons. These narratives routinely and lengthily explore gang members' private and personal thoughts, deliberations, feelings, fears, reflections, and joys about gang life in a way not available to researchers who only rely on social science methodologies. Gang literature and film often extensively cover gang members' lives at home; their romantic and sexual relations and interests; their relationships with their families; and the impact of gang life on the emotional, mental, and physical well-being of those close to and around gang members who may not gangbang, such as gang members' children, siblings, parents, and lovers. How do the values, dangers, and cultures of gang life affect these kin and companions? Do the potential (de)colonial rewards of gangs extend into these people's lives? Or do these (de)colonial projects depend on and heighten the trauma of gang members' families and loved ones? These are questions that law enforcement statistics and highly censored questionnaires and surveys struggle to address and tease out, but that literary and filmic gang narratives may more thoroughly attend to.

(4) Lastly, literary and filmic gang narratives—specifically, the narratives *Clicas* interprets—enable those in critical gang studies to ask new questions and pursue new and imaginative lines of inquiry by studying topics and people vastly underrepresented in social science accounts of gangs—namely women and gay persons. How might these "non-normative" gang members appropriate and transform male-dominated, heterosexual gangs? Despite their common elision, women and gay people reside in these types of gangs. Why might they elect to join, and what might they gain from these subcultures? How might gang literature and film about their lives complicate and rewrite the

universalist narrative of women and gay persons only suffering as abject victims in (and at the hands of) male-dominated, heterosexual gangs?

Clicas pursues these and many other questions through studying a range of literary and filmic forms: poetry, prose, documentary, and feature-length film. While most of these texts are autobiographical or biographically based, this book, at times, interprets fiction to theorize gang subcultures. In doing so, *Clicas* works from the avenue that Stuart Hall established when he used fiction to theorize the "Secondary Modern" generation and the youth gangs that developed in this education system, in his 1959 essay "Absolute Beginnings: Reflections on the Secondary Modern Generation." Although few scholars have published humanities studies of gangs since Hall's essay, Monica Brown continued this trajectory of employing fiction in the analysis of gang subcultures with *Gang Nation: Delinquent Citizens in Puerto Rican, Chicano, and Chicana Narratives*. *Clicas*, likewise, operates in this tradition of using fictional gang narratives in the study of gang subcultures—though, admittedly, some readers will inevitably question the viability of deriving any meaningful takeaways about gang life from fiction. While neither the study of fiction nor humanist methodologies are without limitations, fiction should remain an integral component to the study of any social group or social formation. Fiction possesses the material, psychological, ideological, ontological, and cultural power to shape and produce human behavior and social relations—especially when recognizing, as explained earlier, that even "real" academic accounts of gangs have elements of fiction.

In "Black Men, White Media," Stuart Hall contends that "televisual entertainment" "educates the popular consciousness *informally*; by dealing with real-life problems and situations in fictional terms, it creates images without appearing to do so. And it powerfully attaches feelings and emotions to these images—feelings which can then be triggered in more explosive situations."[29] In US media, film, and television, images of black and brown men as violent criminals who threaten the safety of white institutions, citizens, and property regularly circulate and potentially instruct the "popular consciousness" about "real-life problems and situations" with black and brown men. These images, frequently appearing in gang-exploitation films like *Training Day* (2001) and *Gang Related* (1997), are almost always fictional, yet they have palpable ramifications in shaping "feelings which can then be triggered in more explosive situations." On February 23, 2020, for example, Travis and Gregory McMichael hunted down, shot, and killed Ahmaud

Marquez Arbery, a black man jogging through Satilla Shores, Georgia, whom they suspected of committing a string of robberies. Despite Arbery's innocence, his black body in a predominantly white neighborhood signified criminality for the McMichaels, and these men took this signification as authorization to execute Arbery. Travis and Gregory McMichael's racist actions and rationale arose not necessarily because of an atavistic hatred for black persons present since they inhabited their mothers' wombs. These men's beliefs and actions were a byproduct of cultural interpellation where various ideological and repressive state apparatuses inculcated them consciously and unconsciously to associate black men with violence and crime, in their minds sanctioning and excusing racist vigilantism.

On the one hand, cultural production—whether fictional or not—can contest racist presumptions about people of color that uncritically link them to violence and crime and that potentially inform, precipitate, and "justify" vigilantism and systemic inequality. In this way, because fiction can materially and psychically shape human thought, behavior, and social relations, the form can produce counternarratives that, as critical race theorist Richard Delgado says, may alter the "prevailing mindset by means of which members of the dominant group justify the world as it is, that is, with whites on top and browns and blacks at the bottom."[30] Thus, non-fictional *and* fictional narratives about gang members are, at minimum, worth studying in that they have the potential to intervene constructively in the reformation of dominant perceptions of working-class persons of color, barrios, and people who join gangs. On the other hand, gang narratives about women and gay gang members may also influence the materiality of gang life and gang culture, as well as the psyches, ontologies, epistemologies, cultures, values, and beliefs of gang members. In other words, fictional and non-fictional gang narratives are potentially shaping the gangs and gang cultures that social science methodologies "realistically" study, which in itself makes these narratives worthy in the study of gangs.

Still, perhaps the most consequential upshot of studying gang fiction lies in the form's capacity to enable researchers to imagine and develop novel questions and threads of inquiry, particularly about gender and sexuality in gangs, when the difficulty of accessing human subjects preempts this thinking and investigation. While it goes without saying that I reject the conflation of gang membership with slavery, *Clicas* uses fiction similar to how Orlando Patterson relied on it in his study of social death and slavery. Compensating for the dearth of historical accounts of slavery by enslaved persons, Patterson writes, "In the absence of historical records, one way to explore the inner lives of slaves is to exercise one's literary imagination. Through fiction, I relived the experience, thoughts, and feelings of Jamaican slaves."[31] The queries and thoughts arising from the fiction and other forms this book analyzes enable *Clicas* to mold the future of critical gang studies inside and outside the humanities, influencing the questions researchers ask in interviews and surveys and the conclusions they draw from qualitative and quantitative studies alike.

In no way does this book purport to pit the humanities and social sciences against one another or argue that one methodology works "better" or does not warrant criticism. Indeed, like the social scientists who acknowledge the pitfalls of their methodologies, this book, too, recognizes that humanities methods—as well as gang literature and film as objects of analysis—are imperfect. Some of the criticism about social science methods apply to the humanities and to the study of gang narratives. For example, literary and filmic gang narratives may also feature embellishment and unreliable statistics, and do not offer extensive sample sizes. Nonetheless, as delineated above, these shortcomings do not mean that such narratives have no value—that they cannot offer alternative knowledges to place in conversation with other disciplinary findings. Rather, the weaknesses of humanities and social science methodologies showcase the unfeasibility of pigeonholing critical gang studies into one discipline. As Bruneau explains, the study of gangs "is so diverse that no single discipline or approach could begin to capture it."[32] The humanities and social sciences should, thus, work in tandem in the study of gangs—each building from and influencing each other as scholars work toward a better and more thorough understanding of gang life. This book strives, and urges others, to extend a multidisciplinary conversation on the study of gangs.

Those familiar with literary and film studies, however, will recognize that the book adopts a pointedly deconstructive methodology, exhausting its readings of texts in ways that overlap and sometimes contradict themselves. These contradictions are purposeful and an outgrowth of the type of (de)colonial projects represented in the literature and film this book explores. Because my study argues that (de)colonial projects in gangs often hinge on the contradictory harm of other multiply marginalized persons, the close readings in *Clicas* are inherently paradoxical. They deliberately materialize as antinomies, as a strategy for accentuating the type of (de)colonial projects represented in the gang narratives that this book examines.

Colonialism, Coloniality, and the (De)colonial

In the 1970s, Stuart Hall, John Clarke, and other subcultural theorists established a Marxist framework for theorizing youth subcultures and street gangs as resistant countercultures that respond to class inequalities. Writing on the Teddy Boys, Mods, and other mid-twentieth century British subcultures and gangs, Hall, Clarke, Tony Jefferson, and Brian Roberts contend that these youths, as a "subordinate class," carry to the "'theater of struggle' a repertoire of strategies and responses—ways of coping as well as of resisting."[33] For these theorists, the "ways of coping" and "resisting" that working-class subcultures and gangs develop "are not simply 'ideological' constructs. They, too, *win space* for the young: cultural space in the neighborhood and institutions, real time for leisure and recreation, actual room on the street or street-corner. They serve to mark out and appropriate 'territory' in the localities."[34] Youth street gangs and other subcultures, for these scholars, respond materially, as well as ideologically, to capitalist inequalities. These youths appropriate and "win" public space and territory in a capitalist State that systemically cultivates class imbalances, inhibiting property ownership and resource access for those not of the bourgeoisie and wealthy elite.

These Marxist arguments about youth gangs and subcultures as forms of resistance that react to class inequalities are insightful contributions to the study of gang subcultures, and I do not necessarily find any of these claims made by 1970s subcultural theorists incorrect. I do, however, deem this prior Marxist framework insufficient for theorizing Latina/o/x gang members, especially for a book that centers gay and women gang members. Many of the youth gangs and subcultures Hall and others studied were composed of white working-class Europeans. While a working-class status influences the lives, beliefs, actions, and cultures of many Latina/o/x gang members, the gang members in the literature and film this book interprets respond to racial, gendered, and sexual cruelties as much as to class inequalities. Indeed, their class statuses are inseparable from these other identity categories and are mutually constitutive. But many of the hierarchies, oppressions, and phenomena Latina/o/x gang members circumvent and/or contest originate in colonialism. They persist in the organization of life and aftershocks that remain after the "end" of classic colonialism, such as in marianismo, the imposition of currently dominant understandings of gender and sexuality, and machismo, which is not a synonym for masculinity, but denotes a specifically racialized masculinity that emerges in reaction to the effects and legacy of colonization. In other words, because Latina/o/xs do not navigate class inequalities independent of the legacy of colonization and are, in fact, experiencing the ongoing repercussions of European and US colonialism that remain entrenched in Latina/o/x cultures and spaces, this book's study of Latina/o/x gang literature, film, and subcultures necessitates a turn toward colonial/decolonial methodologies.

So how exactly does this book read Latina/o/x gang members as "colonized" or navigating "colonialism" in the twenty-first century United States? To begin, colonization—regardless of how liberally people may use the expression—at its core features a war in power relations where one party seizes, to use Max Weber's words, "that opportunity existing within a social relationship which permits one to carry out one's will even against resistance and regardless of the basis on which this opportunity rests."[35] Historically racialized, this relationship of domination in colonialism frequently results in exploitive and unequal material conditions between white colonizers and colonized black, brown, and native persons. In *The Wretched of the Earth*, Frantz Fanon describes the materiality of unequal, racialized power relations in colonialism:

> The zone where the natives live is not complementary to the zone inhabited by the settlers.... The settlers' town is a strongly built town, all made of stone and steel. It is a brightly lit town; the streets are covered with asphalt, and the garbage cans swallow all the leavings, unseen, unknown and hardly thought about. The settlers' feet are never visible.... His feet are protected by strong shoes although the streets of his town are clean and even with no holes or stones. The settlers' town is a well-fed town, an easygoing town; its belly is always full of good things. The settlers' town is a town of white people, of foreigners.
>
> The town belonging to the colonized people, or at least the native town, the Negro village, the medina, the reservation, is a place of ill fame, peopled by men of evil repute. They are born there, it matters little where or how; they die there, it matters not where,

nor how. It is a world without spaciousness; men live there on top of each other, and their huts are built one on top of the other. The native town is a hungry town, starved of bread, of meat, of shoes, of coal, of light. The native town is a crouching village, a town on its knees, a town wallowing in the mire.[36]

Whereas the metropole features "well-fed" citizens, an advanced infrastructure, and a hygienic environment that attracts tourism, the colony remains mired in overcrowding and penury, its denizens' lives meaningless and invisible as "it matters not where, nor how" they live or die.

Colonialism, however, does not only involve the material. The process includes the cultural, epistemological, ideological, ontological, and psychological—and, in fact, these racialized, material inequalities that Fanon delineates arise and are "permissible" because of the *imma*terial. Colonial projects always require a narrative that rationalizes the colonizer's appropriation of land, labor, and resources, and the violence the colonizer enacts on the colonized. These narratives often feature a "white man's burden" logic that usually resembles the following: "these people are 'savages' (or another derogatory epithet) and 'uncivilized.' They have no idea how to live adequately or use their resources. Their culture and technology are obsolete, underdeveloped, and inferior. As an advanced civilization, we must help them progress as a society and create a higher standard of living, even if doing so means raping, murdering, and pillaging them for their own betterment."

Charles Mills has dubbed these narratives integral to the "racial contract," a "set of formal or informal agreements ... between the members of one subset of humans ... and coextensive (making due allowance for gender differentiation) with the class of full persons, to categorize the remaining subset of humans as 'nonwhite' and of a different and inferior moral status."[37] Classifying the colonized as "nonwhite" and of "a different and inferior moral status" justifies the colonization of people of color, their resources, and their lands. As Mills elaborates, "the general purpose of the Contract is always the differential privileging of the whites as a group with respect to the nonwhites as a group, the exploitation of their bodies, land, and resources, the denial of equal socioeconomic opportunities to them."[38] White colonizers rationalize the "differential privileging" of whites and the appropriation of resources and labor of the colonized because the racial contract's narrative renders the colonized subpersons. Upon dehumanization, subpersons "have a different and inferior schedule of rights and liberties applying to them. In other words, it is possible to get away with doing things to subpersons that one could not do to persons, because they do not have the same rights as persons."[39]

Once the colonizer creates this colonial narrative and conquers the colonized through material violence, the colonizer institutes cultural violence, what Ngũgĩ wa Thiong'o calls the "cultural bomb." The purpose of the cultural bomb "is to annihilate a people's belief in their names, in their language, in their environment, in their heritage of struggle, in their unity, in their capacities and ultimately in themselves."[40] The racial contract and the cultural bomb that together eradicate and devalue colonized people's language, history, beliefs, customs, religions, and cultural production have psychic consequences for the colonized. The racial contract and cultural bomb sometimes lead to an "inferiority complex," where colonized people believe themselves and their culture inferior to the white colonizer and buy into the righteousness of assimilation, succumbing to the colonizer's psychological power over them as they consent to their own subjugation.

As an example of this psychic phenomenon, Fanon discloses the consequences that colonization, racialization, and racism have on his subjectivity and self-esteem. He writes of a young white child hailing him with the lines "'Dirty nigger!'" or, as Fanon explains in other words, "'Look! A Negro!'"[41] Later disclosing the effects these child's invectives have on his psyche, Fanon says, "Locked in this suffocating reification, I appealed to the Other so that his liberating gaze, gliding over my body suddenly smoothed of rough edges, would give me back the lightness of being I thought I had lost, and taking me out of the world put me back in the world. But just as I get to the other slope I stumble, and the Other fixes me with his gaze, his gestures and attitude, the same way you fix a preparation with a dye."[42] For Fanon, the Other's refusal to grant ontological validation and view him as a full citizen-subject beyond a supposed "Negro" status fractures his identity and imprisons him within his subaltern state, as if he were a "preparation" fixed "with a dye." Incarcerated within this dye, Fanon surrenders to accepting the discourses of the racial contract, of his alleged inferiority. He writes that this child's statements returned his body to him "spread-eagled, disjointed, redone, draped in mourning" as the words "[t]he Negro is an animal, the Negro is bad, the Negro is wicked, the Negro is ugly" reverberated in his mind.[43] This psychological effect reveals how colonialism always implicates intersubjectivity—a process whereby the Other's gaze determines and grants/denies a person's subjectivity through acknowledging/refusing to acknowledge his or her existence as a full citizen-subject and human. Because the colonizer regards the colonized as, and imposes onto them the status of, a "sub-person," an "animal," "bad," "wicked," and "ugly," the colonized may end up psychologically entrenched in a subaltern state and believing these narratives, resulting in colonized ontologies, or what Nelson Maldonado-Torres terms "sub-ontological difference."[44]

For many of the Latin American and Latina/o/x school of decolonial theory, these characteristics of colonialism and the ways that colonialism organizes life materially, culturally, psychologically, epistemologically, ideologically, and ontologically persist contemporarily, even if classic colonialism does not. As Robin D. G. Kelley explains,

> [T]he fact is, while colonialism in its formal sense may have been dismantled, the colonial state has not. Many of the problems of democracy are products of the old colonial state.... The official apparatus might have been removed, but the political, economic, and cultural links established by colonial domination still remain.[45]

These remnants of colonialism are what Aníbal Quijano termed "coloniality" (short for the colonial matrix of power)—an idea that later Latin American and Latina/o/x scholars subsequently built upon.[46] Maldonado-Torres elaborates on the distinctions between colonialism and coloniality: "Colonialism denotes a political and economic relation in which the sovereignty of a nation or a people rests on the power of another nation.... Coloniality, instead, refers to long-standing patterns of power that emerged as a result of colonialism, but that define culture, labor, intersubjective relations, and knowledge production."[47] For Maldonado-Torres, coloniality permeates much of the organization of "post-colonial" life. Coloniality survives in "books, in the criteria for academic performance, in cultural patterns, in common sense, in the self image of peoples, in aspirations of self" and, as Xhercis Méndez says, in the "arrangements of bodies and power, the logics and practices, ways of being and knowing, and racialized capitalism that were born out of formal colonialism."[48]

Coloniality in the United States perhaps most closely resembles formal colonialism in what scholars call "internal colonialism," a concept Eve Tuck and K. Wayne Yang explain as "the biopolitical and geopolitical management of people, land, flora and fauna within the 'domestic' borders of the imperial nation."[49] Internal colonialism "involves the use of particularized modes of control—prisons, ghettoes, minoritizing, schooling, policing—to ensure the ascendancy of a nation and its white elite. These modes of control, imprisonment, and involuntary transport of the human beings across borders—ghettoes, their policing, their economic divestiture, and their dislocatability—are at work to authorize the metropole and conscribe her periphery."[50] For Tuck, Yang, and other scholars like Mario Barrera, Carlos Muñoz, and Charles Ornelas, barrios and "ghettos" are internal colonies—spaces that are the manifestation of coloniality, and where Latina/o/x gang members and working-class persons of color are often relegated to.[51] As such, inhabitants of these sites are, as Wacquant explains, forced to live in "conjugated segregation," and routinely subject to the "corresponding deployment of an intrusive and omnipresent police and penal apparatus."[52]

I am not arguing that coloniality does not exist in the United States. Indeed, the concept provides a valid methodological structure for reading gang life as a (de)colonial response to the inequalities, hierarchies, and systems of oppression and power present in the United States and Latina/o/x barrios. But the theorization of coloniality—like the academic discourse on internal colonialism and colonialism overall—has historically been male-centric and elided questions of gender and sexuality, beyond a cursory observation. Oyèrónké Oyěwùmí, for example, notes that the "histories of both the colonized and the colonizer have been written from the male point of view—women are peripheral if they appear at all."[53] Likewise, Mariana Ortega says of the theorization of coloniality, "Had Maria Lugones not criticized Quijano's work and developed an account of the coloniality of gender, I am not sure that gender would be an issue in the context of Anglo-American Latin American philosophy."[54]

Because this book centers on gay and women Latina/o/x gang members, *Clicas* operates from Lugones's revision of the idea of coloniality that Ortega references. In doing so, this study responds to Oyěwùmí's observation that histories of the colonized have privileged a male—and I would clarify this viewpoint as a heterosexual cis male—perspective. In "The Coloniality of Gender," Lugones argues that European colonialism imposed a binary gender system onto the indigenous peoples of the Americas, a system that perseveres. As Lugones writes, many "Native American tribes were matriarchal, recognized more than two genders, recognized 'third' gendering and homosexuality positively and understood gender in egalitarian terms."[55] Yet because

European colonizers deemed the "behaviors of the colonized and their personalities/souls" as "bestial" and "promiscuous," colonizers classified indigenous persons under the binary categories of male and female, rather than man and woman.[56] Eventually, the colonized moved into the categories of man and woman, but European colonizers only considered indigenous persons as "modified versions" of men and women.[57] When colonizers granted indigenous women the status of the gender of woman, this extension did not involve the "status of white women.... Colonized females got the inferior status of gendering as women, without any of the privileges accompanying that status for white bourgeois women."[58] The imposition of the modern gender system did not just entail the statuses of male/female and man/woman, but also the concept of normative heterosexuality and the perception of alternative sexualities as deviant and criminal. As Lugones writes, prior to colonization, eighty-eight indigenous nations "recognized homosexuality," with many of them conceptualizing "homosexuals in positive terms," including the Aztec and Maya—nations that many Chicana/o/xs trace themselves to.[59]

The imposition of gender and a normative, compulsory heterosexuality onto indigenous persons (and the continuation of this gender/sexual system in coloniality) does not involve just a status of man/woman and hetero/homosexual, but all that these social terms signify. As Lugones elaborates, "the system of gender imposed through colonialism encompasses the subordination of females in every aspect of life."[60] The status of "woman" signifies "economic, political, cognitive inferiorization" and "those who do not have power; those who cannot participate in the public arena."[61] Similarly, heterosexuality signals "the turning of white women into reproducers of 'the [master] race' and 'the class'" and alternative sexualities as "grotesquely sexual and sinful."[62] Thus, for Lugones, the coloniality of gender evokes "not just a classification of people ... but also the process of active reduction of people, the dehumanization that fits them for the classification, the process of subjectification, the attempt to turn the colonized into less than human beings."[63] Lugones's observations about the imposition and significations of modern gender and sexuality do not mean that every pre-conquest indigenous nation was egalitarian and accepting of currently criminalized sexualities. Indeed, as Cherríe Moraga, Gloria Anzaldúa, Norma Alarcón, and a host of other Chicana feminists have shown, patriarchal ideologies infused several areas of Aztec life, even if the nation "recognized homosexuals in positive terms."[64] But, for Lugones, the imposition of the modern gender/sexual system during European colonization transformed and amplified the already present patriarchy and sexual bigotry of some indigenous cultures. As Lugones explains, "collaboration between some Indian men and whites" was a valuable tool that European colonizers used to "construc[t] a powerful inside force" for "undermining the power of women."[65]

Because this gender/sexual system continues after formal colonialism, Lugones reads this system, its logic, its significations, and the hierarchies and violences it enables as integral to coloniality—terming its presence the coloniality of gender. The coloniality of gender does not represent a different type of coloniality than that which Quijano, Maldonado-Torres, Walter Mignolo, and others have theorized. White supremacy, racial capitalism, sub-ontological difference, and the subordination of alternative epistemologies still compose the coloniality of gender. The coloniality of gender is not a separate term that references only how colonialism and coloniality impact gender. Rather, the coloniality of gender signifies the need for more intersectional accounts of how colonialism and coloniality operate. The coloniality of gender is part of coloniality, and vice versa. The two are inseparable. As Lugones clarifies, "The gender system introduced was one thoroughly informed through the coloniality of power.... The imposition of this gender system was as constitutive of the coloniality of power as the coloniality of power was constitutive of it."[66] Just as the coloniality of gender constitutes coloniality (short for the colonial matrix of power), Lugones explains that so, too, does sexuality compose the coloniality of gender: "heterosexuality is not just biologized in a fictional way; it is also compulsory, and it permeates the whole of the coloniality of gender."[67] Race, class, gender, and sexuality are interconnected in coloniality, and these identity categories all intersect "as central constructs of the capitalist world system of power."[68]

When *Clicas* interprets gay and heterosexual male and female gang members as "colonized" subjects, it does so from this intersectional matrix that the coloniality of gender signifies. The book theorizes how Latina/o/x persons navigate the coloniality of gender and how Latina/o/x gang members mobilize material, cultural, ontological, psychological, and ideological (de)colonial projects that allow them to circumvent, undermine, or contest the hierarchies, systems of oppression (and their abstract and physical effects), and overarching organization of life that materialize from the coloniality of gender. This includes: capitalist inequalities, white supremacy, racism, the bigoted and patriarchal ideologies present in the modern gender/sexual system, sub-ontological difference, subordinate identities, and the cultural bomb and imposed assimilation. Gender and sexuality always infuse these just as much as race and class do.

As mentioned earlier, this book's use of the (de)colonial departs from what the word "decolonial" traditionally signifies in European and US academies. In these institutions, decolonial typically connotes decolonization, a term that, according to Mignolo and Catherine E. Walsh, "originally meant freeing a colony to allow it to become self-governing or independent; to build the former-colonized's own nation-state."[69] For some scholars, decolonial should *only* reference reclaiming stolen land, resources, property, and control of the State. Tuck and Yang, for instance, mention that they "wonder whether another settler move to innocence is to focus on decolonizing the mind, or the cultivation of critical consciousness, as if it were the sole activity of decolonization; to allow *conscientization* to stand in for the more uncomfortable task of relinquishing stolen land."[70] For Tuck and Yang, conceptualizing decolonization as a metaphor rather than using the term in its conventional sense "turns decolonization into an empty signifier to be filled by any track towards liberation. In reality, the tracks walk all over land/people in settler contexts."[71]

I do not want to dismiss Tuck and Yang's crucial arguments about recognizing the US occupation of stolen land, the importance of land repatriation, and the role of using decolonization as a metaphor in allowing people to forget their complicity in settler colonialism. At the same time, I find Tuck and Yang's essay on the use of the terms decolonial/decolonization insufficient in its understanding of how colonialism operates. Although land appropriation is a core component of colonialism, this land appropriation, as I previously delineated, cannot transpire without—and does not exist independent of—ontological, epistemological, psychological, and cultural violences. Colonization of the mind, of subjectivity, of being, and of knowledge occurs in all forms of colonialism, and decolonizing these components of colonialism is not a move to take lightly. Moreover, land repatriation does not nullify or even account for coloniality, which—as decolonized states in Asia, Africa, and Latin America show—still persists after decolonization.[72]

As I am insinuating, this assumption that the decolonial should only reference land repatriation also ignores the entire Latin American and (somewhat) Latina/o/x school of thought on decolonial theory and on the colonization of the Americas. In fact, Tuck and Yang never once engage with, let alone acknowledge, the Latin American tradition that theorizes the decolonial much differently than does the US-European academic status quo. Admittedly, this elision (both by Tuck and Yang and the US-European academy) may arise from the fact that much of the early Latin American work on the decolonial originally appeared in Spanish. Nevertheless, as Mignolo says, "The American and the European Academy are not hubs of the decolonial."[73] For the decolonial theorists of the Latin American and Latina/o/x tradition, decolonization—in the sense of colonized nations obtaining their stolen land and developing into sovereign nation-states—"was successful in sending the colonizer home, but it was a failure, for it ended up creating nation-states that remained within the management of the CMP [colonial matrix of power] even if settlers were no longer in the terrain."[74] Because coloniality remained after the colonized attained their freedom, decolonization failed in that it left the organization of life that colonialism produced intact. For this reason, the Latin American and Latina/o/x tradition has emphasized epistemological and ontological decolonization that targets coloniality. This is especially so since, for some, decolonization from the US and Europe, in the original sense of the word, does not appear viable. As Mignolo and Walsh write, after the Cold War and upon "the beginning of neoliberal global dreams," "it became evident that the state can be neither decolonized nor democratized.... We are living on the planet in the concerted Western effort (the United States and the European Union) to manage and control the colonial matrix of power."[75]

Lugones, Mignolo, Walsh, Quijano, Maldonado-Torres, and others of this school of thought have developed the idea of decoloniality in response to decolonization's failures. For Maldonado-Torres, the decolonial should not just reference "simply the end of formal colonial relations," but instead "a confrontation with the racial, gender, and sexual hierarchies that were put in place or strengthened by European modernity."[76] Contesting these hierarchies and how they inform the ontological and epistemological shapes the bedrock of decoloniality. As Mignolo and Walsh elaborate, decoloniality "is the exercise of power within the colonial matrix to undermine the mechanism that keeps it in place requiring obeisance. Such a mechanism is epistemic, and so decolonial liberation implies epistemic disobedience."[77] Decoloniality, thus, "is a form of struggle and survival, an epistemic and existence-based response and practice.... Decoloniality denotes ways of thinking, knowing, being, and doing.... It implies the recognition and undoing of the hierarchical structures of race, gender, heteropatriarchy, and class that continue to control life."[78]

This book uses the concept of (de)colonial in a manner that more closely approximates decoloniality than decolonization. In arguing that the gang members of the literature and film this book studies are (de)colonial, I am not contending that gang members are overthrowing US empire to seize land and sovereignty. Instead, I use the term (de)colonial similar to (though not entirely the same as) the way the Latin American and Latina/o/x tradition has conceptualized decoloniality. The gang members of the narratives I interpret engage in struggles of survival that contest, circumvent, or undermine the abstract and material inequalities, hierarchies, and oppressions that materialize in the coloniality of gender. Their gang lives enable the development of alternative subjectivities and ontologies—what Fanon might refer to as "the veritable creation of new men [and women]"—that allow them to resist the power the coloniality of gender exerts over their psyches, bodies, and lives.[79] They develop means of defying the cultural bomb, and circumventing capitalist inequalities, in abstract and material ways that implicate gender, sexuality, race, and class. In some cases, the gay and women gang members of these narratives recognize how the coloniality of gender structures their Latina/o/x communities and gangs, and refuse and/or reconfigure its ideologies. In theorizing these gang members as (de)colonial in these ways, this book follows the trajectory that scholars of decoloniality like Quijano and Mignolo first established, and that was continued by later Latina/o/x studies works, such as Emma Pérez's *The Decolonial Imaginary* and the essays featured in Arturo J. Aldama and Frederick Luis Aldama's *Decolonizing Latinx Masculinities*—especially T. Jackie Cuevas's "Fighting the Good Fight: Grappling with Queerness, Masculinities, and Violence in Contemporary Latinx Literature and Film." Collectively, these later texts theorize methods and cultural paradigms for how to decolonize ourselves from the harmful effects that the coloniality of gender has imposed on our masculinities and our means of writing Chicana histories.

Because the gang members in this book do not *fully* work to undo "the hierarchical structures of race, gender, heteropatriarchy, and class that continue to control life," they—to use the language of decoloniality theorists—do not entirely "delink" from the coloniality of gender.[80] This idea of "delinking" from the coloniality of gender is one that Cuevas has recently advanced in her theorization of "new forms of queer

Latinx masculinities" and their capacity to work "toward delinking the toxic from masculinities to create more expansive experiences and performances."[81] Studying the contemporary queer Latina/o/x films *La Mission* (2009), *Bruising for Besos* (2016), and *We the Animals* (2018), Cuevas shows how these movies "delink masculinity from violence and the imperative to use it to enforce dominance."[82] In doing so, the queer figures of these films "construct new forms of queer Latinx masculinities that leave violence and violent patriarchs behind," to instead pursue "Latinx queer worldmaking."[83] In many ways, Cuevas's revelation of how contemporary queer Latina/o/x films envision alternate masculinities that delink from the heteropatriarchal violence of the coloniality of gender serves as the barometer for the gang masculinities this book studies. Unlike the queer figures Cuevas theorizes, the gang members in this book might perform non-hegemonic masculinities in order to help circumvent the abstract and physical effects of the coloniality of gender, but they do not fully delink from this coloniality or its patriarchal violence. Rather, they transform—but still employ—masculinity's "imperative to use [violence] to enforce dominance."[84] They thereby recuperate the violence of masculinity to win material, abstract, economic, and cultural space, but in a manner that hinges on exacerbating coloniality for other multiply marginalized persons.

In this way, the gang members of the cultural texts this book interprets epitomize the (de)colonial in their contradictory actions that are generative for them but, in some way, depend on reproducing the effects of the coloniality of gender for other subaltern people. As such, while the (de)colonial does not resemble decolonization, the concept does not truly encapsulate decoloniality either, since decoloniality would signal a complete delinking from the coloniality of gender. This simultaneous approximation to and departure from decoloniality—of thinking through how decoloniality might shift or struggle to completely materialize in certain contexts—is an idea that Mignolo and Walsh have welcomed. They note that "there is no proprietor or privileged master plan for decoloniality," and that we should "not take seriously any decolonial project that postulates itself (implicitly or explicitly) to be the guiding light of decoloniality."[85] In theorizing working-class youth subcultures and gangs, Clarke et al. write that "[w]e must try to understand, instead, how, under what conditions, the class has been able to use its material and cultural 'raw materials' to construct a whole *range* of responses."[86] The idea of the (de)colonial aids in pursuing this goal that Clarke and others identify. The (de)colonial provides a hermeneutic for comprehending the ontological, cultural, psychological, ideological, and material components of gang life, and for considering how Latina/o/x gang literature and film might contribute to our understanding about impetuses for gang membership, violence, and crime that implicate gender and sexuality as much as they do race and class.

(De)colonial Clicas

Those familiar with critical gang studies and Latina/o/x gang culture will recognize the specificity of this book's title. Sometimes spelled clikas or cliques, clicas are relatively autonomous cells that collectively form an overarching gang. Clicas are usually made up of teenagers and young adults from working-class or low-income backgrounds. They often have shared and shifting leadership, and feature close bonds among their members. Clicas are the most important units of a gang, especially for theorizing (de)colonial projects in gangs, because gang members usually spend most of their "gang time" with members of their clica. Gang members' closest friends, confidants, and romantic partners are often in their clica. Gang members claim territory, participate in violent and criminal activity, and hold recreational get-togethers with their clica. They fight (alongside and against), mourn, love, laugh, and often live with each other. The (de)colonial projects in gangs that this book theorizes transpire in and at the level of clicas. For this reason, unless otherwise specified, the term "gang" in this book acts as a synonym for clica.

Many often confuse clicas with organized crime. Neither clicas, nor the overarching gangs they form, are organized crime. Mafias, cartels, and other organized crime syndicates are criminal enterprises that have distinct hierarchies, memberships, relationships, and delinquent practices. As Sonja Wolf explains, these enterprises "require mature, professional members with organizational skills" and feature "a well-defined leadership" and "division of labor."[87] Mafias and cartels usually "develop relationships with legitimate, political, and legal institutions" and have the capacity to launder money.[88] In contrast, street gangs generally feature "younger members, a shifting and shared leadership," and only "intermediate levels of organization."[89] Many mafias and cartels are also transnational and international, whereas clicas are local to their neighborhoods, and organized crime leadership rarely participates in violence, instead contracting foot soldiers to enact violence in the name of the criminal enterprise. On the other hand, clicas often expect each member to engage in violence, and violence has a crucial role in the creation and maintenance of clicas and their internal bonds and territories. In short, much of clicas' capacity to challenge and circumvent coloniality hinges on violence.

Gangs or clicas are not inherently (de)colonial. As much as gangs might enable (de)colonial projects, they may also *only* operate as groups that amplify racialized inequalities and uphold the wages of whiteness. The persons who populate a gang determine if the gang and its activities have the potential for (de)colonial projects for its members. For example, the lone purpose of police gangs (like the Los Angeles Executioners or Lynwood Vikings) or neo–white supremacist gangs (like the Proud Boys or Boogaloo Boys) is to maximize US white supremacy and power over subaltern persons of color.[90] This agenda recently materialized when the Executioners—a gang in the Los Angeles County Sheriff's Department whose members brazenly sport Nazi tattoos—continued their custom of initiating members through having them kill black and Latina/o/x people.[91] One was Andres Guardado, who died on June 18, 2020, after a prospective Executioner murdered him.

The working-class Latina/o/x gangs that this book studies, however, are often (de)colonial responses to the coloniality of gender in the United States. Furthermore, the gay and women gang members in the film and literature this book extrapolates appropriate and transform their male-dominated, heterosexual gangs to also challenge and bypass how the coloniality of gender infuses their Latina/o/x families and communities. While their (de)colonial projects simultaneously depend on exacerbating the trauma and precarity of other multiply marginalized persons, working-class Latina/o/x gangs primarily form for psychologically, ontologically, culturally, and materially (de)colonial reasons. In contrast, police and white supremacist gangs arise *only* to perpetuate US empire, power, and hegemony.

The (de)colonial projects that Latina/o/x gangs may enable in part center on these gangs' statuses as countercultures that embrace Latina/o/x heritage, culture, and identity. Latina/o/x gangs often cherish the concept of familia that many Latina/o/x cultures idealize. Clicas practice familia through the ideology of carnalismo, which involves gang members regarding and treating their fellow gang members as "blood brothers," and through what Vigil calls the "cohorting tradition"—the expectation that the clica does as much as possible together.[92] Latina/o/x gangs also typically speak an argot, usually a slang that involves Spanish or Spanglish, which, in the Southwest, is often Caló—a type of Spanglish patois featuring rhyme-scheme, the conjugation of English verbs with Spanish tenses, and neologisms like vato, ruca, chale, simón, and esé or esá. Latina/o/x clicas have their own style and aesthetics as well. Richard T. Rodríguez has referred to this image as the "homeboy aesthetic," which references further "designations such as cholo, vato, and gangster."[93] For Rodríguez, this aesthetic features "an assemblage of key signifiers: clothing (baggy pants and undershirts are perhaps the most significant), hair (or, in the current moment of the aesthetic, lack of hair), bold stance, and distinct language."[94] Beyond these categories, I would specify and elaborate a contemporary Latina/o/x cholo/homeboy aesthetic as entailing a shaved head, greased pompadour, or slick-back; billowing Dickies and Ben Davis khakis; Pendleton flannels, oversized white or black tees, and "wife beaters"; Nike Cortez and Converse Chuck Taylor sneakers; paños (bandanas); Locs sunglasses; sporting apparel bearing team colors or letters used to represent cities associated with the gang; and many tattoos that symbolically mark the gang as familia, normally the gang's name or emblem (sometimes etched on clothing) and the "pachuco cross" or tres puntos triangle.

This style is not exclusive to men. Homegirls or cholas don many parts of this aesthetic, particularly the khakis, flannels, sneakers, paños, sunglasses, sporting apparel, and tattoos. While these items might render the chola/homegirl aesthetic primarily masculine, gang girls also infuse the style with elements of what Catherine S. Ramírez might call "aberrant femininity."[95] The chola/homegirl aesthetic routinely includes teased and dyed hair (often red or black in California), hoop earrings, and dark, heavy makeup styles that convey meaning to those aware of the semiotics of gang life. Norma Mendoza-Denton, for example, identifies one paramount element of the chola aesthetic in dark eyeliner, which signals truculence. As Mendoza-Denton explains, "length of eyeliner" typically signifies "intention as well as willingness to fight," and many gang girls read "long eyeliner as a provocation."[96]

Like the meanings of chola eyeliner suggest, this aesthetic for men and women in gangs is, as Nadiah Rivera Fellah says, a strategy for "confront[ing] the hostile, urban environment outside their home."[97] The chola/o/x aesthetic conveys power and an intimidating persona, and simultaneously helps to unify the gang. At the same time, the style also connotes dissent at the level of the sign. In *Subculture: The Meaning of Style,* Dick Hebdige argues that the "struggle between different discourses, different definitions and meanings within ideology is therefore always, at the same time, a struggle within signification: a struggle for the possession of the sign which extends to even the most mundane areas of everyday life."[98] For Hebdige, every signifier, no matter how "mundane," signifies an ideology, discourse, and meaning, and he consequently views non-normative, subcultural fashion styles as in conflict with hegemonic culture and its ideologies. Thus, subcultural resistance, in Hebdige's mind, manifests not solely through material violence, but "is expressed obliquely, in style."[99] Because hegemonic fashion often evokes white supremacy, aristocratic elitism, a politics of middle-class respectability, and/or heteronormativity, the subcultural appropriation and re-deployment of banal items in a non-normative style functions as a "form of Refusal" by signaling "noise" and "semantic disorder" within the ruling ideology that rationalizes the suppression of the subaltern subject.[100]

Latina/o/x gangs do not necessarily co-opt normative clothing in the same ways that the punks and Teddy Boys adorned themselves in lavatory chains or trashy fabrics with loud designs. If, however, as Hebdige says, signs and style are always ideological, then this Latina/o/x gang aesthetic signifies the clica's rejection of contemporary "cultural bombs" and racial contracts that aim to destroy and devalue Latina/o/x culture, heritage, and people. The aesthetic symbolically voices the gang's defying ideologies and practices—such as Caló, carnalismo, and the "cohorting tradition"—that resist imposed assimilation, the devaluation of Latina/o/x culture, and the hegemony of the US nation-state. Mendoza-Denton, for instance, notes how Chicana gang members intentionally adopt makeup shades that foreground their anti-assimilationist stances. She writes that Chicana girl gangs prized "a (Mestiza) Mexican-based identity of some sort," and, thus, "dark skin was something that was valued."[101] As a Chicana of Mendoza-Denton's ethnography advises on makeup shades, "Always wear brown 'cause that's the color of your skin. . . . You have to use darker cover-up. You can't wear cover-up lighter than you 'cause they tell you that you want to be white."[102] In this way, this young woman imbues the aberrant femininity of her chola aesthetic with what Jillian Hernández terms an "aesthetics of excess"—a modality of style, fashion, and performance that black and Latina women employ to signal "ethnic pride, sexual autonomy, and indifference toward assimilating to whiteness."[103] Despite this Chicana gang girl's desires, Latina/o/x gang members cannot completely resist assimilation. Nevertheless, their languages, style, and carnalismo indicate they reject and inhibit total acculturation.

The style, language, and ideology that permeate many Latina/o/x gangs also have social, psychological, ontological, and intersubjective ramifications. The close bonds in clicas, and the esteem gang members have for their shared culture and each other, circumvent the othering, dehumanizing feelings many subaltern persons may experience in all forms of coloniality. By participating in a gang where other people recognize their subjectivity, humanity, and worth, and identify with them, gang members resist the psychological, ontological, and social consequences that accompany a subaltern status in the US nation-state. They thereby undermine the potential inferiority complexes and meager self-esteem that arise from that nation-state's habit of viewing the racial Other as an abject subperson. As many in critical gang studies have explained, some members also come from toxic and abusive homes filled with domestic violence, child abuse, sexual violence, and emotional and mental abuse, and consequently have fragile egos and suffer depression.[104] Gangs, thus, provide an avenue for remedying the psychological and emotional trauma gang members may experience at the hands of both the US nation-state and their Latina/o/x communities and families. Gang members' clicas can supply them with social-familial meaning and value through fellow members' acknowledgment and appreciation of their personhood, and subcultural citizenship.

Violence plays a paramount role in establishing the psychological, emotional, social, and familial rewards of gang life. Gang members often initiate prospective members through violence, jumping them in with a beating that usually lasts from thirteen to eighteen seconds. After this beating that symbolically births the new member into the family, gang members congratulate and welcome their new colleague, granting the person membership in a subculture that values his or her personhood and culture. This status and the familial bonds that the violent "baptism" bestows increase and strengthen through shared violent activities. Gang members participate in fistfights, rumbles, robberies, and attacks on rivals together. These actions intensify the kinship ties between members, as well as the standing of each person and of the gang, to create what Wacquant calls the "currency of honour."[105] As Wolf elaborates, through partaking in these violent crimes together, gang members "can acquire the status and respect that are otherwise unobtainable" both as second-class citizens in the United States and in some of their families.[106] This violence also acts as therapeutic catharsis from the psychological trauma that results from the treatment gang members experience from the US nation-state and, potentially, their communities. For instance, in T. W. Ward's study of Southern California gangs, a member named Psycho—his name suggesting his mental and emotional distress—said that fighting "provided catharsis, a physical release from psychological stress or pent up emotions."[107] In short, gang violence may act as (de)colonial violence in its capacity to enable gang members to reject and circumvent the abstract and psychological power of the US nation-state through: providing emotional and mental release, aggrandizing the social stature of people whom the nation routinely demeans as subpersons, and creating and strengthening familial bonds between gang members who recognize each other's subjectivity, humanity, and worth.[108]

Violence also enables gang members to circumvent the material trauma of a capitalist colonial structure that inhibits property ownership and instead cultivates mass poverty for many Latina/o/x people. As Wacquant argues, in the "criminal economy" of the streets, "routine displays of violence are a business requirement," serving to "establish credibility and avert being taken over by competitors or robbed by intruders, customers or police."[109] Gang members claim and hold their territory through violence, initiating wars against rival gangs as they harness land—or, as Stuart Hall might say, "win space." Within their territory, gang members use violence—or the threat of violence—to engage in their own capitalist ventures, thereby ameliorating their financial poverty. They will often charge small business owners in their territories renta or war taxes, a type of extortion or strong-arm robbery where a gang demands payment of a monthly fee for protection from rival gangs or for the right to operate a business in the gang's territory. In their territories, gang members also participate in other "criminal economies," such as selling guns and drugs, trades that normally require violence, or the threat of violence, to ensure success. The amount and location of a gang's territory influence its capacity to charge renta or participate in the drug and gun trade, because a gang can normally only conduct these crimes in its own territory. Thus, the arrogation of land and the obstacles to property ownership imposed by the US capitalist colonial system incentivize gangs to expand and protect their territory continually through violence. By holding territory, gang members can circumvent the economic inequality they might experience in rising property costs, gentrification, redlining, and other forms of forced displacement.

In reading gangs as (de)colonial subcultures, this book extends and complicates preceding scholarship that regards Latina/o/x gangs—and criminality more broadly—as liberating, subaltern agency. In *Gringo Justice*, Mirandé examines Chicano (not Chicana) criminality in the nineteenth and twentieth centuries. He argues that Chicano crime, such as banditry, is oppositional because Chicano criminality violates US law and, in some instances (like that of the bandido Gregorio Cortez), challenges US empire.[110] Other scholars across a range of disciplines have also interpreted Chicano (again, not Chicana) banditry and criminality as resistance, such as Rodolfo Acuña in *Occupied America* and Julian Samora et al. in *Gunpowder Justice*. Many academics in the social sciences and humanities have also focused on less pastoral forms of Latina/o/x criminality, instead reading gang membership, crime, and violence as empowering. José Navarro, for instance, argues that gangs are "responses to State discursive and material violence" and, thus, Latina/o/x social movements and cultural production have perceived gangs "as a conduit of Chicano nationalist resistance," such as in Luis Valdez's 1978 play *Zoot Suit* or the Chicano Movement's incorporation of gangs into its marches.[111] Vigil, Sánchez-Jankowski, Josephine Metcalf, Ward, Venkatesh, and Robert J. Durán—among many others—have also all documented gangs' participation in criminal economies, their violence, and their ability to create group cohesion and identification as liberating responses that stymie white capitalism, systemic racism, and trauma in their childhood homes. Similarly, in *Gang Nation*, Brown interprets gangs as "counternations" in their ability to flout partially the discriminatory power of the US nation-state. As Brown summarizes, gang counternations enable their members to form "an alternative citizenship"—"one that fulfills fundamental needs not accorded by the state, one that provides a sense of economic security (most often through delinquent behavior), one that establishes its own moral and juridical authority with a history tied to territory, and one that provides a sense of communal identity and belonging."[112]

Much of critical gang studies that interprets gang life and culture as oppositional—and even scholarship that does not—often considers gang life available only to straight men. If scholars acknowledge women and gay persons, they often deem these persons unable to participate in male-dominated, heterosexual gangs except as abject objects.[113] *Clicas* does not argue that women and gay gang members *never* encounter violence and marginalization in male-dominated, heterosexual gangs. Indeed, many gang narratives feature heterosexual male gang members assaulting women and gay persons that are involved in gangs and those that are not—such as in Luis J. Rodriguez's *Always Running*, Piri Thomas's *Down These Mean Streets*, Miguel Durán's *Don't Spit on My Corner*, Reymundo Sanchez's *My Bloody Life*, Warren Miller's *The Cool World*, Irving Shulman's *The Amboy Dukes*, Luis Valdez's *Zoot Suit*, and the films *American Me* (1992), *Bound by Honor* (1993), and *Sin Nombre* (2009).

While I recognize the bigotry and violence women and gay gang members might encounter in male-dominated heterosexual gangs, this book rejects the belief that such individuals are invariably passive victims, and it refuses to regard these gangs as always useless for women and gay people. On the contrary, I hope to show that gang narratives by and/or about women and gay gang members reveal how these persons may receive the same material, psychological, cultural, and ontological (de)colonial rewards in male-dominated heterosexual gangs that heterosexual men do. Furthermore, women and gay gang members experience the violence, trauma, and hierarchies of the coloniality of gender to different and far more oppressive degrees than do heterosexual men. But through close readings of Latina/o/x gang literature and film, this book shows how these gang narratives visualize strategies that many women and gay gang members perhaps employ to appropriate and transform heterosexual male gangs. In doing so, they use these gangs to circumvent the psychological, cultural, ideological, ontological, and material effects of the coloniality of gender. In the gang narratives I study, Latina gang members use gang membership, culture, violence, crime, and masculinity to resist sexual and domestic violence when the State refuses to protect them. These same aspects of gang life also help them challenge the heteropatriarchal regulation of their autonomy, gender, and sexuality they experience inside and outside their Latina/o/x communities and families. The gay gang members also use and reconfigure these heterosexual gangs to not only challenge the sexual violence and homophobia they encounter from the US nation-state and Latina/o/x spaces, but to explore their sexual identities as well. Both the women and gay male gang members also develop alternative ontologies that contest intolerant ideologies that homogenize them as weak, powerless, fragile, and antithetical to hypermasculinity.

In sum, though gangs potentially lead to other forms of, or heighten, oppression and trauma—such as through police violence or the prison industrial complex—the gay and women gang members of the literature and film I explore use gang membership, violence, crime, culture, and masculinity to attain psychological, cultural, ontological, and material (de)colonial rewards, even if gang life only temporarily provides these. Through reshaping or strategically navigating male-dominated heterosexual gangs, the women and gay gang members in these narratives circumvent and challenge the abstract and physical manifestations of the coloniality of gender, thereby achieving status, power, recognition, belonging, respect, value, protection, security against sexual violence, a level of sovereignty, and improved financial stability.

Gang Girls, from la Pachuca to la Chola

While much of social science and humanities scholarship on women gang members has revolved around their alleged abjection, some scholars have begun to acknowledge women in gangs as full citizen-subjects. In Latina/o/x literary and cultural studies, theorizing gang girls as more than subordinate objects begins with la pachuca. The pachuca/os were a Mexican American counterculture that arose in the late 1930s in Los Angeles, and were famous for wearing the zoot suit and speaking Caló. The zoot suit style featured an excessively baggy suit jacket, trousers, and dress shirts, as well as a tando (fedora), calcos (shiny, pointy leather shoes), a lengthy watch chain that extended past the knee, and pompadour hairstyles. Mexican American women also wore a female version of the zoot suit, maintaining the pompadour and billowing jacket, but replacing the pants with tight and revealing skirts. During World War II, the US nation-state took the zoot suit as another reason to criminalize Mexican Americans. Because of wartime fabric shortages, many Americans viewed zoot suiters as unpatriotic and an internal enemy—especially since many zoot suiters were pachuca/o gang members, though pachuca/o gangs were less violent than contemporary gangs. The unpatriotic and internal enemy accusations contributed to the Zoot Suit Riots in June 1943, a week-long event where marines and sailors stalked through Los Angeles, hunting, beating, and raping Mexican American zoot suiters under the pretense of defending American citizens from the internal enemy.[114]

As with late-twentieth century gang members, Chicana/o/x culture, history, and cultural production often lionize el pachuco as an icon of nationalist resistance. As Rosa Linda Fregoso explains, the "pachuco is one of the principal actors in the Chicano narrative of cultural affirmation and resistance. He performs as a legendary figure of counterhegemonic masculinity for Chicano nationalists who see in him the embodiment of revolutionary identity and identification."[115] Because of the gang history of pachuca/os, the cultural, literary, and scholarly valorization of el pachuco as "the embodiment of revolutionary identity" points to gang membership as a (de)colonial practice. But the cultural and academic representation of the pachuca/o subculture concentrates on a male, heterosexual ideal that subsumes la pachuca. As Fregoso elaborates, la pachuca "remains his [el pachuco's] dangling object, unseen and unnamed within Chicano movement strategies insofar as their asymmetrical constructions of cultural and political resistance identities relegate the pachuca to an exotic image for public and private consumption."[116] Although la pachuca materializes in Chicana/o/x literary and cultural production, she usually appears only as a fetishized, sexualized object for consumer consumption, perpetuating stereotypical discourses about women participating in gangs solely as sexual labor for their male counterparts.

In *The Woman in the Zoot Suit*, however, Catherine S. Ramírez uncovers pachuca histories to divulge how pachuca gangs facilitated women's "incursions into the public sphere."[117] Ramírez illuminates how pachucas used fashion, language, and media representation to blur "the distinction between public and private" and combat "gender norms both within and beyond spaces of domesticity."[118] Other scholars have built from Ramírez in revealing how la pachuca's modern successor, la chola, similarly challenges Chicana/o/x heteropatriarchy through gang culture, crime, and violence. Fregoso, for instance, interprets Carmen Tafolla's poem "and when I dream dreams" and the film *Mi Vida Loca* (1993) to illustrate how these representations show how contemporary gangs accord the same liberation for women as did pachuca gangs of the past. Fregoso writes that *Mi Vida Loca* positively depicts "Chicana homegirls" as "independent and self-sufficient" because their girl gang "challenges the artificial divisions between the public and private sphere."[119] Like the pachucas of the early- and mid-twentieth century who rejected "proper" gender decorum through breaching domesticity, *Mi Vida Loca*, according to Fregoso, discloses how girl gangs enable Chicanas to construct new identities in the private and public spheres, and disrupt ideologies of "proper" gender decorum.

Additionally, in *Gang Nation*, Brown writes a chapter about gang girl narratives to build upon her observations that women in male-dominated heterosexual gangs are "consistently objectified and denied agency, reduced to poverty to be exchanged between men, their bodies receptacles of violence, territories on which the acts of war are played out."[120] By examining Yxta Maya Murray's novel *Locas* and Mona Ruiz's autobiography *Two Badges*, Brown unfurls these books' "representation of girl gang members' sense of resistance to and critique of oppressive forces emanating from the inherent contradiction of dominant US nationalism *as well as* the cause and effects of sexism within Chicano culture."[121] For Brown, the women in these texts create girl gangs to challenge heteropatriarchy in the nation-state and in their Latina/o/x communities.

While Ramírez, Fregoso, and Brown primarily employ humanities methodologies, and focus on a range of cultural forms (literature, film, poetry, media, performance), some social science scholarship on women in gangs corroborates much of their insistence on women finding gang membership generative. Vigil, for example, notes that gang violence and crime are potentially cathartic for female gang members. He writes that because "female youths" might experience "culture conflict, poverty, and associated family and school problems," "stricter childrearing experiences, tension-filled gender role expectations, and problems with self-esteem," "young females are now channeling that rage into holding their own in the violence of the street gang world."[122] Marie "Keta" Miranda works from Vigil's contentions to explain more explicitly how gangs are possibly productive for women, constructing an argument related to Fregoso's and Ramírez's, but from a social science perspective. In *Homegirls in the Public Sphere*, Miranda examines two Northern California girl gangs to reveal how female gang members "resist their localization and objectification" and "challenge prevailing representations of Latina/o youth, gang youth, and girls in particular."[123] Contesting the rote argument that gang membership arises from cultural deficiency, Miranda argues that the "bonds of friendship and solidarity found in the girls' gang" are "subjective responses to a social world that relegates youth in general to the margins."[124] For Miranda, this impetus for the formation of girl gangs signifies intersubjectivity, as a part of the benefits of girl gangs centers on "creating a group of street peers for social support and recreation" to "validate one's identity as inviolably superior to other groups in public space."[125]

Vigil, Miranda, Fregoso, Brown, Ramírez, and others have contributed excellent work in explaining how women achieve empowerment through gangs, but much of this scholarship focuses only on girl gangs, subsuming women who participate in mixed-gender or predominantly male gangs and, in the process, insinuating that women find only girl gangs emancipating. Al Valdez and Dana Peterson are two of the rare few who briefly consider that women in male-dominated gangs are not always marginal. In his history of Southern California Latina/o/x gangs, Valdez writes that in "some Latino street gangs, the gender barrier was broken.... In some cases, girls or women even became co-leaders of their gang" and "were involved in drive-by shootings, robberies, carjackings, and murders, and in some cases, they shared equal responsibility with their male cohorts for the protection of gang turf."[126] Similar to Valdez, Peterson observes that some predominantly male gangs in her study reject misogyny, enabling their female members to liberate themselves from patriarchal cultures through gang membership.[127]

While Peterson and Valdez recognize that predominantly male gangs are potentially rewarding for women, these contentions are either conditional on gangs that are not sexist, or they gloss over how "the gender barrier was broken" in Latina/o/x gangs. As such, analyses of the alienation and bigotry women may encounter in male-dominated gangs *and* of how women work within these parameters to claim citizenship and mobilize (de)colonial projects remain absent. In *Going Down to the Barrio: Homeboys and Homegirls in Change*, Moore briefly begins to allude to this topic when she describes the gender dynamics of the longstanding Chicana/o/x gangs El Hoyo Maravilla and White Fence. She notes that women from each gang claim that "[w]e didn't let the guys tell us what to do," and instead "used to boss the guys."[128] But though Moore hints at gendered tensions within the gangs and at women's success in navigating these obstacles, she never pursues the topic further, leaving unaddressed the role of violence in "boss[ing] the guys," *how* women achieve a non-second-class status in these primarily male gangs, or *how* women's power in White Fence and El Hoyo Maravilla may rely on harmful methods that depend on exacerbating the trauma of other multiply marginalized persons, something Moore has in common with previous scholarship on women in gangs.

Queering the Gang, or the Lack Thereof

Like scholarship on women in gangs, studies of gay gang members or members who "queer" gender and sexual norms in gang life are also lacking, perhaps more so. Nonetheless, a few scholars have recently attempted to initiate this conversation, and have produced invaluable insights that this book builds on. Lorena Galván, for example, studies Murray's *Locas* and Helena Maria Viramontes's *Their Dogs Came with Them* to show how the two books queer gang girl gender performativity. As Galván says, the novels "problematize gender norms by appropriating the tough defiant *Cholo* stance to redefine the *Chola*, thus positioning the *Chola* as both feminine and masculine."[129] Because the gang girls in these novels maintain some of their femininity while cholas, Galván views these characters as embodying a queer subject position that destabilizes gender normativity in Chicana/o/x cultural production, the "gender system in gang subculture," and "dominant patriarchal ideologies in an experimental way."[130] Rivera Fellah supplies a similar argument in her analysis of the duality of chola masculinity and femininity in Graciela Iturbide's photography series *Cholos/as*, contending that the cholas Iturbide photographs combine "their overdone hair and makeup" with "masculine attitudes and language of signs" to "problematise binary gender systems."[131]

Dovetailing with Galván's and Rivera Fellah's postulations on cholas queering gender, Dominique Johnson examines lesbian gang members who queer gender and sexual normativity in gang culture. Writing on the Philadelphia, African American, butch lesbian gang Dykes Taking Over (DTO), Johnson responds to what she considers a smear campaign against the DTO, as local television and print media copiously covered a "series of alleged incidents of same-sex sexual harassment by [DTO] gang members on heterosexual students."[132] According to Johnson, "Although the media coverage framed these incidents as sexual harassment, LGBT community members saw them as, at best, sensationalized and, at worse, fabricated by nervous parents and fanned by an overzealous local news media."[133] Without excusing the DTO's alleged actions, Johnson contemplates that the "lesbian students' behavior was the result of a lack of programs and services available for LGBTQ youth."[134] Although Johnson spends the crux of her article delineating the homophobia lesbian students encounter in secondary education, and the lack of institutional support available to them, she conjectures about the possibility of the DTO's sexual harassment of other students as reactions to bigotry: "Formation of gangs and their same sex sexual harassment of other students may be weapons against homophobia and a means by which they assert themselves in their masculinities."[135] With this line, Johnson insinuates the potential for (de)colonial projects in gangs that depend on violence against other women, and accounts for how an impetus for gang violence coagulates at race, gender, and sexuality. While Johnson never fully fleshes out this subject and limits her contentions to lesbian gangs, she valiantly constructs an avenue for further pursuing scholarship on this matter, and for applying her ponderances to gay men in gangs.

Cultural representations of gay men in gangs far outnumber depictions of lesbian gang members. Consequently, scholarship on gay male gang members exceeds the scant material on lesbian gang members, though the amount still remains small. Much of this scholarship on the representation of gay men in gangs, however, centers on outing the same-sex desire that gang literature and film often displace, not necessarily on the empowerment gay men may achieve—or their reasons for joining gangs. For instance, the two most popular gang texts in Latina/o/x literary and cultural studies that have amassed queer studies readings are Piri Thomas's memoir *Down These Mean Streets* and Edward James Olmos's *American Me*, a filmic adaption on the rise of the prison gang the Mexican Mafia. In explicating *American Me*, Daniel Enrique Pérez explores how its diegesis and its editing queer the film's antihero, Montoya Santana. Pérez observes that upon release from prison after serving a twenty-year sentence, Santana returns to the barrio and courts a Chicana named Julie. But, because Santana has spent most of his life in prison and has rarely interacted with women in a romantic way, "he is utterly unsuccessful at performing as a heteronormative male. He does not know how to dance, drive a car, or kiss Julie intimately."[136] Outside of prison and its activo/pasivo (penetrator/penetrated) gender and sexual system, which uses male-on-male sexual violence to achieve heterosexual masculinity and power, Santana struggles to perform as a heteronormative man in the barrio.[137]

According to Pérez, Santana's inability to adapt to the barrio's cultural codes and an environment with a larger population of women queer not only his gender, but also his sexuality. When trying to have sex with Julie—the first time he ever has sex with a woman—Santana cannot climax through vaginal intercourse and forcibly turns Julie over to sodomize her, as if he were having sex with a man in prison. During Santana's rape of Julie, the camera crosscuts between this scene and an all-male gang rape in prison. Pérez asserts that "Santana's homoerotic desire is expressed through the juxtaposition of the images of the male-on-male rape scene and his sexual encounter with Julie where he simulates homoerotic acts. . . . The closer the gang gets to raping their victim, the more aroused Santana gets."[138] For Pérez, these two scenes problematize activo/pasivo reasoning through insinuating that the activo sexual position indicates gay desire—a connotation that in many homophobic rationales only the pasivo carries—by juxtaposing same-sex and heterosexual rape and in Santana's preference for a rectum over a vagina.

Similarly, Frederick Luis Aldama reconsiders Santana's assumed heterosexuality by thinking through *American Me*'s incorporation of the activo/pasivo sexual system and the homoeroticism present in Santana's relationship with J. D., Santana's best "crime partner." Aldama argues that Santana inhabits a metaphorical activo position with various members of his gang as their hypermasculine, unmerciful, and truculent jefe but, over the course of the film, slowly deteriorates into a pasivo in his relations with J. D. As Aldama says, Santana "comes into an in-between ethnosexual identity that is both bully/top (the heterosexual macho anal penetrator) and also sissy/bottom (anally penetrated)."[139] Informing Aldama's reading, J. D. eventually betrays Santana and orders his death, which fellow gang members carry out via stabbing, signifying J. D.'s figurative penetration of Santana.[140]

Thomas's *Down These Mean Streets* also invokes a version of the activo/pasivo ideology to displace same-sex desire in gangs. Covering Thomas's journey as a gang member in Spanish Harlem during the mid-twentieth century, *Down These Mean Streets* features a sexual gang initiation that marks Thomas's evolution from an affiliate to a citizen-subject of his local clica. As a test of hypermasculinity, the gang and Thomas visit male-to-female crossdressers to receive oral sex. Before entering the crossdressers' apartment, Thomas remarks, "*I don't wanna go—but I gotta, or else I'm out, I don't belong in. And I wanna belong in! Put cara palo on, like it don't move you.*"[141] Although Thomas does not wish to receive oral sex from these crossdressers, he wants to earn membership in his gang and, thus, must wear a "cara palo" and prove his toughness, that he "wasn't gonna punk out first."[142] Because Thomas and his gang occupy activo positions in this scene (receiving, rather than performing, oral sex), Thomas displaces any potential for sexually desiring these crossdressers, instead viewing oral sex with them as a performance and validation of his hypermasculinity, and thereby demonstrating a pedigree worthy of full membership in his gang. As Brown elaborates on the gang and Thomas's mindset, "This 'transgression' serves to confirm their masculinity and heterosexuality and is evident throughout the scene, as Thomas and his boys refer to these men as 'faggots' and 'maricones,' further distancing the transvestites from themselves and strengthening through language the dichotomy of 'us' and 'them.'"[143] Though Thomas adopts an activo/pasivo rationale to reject the possibility of sexually desiring male-to-female crossdressers, Brown draws from Eve Sedgwick's concept of "erotic triangles" to disclose how the homosociality and homoeroticism of this scene cross into sexual desire between men, regardless of activo/pasivo displacement. According to Brown, "Homosocial bonding between the boys in the gang underwrites these sexual exchanges involving the transvestites as passive caricatures—bodies used in a ritual of proving who has 'heart' in the gang. But it is taken a step further, and the 'boys'' desire for each other is triangulated through the body of the transvestite."[144] Like many critics of *Down These Mean Streets*, Brown reads same-sex desire not between the crossdressers and the gang but between the men of the gang. The crossdressers mediate and facilitate the gang members' sexual desire for each other that their gay panic and homophobia disallow them from expressing.[145]

In contributing these interpretations, Pérez, Aldama, and Brown valuably show how gang narratives are mired in homophobic ideologies that de-suture sex from sexuality solely to displace the possibility of gay sexuality. But because cultural products like *American Me* and *Down These Mean Streets* displace sexual desire between men and never engage gay sexuality as a serious subject, these types of texts limit the theorization of how gay sexuality implicates gang life, violence, and masculinity. Although *Down These Mean Streets* and *American Me* include "queer" scenes, the homoerotic actions in these texts only act as *methods* through which gang members form the kinship bonds, hypermasculinity, and power of their gang. Gay sexuality never figures as a *reason* for a gang's emergence or violence.

While most scholarship on gay men in gangs focuses on their representation in cultural production, Vanessa R. Panfil has contributed the first study on actual gay men in gangs. In *The Gang's All Queer*, Panfil studies gay African American male gang members in Columbus, Ohio, to respond to what she calls the "heterosexual imaginary" in criminology.[146] Although Panfil recognizes that "gay gang- and crime-involved men have entered the broader consciousness thanks to popular culture"—such as the art of Hector Silva and Alex Donis that depicts homeboys in homoerotic positions—she contends that "criminology scholars remain stuck in a 'heterosexual imaginary' where assumed heterosexuality is not questioned, where queer folk don't exist."[147] Although unsatisfied with an academic propensity for imposing heterosexuality, Panfil also critiques criminal justice and criminology research that attempts to account for gay sexuality, arguing that this "literature focuses on gay men's victimization and thus implies gay men have little agency."[148] As such, *The Gang's All Queer* begins to uncover the agency and power gay men in gangs attain—how they might use gangs to "fight back" against "bias crimes, intimate partner violence, or homophobic bullying."[149] Panfil's work, thus, constructs a key route for interpreting gay gang members as (de)colonial, as she shows that gay sexuality does not negate men's capacity to participate in gang life. Though indispensable, Panfil's work on gay men achieving power and citizenship in gangs parallels past scholarship on girl gangs insofar as it conditions these observations on gay gangs only. Although Panfil condemns scholarship that exclusively centers on gay victimization, her discussion of gay men in heterosexual gangs only documents the trauma they encounter in these subcultures, finding that, in these gangs, "[g]ay men have been tortured by gang members," and "some gangs have formal rules against same-sex activity."[150] Panfil's book allocates no attention to the possibility of gay men successfully navigating, and achieving citizenship in, heterosexual gangs.

Furthermore, some scholars have questioned the validity of Panfil's study. Vernon Rosario, for example, criticizes Panfil's generalizing definition of a gang: "durable, street-oriented youth groups whose identity includes involvement in illegal activity."[151] As Rosario recognizes, under Panfil's definition of a "gang," she may dub gay men as gang members without them participating in an actual gang, but only partaking in "illegal activity." Correspondingly, Rosario points out that the gay gangs Panfil examines differ considerably from traditional gangs in that they "are not armed and have no territory to defend."[152] Because these gay gangs do not own territory in their barrios and might not engage in violence, many scholars reject deeming them gangs. Brown, for instance, likely would not consider these gay clicas counternations, as territory has an integral role in her counternation theory. Despite these critiques, Panfil's book is part of the corpus—including the work of Galván, Johnson, Brown, Pérez, and Aldama—that establishes the crucial foundation *Clicas* builds from in its theorization of gender and sexual "non-normativity" in heterosexual male gangs.

Organization of the Book

This book considers how Latina/o/x gang literature and film reveal how women and gay gang members appropriate, reinvent, and rearticulate gang violence, crime, culture, and masculinity to circumvent, undermine, and challenge the abstract and material effects of the coloniality of gender. Readers should note, however, that *Clicas* does not act as a catalog of narratives by and/or about women and gay gang members. Instead, it selects representative gang narratives that enable the theorization of how gender, sexuality, race, and class converge in (de)colonial projects in and through gangs, and that build off each other to complicate and expand the findings each text offers.[153]

I have organized the book in a manner that enables each successive chapter to further *Clicas*'s departure from the normative discussions permeating the scholarship on gangs. Chapter 2 focuses on Ana Castillo's *My Father Was a Toltec*, a poetic reflection on her father in a 1950s and 60s Chicago gang, and her own entrance into Chicago gang life. This chapter reimagines the boundaries of what academics might study when researching gangs. It elects to center the shared, gendered experience of (de)colonial gangs amongst gang members' families—what this book terms their "socialities"—pondering how gang life and culture shape the experiences of these socialities in the private and public spheres. Through a close reading of Castillo's poems, Chapter 2 discloses how Chicanas in the private sphere may appropriate the gang fashion, culture, and violence that seep into the home as an antiassimilationist strategy for circumventing mass poverty, vigilante violence, and Chicano patriarchy's regulation of their sexuality, gender, and autonomy. Furthermore, the chapter uncovers how the daughter-speaker of *My Father Was a Toltec* transforms the normative heterosexual hypermasculinity of conventional gang life into a queer homoerotic that acts as an ontological and a psychological (de)colonial politics for women uninvolved in gangs and relegated to the private sphere. In this way, Chapter 2 elucidates how Chicanas might use gang culture, violence, and masculinity to challenge the racialized, heteropatriarchal, and classed structures that compose the coloniality of gender.

Chapter 3 concentrates on concerns that *My Father Was a Toltec* and much of the scholarship on gang girls overlook—namely, the romanticization of gang violence, crime, and masculinity as (de)colonial praxis for women, and *how* female gang members attain citizenship and mobilize (de)colonial projects in heteropatriarchal, misogynist gangs. In addressing this aperture, Chapter 3 studies Yxta Maya Murray's *Locas* to show how women in Murray's novel perform racialized female masculinity to aggrandize their standing in their male-dominated gang so that they may bypass the harmful effects of the coloniality of gender for working-class Latinas in Echo Park, Los Angeles during the 1980s and 90s, such as domestic violence, psychological abuse, menial labor, and State neglect. In doing so, the chapter advances the overarching discussion of female masculinity by theorizing the masculinity that women gang members perform in *Locas* as a toxified, racialized female masculinity predicated on the violent abuse and devaluation of other working-class Latinas. Calling for an expanded understanding of how class and race intersect with female masculinity, the chapter argues that *Locas* identifies the toxicity of this type of racialized female masculinity as arising from the vulnerability and violability that the coloniality of gender imposes on Latinas.

Chapter 3 also refuses the frequent assertion that femininity automatically results in marginalization and ineligibility for citizenship in hypermasculine, male-dominated gangs. Rather, insofar as it examines racialized female masculinity as a (de)colonial performance, the chapter also identifies a (de)colonial femininity in illuminating how the female gang members in *Locas* use the performance to manipulate male gang members and heterosexual masculinity in order to secure avenues for citizenship and power in gangs. In this manner, Chapter 3 explains how women gang members might co-opt predominantly male gangs to initiate (de)colonial projects, and it unravels how the State and patriarchy contribute to subaltern persons relying on toxified (de)colonial projects.

Chapter 4 segues to further strategies that non-normative gang members employ for metamorphosing bigoted heterosexual gangs into (de)colonial subcultures, in this case focusing on gay men. The chapter centers on how gay men in gangs navigate and alter the logic of the modern gender/sexual system that informs heterosexual gang life, thus circumventing the abstract and material power coloniality wields over their lives. Primarily examining Dino Dinco's *Homeboy*, a documentary about Southern California gay Latino gang members, Chapter 4 draws from José Esteban Muñoz's theory of disidentification to contemplate how these men psychologically persist in their homophobic gangs and rearticulate gay sexuality into a signifier for violent hypermasculinity. In doing so, these gang members develop alternative ontologies and epistemologies that reject the homophobic ideologies of the coloniality of gender that regard gay men as fragile, weak, feminine, and subordinate. For these men, their sexuality does not render them failures in heterosexual gang life. The chapter thereby unearths how these gang members ironically find community in their heterosexual gangs to enact (de)colonial projects that combat the hate crimes and social and familial ostracism they encounter *outside* those gangs, though in a way that still reproduces toxified masculinities. Additionally, Chapter 4 charts how the exhibition of *Homeboy* operates as a (de)colonial performance through its establishment of a counterpublic that destabilizes normative gender and sexuality, and helps gay men in and outside of gangs attain feelings of belonging and catharsis.

Whereas the previous chapters focus on supposedly atypical gang members who succeed in heterosexual male-dominated gangs, Chapter 5 reconceptualizes gang violence, crime, and heterosexual hypermasculinity to contemplate how failure in gangs that espouse these ideals may also contribute to a sense of (de)colonial freedom. The chapter pursues this idea through interpreting Tadeo García's *On the Downlow* (2004)—a film about two gay men who fall in love with one another, despite their membership in rival Little Village, Chicago gangs: the Two Six and Latin Kings. This chapter reveals how the film shows that failure to meet gang expectations of violent, heterosexual hypermasculinity may not foreclose, but rather paradoxically enable, a sense of (de)colonial liberation for gay men in gangs. Chapter 5 unfurls this antinomy by exploring how the gay men of this film embrace their failure in gangs and in their barrio as a method for constructing a utopian futurity. In this utopian futurity, these men attain a sense of psychological and affective freedom through fantasizing about a world where they can escape the capitalist and sexual inequalities of the coloniality of gender. Chapter 5 thus shows how (de)colonial projects need not always entail conventional notions of success—that gangs might facilitate them through failure. Nonetheless, as much as these gay gang members develop utopian futurities that allow *them* to circumvent the coloniality of gender, these (de)colonial projects—like much of the (de)colonial work in gangs the previous chapters delineate—are not systemically revolutionary. The utopian futurities ironically hinge on an overarching investment in white capitalism (even if these men escape its inequalities) and ethnic and cultural betrayal, resulting in *On the Downlow* revising the anti-assimilationist ideals of Latina/o/x gang subcultures.

Clicas concludes with the specter that haunts this entire book, the terror that stands in as *the* Latin American gang, the gang US politicians, nativists, and racists constantly invoke to pathologize Latina/o/xs and Latin American immigrants: Mara Salvatrucha. Focusing on Javier Zamora's poetry collection *Unaccompanied*, which covers his migration from El Salvador to the United States, I reveal how Zamora's poems rearticulate the figure and masculinity of the Mara Salvatrucha gang member in a way that rejects the gang member/immigrant trope in Latina/o/x literature and film. As much as gang subcultures may enable their members to circumvent the extent to which coloniality regulates their lives, the State often recuperates the image of the gang member to demonize Latin American immigration and garner support for anti-immigrant legislation, suggesting that Latin American immigrants are ruthless, murderous gang members seeking to harm US citizens. For this reason, the book's afterword shows how the mere existence of Latina/o/x gang subcultures constitutes the paradoxical contradictions of what I am calling the (de)colonial.

Latina/o/x literature and film frequently attempt to challenge this gang stigma affecting Latin American immigrants, and engage the immigrant rights struggle through disassociating immigrants from gang members, often featuring a binary of a "good, hardworking" immigrant who contrasts with the "violent, bad" gang member. This trope, however, relies on what Lisa Marie Cacho terms valuing, a harmful process that ascribes "readily recognizable social value" through the "devaluation of an/other" who also often occupies a "poor, racialized, criminalized, segregated, legally vulnerable, and unprotected" status.[154] Zamora's poetic exploration of Mara Salvatrucha masculinity and gang members, however, departs from this binary, unveiling how Latina/o/x literature and immigrant rights discourse might bring these two figures together in productive ways that reveal and critique the coloniality afflicting both groups.

2 | THE SHARED EXPERIENCE OF (DE)COLONIAL GANG LIFE

IN 2016, JUAN JOSÉ MARTÍNEZ D'AUBUISSON INTERVIEWED A WOMAN named Medea about her experiences with gangs. Medea explains that she began dating a gang member who was renowned for murdering a rival leader "dos veces" (two times), shooting him to death and later exhuming his body to decapitate him.[1] Although not a gang member when she began dating this man, Medea in part continued her relationship with him because she felt "protegida con él" (protected with him).[2] Eventually, Medea's relationship with her partner facilitated her own gang membership, as the extensions of gang life became too tempting for her to resist. Medea's transition into a gang reveals how the clutches of gang membership extend far beyond the actual clica, implicating those uninvolved in gangs but in proximity to people in them.

Medea's story is not alone in attending to the shared experience of gang life. Many novels, poems, and memoirs attest to gang life affecting members' families, even if their kin refuse to gangbang, such as Ernesto Quiñonez's *Bodega Dreams*, Luis J. Rodriguez's *Always Running*, Sister Souljah's *The Coldest Winter Ever*, Jesmyn Ward's *Men We Reaped*, and Ana Castillo's *My Father Was a Toltec*. The shared experience of gangs that many of these narratives recognize often means a shared experience amongst women because of the frequency of these subcultures as male-dominated organizations. Although many literary writers address women's shared experience of gangs, scholarship and US media rarely observe or take seriously the psychological, emotional, ontological, and material ordeals women undergo alongside their gangbanging husbands, boyfriends, fathers, brothers, and sons.[3] Indeed, the scholarly acknowledgement of gang members' families primarily centers only on how abusive homes compel at-risk youth to join gangs.

This chapter fills the lacuna by building from Ernesto Javier Martínez's contention that queer persons have a *"muted sociality* of queerness," that queerness "is a social and shared experience, even as oppressive ideologies work at making it seem less real and shared, and even if the queer subject often seems isolated in the process."[4] In examining how queer of color literatures have shifted from narrating from the perspective of the queer subject of color to the queer's sociality, which consists of "the queer subject's siblings, friends, parents, and neighbors" and "relationship to various people, places, [and] histories," Martínez argues that queers' socialities can provide "a deeper understanding of the intersubjective and social contexts in which queer subjects come into being" and the "shared quality of queer experience."[5] Working from Martínez's suggestion that the overlooked socialities of queers inform, influence, and experience queer identity, this chapter explores male and female gang members' female socialities, and how gangs and gang culture shape and determine these women's life chances and experiences in the private and public spheres.

This chapter pursues this endeavor by interpreting Ana Castillo's *My Father Was a Toltec*, a poetry collection that, amongst other topics, chronicles Castillo's childhood experience of her father in a mid-twentieth century Chicago gang (the Toltecs), as well as her own teenage entrance into a gang. On the one hand, *My Father Was a Toltec* suggests that many of the (de)colonial possibilities that gangs accord Latino men hinge on exacerbating the hardship of their female family members who do not participate in gangs. The book reveals how male gang members may relegate women to the private sphere and inundate them with domestic labor so these men can reap the (de)colonial benefits of gang life. Yet on the other hand, private life and the public life that gangs facilitate are not always oppositional, but rather hybrid, in *My Father Was a Toltec*. As much as the (de)colonial projects Castillo's father enacts in the Toltecs depend on the suppression of his female kin, his presence in their home also admits gang culture into their lives. Ironically, this admittance creates an avenue for his daughter to enter gangs and use them to circumvent and resist the effects of the coloniality of gender, including racialized sexualized violence, patriarchal subordination, and financial penury. In this way, *My Father Was a Toltec* suggests that the anti-assimilationist ideologies of Latina/o/x gang culture potentially enable Latinas to challenge sexism in their communities without facing the agringada accusations they commonly encounter when partaking in feminist projects.[6]

The Racial Cultural Politics of Twentieth Century Chicago Gang Life

Written across a fifteen-year period in the late-twentieth century, Castillo's *My Father Was a Toltec* features eight chapters, each working to create a chronological narrative of Castillo's maturation from a young girl to the Chicana feminist writer many now perceive her as. *Clicas* focuses on the first chapter of her collection—the one that addresses gang life. The first chapter's eight poems, which I interpret collectively as a sequential ensemble, depict gangs as (de)colonial for their members, but in a way that often depends on the suppression of their female socialities. In doing so, *My Father Was a Toltec* traces Castillo's and her mother's shared experiences of her father in the Toltecs, and her development into the appellation she adopts as a teenager: la Heredera (the heiress), her father's successor to the Toltec throne.

Set in the 1950s, 60s, and 70s, Castillo's Toltec poems center the racial and sartorial politics of the Irish, Italian, and Mexican American gang scene in the Near West, Lower West, and South Sides of Chicago. Irish and Italian gangs in Chicago arose with these two groups' immigration to the city in the nineteenth and twentieth centuries, but Irish and Italian gang membership and culture did not peak until the 1950s and 60s. During this era, these two ethnic groups were known for developing "greaser gangs" like the Playboys, Taylor Street Jousters, Ventures, C-Note$, Simon City Royals (now primarily a prison gang), and the famed Gaylords. Although not synonymous with the greaser subculture, many of these white greaser gangs borrowed cultural aesthetics from the greaser scene. As James O'Connor and Damen Corrado explain, "[B]eing a greaser didn't mean you were a gang member. To be a greaser was to be a man, to like a particular type of music, to build or drive or race hotrods, or just preserve a lifestyle of years past."[7] In contrast, white Chicago greaser gangs were more concerned with mimicking the sartorial image of the greaser and with developing anti-Latina/o/x, anti-black, and white supremacist ideologies. Members of greaser gangs were predominantly from working-class European immigrant enclaves in Chicago, such as Bridgeport of the South Side and Little Italy of the Near West Side, and they adopted the "greasy hair, black or white fitted T-shirts, leather jacket, denim jeans, and black boots" of the greaser subculture.[8]

Beyond the iconic leather jacket, white greaser gangs also wore varsity sweaters to signal the semiotics of mid-twentieth century Chicago gang life. These gangs would attach onto their sweaters symbols or lettering they associated with their gang, such as the Playboy bunny (an image that multiple gangs, including Latina/o/x gangs, have used) or a Ku Klux Klansman (a mascot that the Italian C-Note$ and Gaylords each embraced).[9] Gangs of this era wore two styles of sweaters, black-body ones with colored trim and the inverse of this scheme. The colored-body sweaters were "party sweaters" that gang members wore in recreational settings to represent their gang, whereas the black-body sweaters were "war sweaters" that gangs donned during battles with rivals (Figures 2.1 and 2.2).[10] In addition to the colors of their sweaters, gang members also wore them in specific ways to convey their intentions when in another gang's territory. As Erica Gunderson writes, "Gang members would drape their sweaters over their arms when entering enemy territory to indicate they were not looking for a fight."[11] Oftentimes, gang members would attempt to disrespect rivals through stealing and remodeling rivals' sweaters, usually turning the patches on the sweater upside down. Chicago gang historian Zach Jones illuminates the competition over and importance of these sweaters: "It was just as coveted to beat up and steal a rival gang member's sweater as it was to hold onto your own. . . . Gangs would have prized collections of stolen sweaters that some guys hung onto for many years. . . . [T]he more you get, the more of a badass you are."[12] Eventually, the sweater practice ended after gangs came to consider them a liability, realizing that police used them to identify and harass gang members.[13] By the 1990s, the sweater game would fall out of fashion in favor of Starter sports jackets and caps.[14]

The greaser and sweater style were features not only of the Italian and Irish gangs of this era, but were also typical of the Latina/o/x gangs that formed in response to Irish and Italian racism.[15] During World War II, many Mexicans immigrated to the Near West Side and later to the Lower West Side, after the construction of the Eisenhower and Dan Ryan Expressways and the expansion of the University of Illinois, Chicago campus pushed them south.[16] These migration patterns meant that once predominantly Italian, Irish, Czech, and Polish areas were transforming into Mexican American enclaves. By the 1970s, Pilsen of the Lower West Side would become primarily Mexican American. Italian and Irish gangs, which were already largely racist (evident in the usage of KKK iconography), reacted to a growing Mexican American presence and cultural differences by violently lashing out against Mexican Americans—seemingly attempting to drive them out of the city. For instance, Mark Watson, a former member of the Simon City Royals, elucidates the

Figure 2.1 *Party sweater of the Cicero Noble Knights, a gang that lasted for almost forty years. Courtesy & copyright © by Jinx.*

resentment the Irish and Italians held toward Latina/o/xs. He claims that "immigrants from Mexico and Puerto Rico outnumbered the immigrants coming from all the other countries on the Earth combined," and constituted a "Hispanic invasion" that ultimately brought "guns, drugs, and violence."[17] For Watson, Puerto Ricans and Mexican Americans not

Figure 2.2 *Palmer Street Gaylords war sweater, its tipped cross showcasing the gang's investments in white supremacist, Ku Klux Klan imagery. Courtesy & copyright © by Jinx.*

only imported violence and crime into Chicago but culturally and economically altered the city in a way that harmed white populations. As he writes, "[E]ntire sections of Chicago went from English-speaking to Spanish-only.... It was as if half of Chicago was off-limits to us."[18] These geographic/cultural boundaries that Latina/o/xs supposedly created, in Watson's mind, cut whites out of the workforce because Chicago "insisted that all city departments have Spanish-speaking staff on hand at all times," which meant "locking us out of many of the good city jobs," an issue that built upon the problem of post-deindustrialization factory jobs apparently only "going to the Mexicans."[19] Beliefs about Latina/o/x immigrants similar to Watson's resulted in many Irish and Italian gangs forming a coalition, operating under the name the United Fighting Organization (UFO), to attempt to curtail "the spread of Hispanic Immigration."[20] In the 1970s, the Gaylords would even revise the meaning of their acronym, dubbing Gaylords as standing for Great American Youth Leading Our Right Destroying Spics.

After experiencing this racist harassment in the mid-twentieth century, many Mexican Americans in the Lower West and Near West Sides formed their own street gangs, such as Ambrose, the Latin Counts, the Spartans, and the Rampants, to fight off Italian and Irish attacks. These gangs would not only mirror Italian and Irish gangs in adopting greaser aesthetics and the varsity sweater style, but they would also form their own coalition to combat the UFO and to protect Latina/o/xs: the United Latino Organization (ULO).[21] Later in the twentieth century, many of the smaller Latina/o/x gangs that had emerged in the Near and Lower West Sides would become extinct, subsumed by larger Latina/o/x gangs that reign over the gang scene in this space today, such as the Latin Counts, Ambrose, the Bishops, Party People, the Satan Disciples, and La Raza.

The Toltecs that Castillo writes about were one of the many smaller Mexican American gangs that formed in response to Irish and Italian racism. They inhabited approximately the Lower and Near West Sides of Chicago before eventually fading out. The Toltecs appropriated their name from the indigenous Toltec civilization that prospered in now Central America during the tenth through twelfth centuries CE. The later Maya and Aztecs regarded the Toltecs with immense prestige; the Aztecs claimed the Toltecs as their ancestors and conveyed their reverence for the nation with the Nahuatl expression Toltecayotl, which denoted having a "Toltec heart" and excelling in every facet of life.[22] As Castillo more colloquially explains, "No Aztec worth his salt did not claim lineage to that civilization."[23] Moreover, Elizabeth Salas claims that the Toltecs espoused gender egalitarian ideals, as Toltec queens not only often ruled the civilization, but Toltec women also fought alongside men in war.[24] Toltec legends even suggest that when

Queen Xochitl died, her spilt blood formed the phrase "This is the end of the Toltecs."[25] While the modern gang built from the Aztec tradition of idealizing the Toltecs by associating the name Toltec with resistance and prestige, the gang bearing this name partially departed from the indigenous nation's gender egalitarianism—a topic Castillo broaches in her collection's first poem: "The Toltec."

Set in the 1950s, "The Toltec" represents gangs as materially, ontologically, and psychologically liberating for the daughter-speaker's father, with violence and mid-twentieth century Chicago gang fashion having pivotal roles in his gang life. In its entirety, the poem reads:

> My father was a Toltec.
> Everyone knows he was *bad*,
> Kicked the Irish-boys-from-Bridgeport's
> ass. Once went down to South Chicago
> to stick someone
> got chased to the hood
> running through the gangway
> swish of blade in his back
> the emblemed jacket split in half.
>
> Next morning, Mami
> threw it away.[26]

The father's "emblemed jacket split in half" connotes either the Chicago gang practice of emblazoning gang insignias onto varsity sweaters or the leather jacket of the greaser image that Latina/o/x (as much as Italian and Irish) gangs adopted. With the split jacket, this opening poem begins to suture style and aesthetics to the Toltecs and the father's public life, a theme manifesting throughout much of the first chapter of *My Father Was a Toltec*. For instance, in a later poem called "Saturdays," the daughter-speaker also defines the father by fashion, commenting on his habit of donning a "tailor-made silk suit."[27] These repeated references to the father's clothing accent the connection between style and ideology and how, in the first chapter of Castillo's poetry collection, fashion often signals counterhegemonic ideologies that materialize through violence.

In "The Toltec," the "swish of a blade in his back" of his "emblemed jacket" might accent the precariousness of gang life, but the father earning this rip in Bridgeport of the South Side of Chicago elucidates the (de)colonial projects he enacts against the US capitalist colonial structure and the racist Irish gangs working to uphold this white supremacist regime. Throughout most of the nineteenth and twentieth centuries, Bridgeport had historically been an Irish enclave entrenched in anti-black and anti-Latina/o/x racism. Town residents often held pro-Confederate rallies during the Civil War, and targeted black Americans during the Great Migration.[28] As Mike Amezcua says, black Americans migrating to the "Black Belt" of South Chicago "during the Great Migration on the promise of freedom from Jim Crow encountered a deeply entrenched localism and a white populace ready to preserve a hierarchical racial order."[29] Bridgeport's Irish gangs were integral in upholding this town's "entrenched localism" and "hierarchical racial order," perhaps most famously in the 1919 race riots when the Hamburg Club and Ragen's Colts gangs hunted and fought blacks who were protesting the killing of Eugene Williams, a seventeen-year-old boy who was stoned to death after swimming at an all-white beach in South Chicago. The Hamburg Club and Ragen's Colts also partook in political corruption and voter intimidation. Operating under the directives of Cook County Commissioner Frank Ragen, Ragen's Colts engaged in ballot-stuffing, whereas Richard Joseph Daley, a member of the Hamburg Club who became mayor of Chicago from 1955 through 1976, used the gang as "Irish toughs" who "terrorized and beat people senseless" to manipulate votes and ensure that the Irish controlled political offices.[30] Bridgeport would later see the development of other racist white gangs called HEADS, an acronym for Help Eliminate and Destroy Spics.

With this racist climate in mind, the father of "The Toltec" venturing south to "Kic[k] the Irish-boys-from-Bridgeport's / ass" during the 1950s suggests that gang life has multiple (de)colonial consequences for the father and Toltecs. Because of Irish gangs' racism toward Latina/o/xs in the mid-to-late twentieth century and Bridgeport as a haven for this racial animus, the father's violence toward these Irish acts as a (de)colonial violence against agents of US white supremacy and racism. The father deploys violence as a means of defying the subaltern status that white Atlantic immigrants and the US nation-state impose on him and, in the process, helps his gang "win space," expanding its territory and defending its sovereignty from Irish gangs. In this way, the father and the Toltecs respond to the material conditions of a US capitalist colonial structure that denies and inhibits property ownership for working-class Latina/o/xs. By partaking in a gang war against an ethnic group that works to suppress Latina/o/xs to ascend into whiteness, the father and the Toltecs strive to amass land and territory to call their own. They thereby potentially augment the space where the gang can further circumvent the racialized poverty present in coloniality through participating in black market economies, as well as through claiming territory in the face of 1950s urban renewal pushing Mexican Americans out of the Near West Side.[31]

Additionally, this poem's representation of the father suggests that he also attains ontological and psychological (de)colonial rewards through his gang fashion and violence against the Irish. As the speaker of the poem says, "My father was a Toltec. / Everyone knows he was *bad*."[32] The Irish are not the only persons aware of the father's reputation, as "Everyone" accounts for all persons in the father's barrio. This sociality does not acknowledge the father's existence with a Fanonian "Look! A Negro" hailing that dehumanizes him, but instead regards the father as exemplifying the "bad." In this line, "bad" functions in the way the word operates in slang dialects in working-class communities of color—often signaling an attractive style or impressively combative, tough, and dangerous person who provokes awe or admiration. The connotations of an appealing style and a rowdy and truculent persona align with the father's actions and fashion, as in his violence against the Irish and in his shredded jacket bearing gang insignias that telecast his (de)colonial ideology. When the daughter-speaker attests that everyone deems her father "*bad*," she is expressing that these particular socialities find him a person to admire because of how he stylishly throws down in his gang jacket against white ethnic groups that strive to maintain many Mexican Americans' alterity. Consequently, his reputation for fashion and violence enables the father to attain a status, recognition, power, and fame in his barrio that contest and compensate for the potential debasement, meager social standing, and inferiority that accompany his racialized social status in the 1950s/60s United States.

Violence, Masculinity, and Colonization/Coloniality

In *The Wretched of the Earth*, Fanon argues that decolonial violence "is a cleansing force" that "frees the native from his inferiority complex," making "him fearless and restor[ing] his self-respect."[33] In addition to violence, women's bodies are often central to subaltern heteropatriarchal persons shedding inferiority complexes. Indeed, in a more extreme length, these persons often develop new ontologies and a perverse sense of "self-respect" through enacting violence against women. Many psycho-sexual (de)colonial projects often work through the symbolic possession of women's bodies because of the racialized sexualized violence of colonialism. This is a type of violence that persists in present day coloniality, such as in the high occurrence of rape against black women and in the poor prosecution rates of their abusers. Colonial projects normatively rely on violence (especially sexual) against women not only to create psychological and material terror for women, but also to fracture the psyches of, and emasculate, rulers of heteropatriarchal societies. For example, in *An Account, Much Abbreviated, of the Destruction of the Indies*, Bartolomé de las Casas writes of the role of racialized sexualized violence during the Spanish Conquest of the New World: "The Christians would smite them [native Americans] with their hands and strike them with their fists and beat them with sticks and cudgels, until they finally laid hands upon the lords of the villages. And this practice came to such great temerity and shamelessness and ignominy that a Christian captain did violate the wife of the greatest king, the lord of all the island."[34] According to Las Casas, Spanish soldiers tactically rape the wife of the most powerful native American king, presuming an ideology of heteropatriarchal control and trying to imply that the "lord of all the island" cannot halt the Spanish from arrogating his "possessions," including land and women. For this reason, while the racialized sexualized violence of colonialism primarily targets women, Maldonado-Torres argues that this type of violence symbolically renders colonized men "feminized" and "penetrable subjects,"—a status implicitly continuing in the coloniality of gender.[35] Emma Pérez has termed this racial-sexual dynamic amongst the colonizer and colonized the "Oedipal-conquest-triangle," which she, similar to Maldonado-Torres's contention, interprets as rendering "the mestizo male" a "castrated man in relation to the white-male-colonizer father."[36] For Pérez, racially subaltern men develop a castration anxiety over "losing it [the masculinity and power that the penis symbolically connotes in heteropatriarchal societies]" and over the "fear that his will never match the supreme power of the white man's."[37]

Colonialism relies on racialized sexualized violence for psychological and physical conquest, and symbolically renders colonized men "feminized," "penetrable" persons insecure over their masculinity's capacity to match "the power of the white man's." Certain (de)colonial projects might therefore also operate through the logic of the coloniality of gender. In so doing, they compensate for, or nullify, the "castration anxiety" of the Oedipal-conquest-triangle, often materializing through the symbolic repossession of stolen "property"—again, land and women. Pérez sees an obsession with pornography as one of the avenues through which colonized men might psycho-sexually repair fragile masculinities in an attempt to mimic the hegemonic masculinities of the "white-male-colonizer father." She writes that pornography "helps him swear that he no longer suffers from Oedipal anxiety. Women become his idea—castrated, passive, and eternally feminine in his eyes, in his gaze."[38] This dynamic between patriarchal subaltern masculinities and the symbolic collection of women via pornography manifests in other sexual practices as well, such as in womanizing. As in collecting pornography, certain subaltern masculinities may entail womanizing or the "possession" of both subaltern and/or hegemonic (read white) women to prove symbolically and psycho-sexually that the colonizer has not rendered the masculine racial Other inferior or effeminate.[39] Regarding the "possessing" of hegemonic women specifically, subaltern persons performing these types of masculinities also gender (de)colonial "violence." They reverse colonization's/coloniality's use of racialized sexualized violence by carrying out an offensive and emasculating attack on colonizers (or those occupying a hegemonic status in coloniality) through philandering with—or "stealing"— white women. As Pérez says, "Chicanos are usually incensed when Chicanas marry the 'enemy'—white men," but they, "on the other hand, practice male prerogative and marry white women to defy, and collaborate with, the white father."[40] As such, whether philandering with white women or women of color, the subaltern subject subscribing to this toxified understanding of masculinity uses women to respond to colonial history and its legacy, proving that masculinity and power remain intact.[41]

Castillo's Toltec poems represent this type of subaltern masculinity as part of the father's gang persona, which not only entails (de)colonial violence against whites, but also includes maintaining a dandyish visage to attract and carouse with other (possibly white) women in the public sphere, despite having a wife at home. For instance, in "Saturdays," the daughter-speaker remarks that the father "donned the tailor-made silk suit" before leaving for a night out—without his wife.[42] As the daughter-speaker says, her father "married her, a Mexican / woman, like his mother, not like / they were in Chicago, not like / the one he was going out to meet."[43] The father forsakes his Mexican wife in favor of another woman unlike her. While this contrast between his paramour and his wife may involve multiple distinctions, these include the possibility of the father having a white lover. This is even more likely when considering his other (de)colonial actions in gang life, and the ways that philandering with white women potentially defies the symbolic "white-male-colonizer father" and provides a sense of psycho-sexual restoration to men idealizing certain patriarchal subaltern masculinities.

The father's philandering, however, discloses a divide between his heterosexual gang persona and his female sociality, a point that the final stanza of "The Toltec" underscores. In "The Toltec," the mother remains separate from and opposed to gang life and culture. This is indicated by her throwing out her husband's emblemed gang jacket ("Next morning, Mami / threw it away"), and the bracketing of her character in a separate stanza, so that she never comes into contact, either in content or in form, with her husband.[44] Furthermore, her seemingly minor presence in a discrete, two-line stanza implies her marginality and invisibility, both amongst her barrio and to her husband (though not to the daughter-speaker and, perhaps, not to girls and women). Whereas "Everyone" knows the daughter-speaker's father, no one in this poem—not even her husband—engages the mother or acknowledges her existence. Instead, she remains like an afterthought in the poem, as her narrative action consists solely of trashing the father's gang jacket—a deed that, while minor, may connote her symbolic resistance to the way her husband's Toltec lifestyle alienates her.

In his explication of "The Toltec," Rafael Pérez-Torres measures how the poem engages Chicana/o/x cultural memory, contending that "The Toltec" follows the Chicana/o/x literary tradition of mythologizing the male gang member as "the quintessence of nonconformity and resistance."[45] While "The Toltec" does romanticize the male gang member as (de)colonial, this poem and "Saturdays" also simultaneously criticize this figure. Both poems reveal how his (de)colonial gang life also depends on the marginalization of his female sociality, the father forsaking and neglecting his wife as he carouses with other women and attains fame, status, and territory through gang life. However, as with *Clicas* more generally, my analysis extends beyond the observation that female socialities are antithetical to gang life, and the resulting scholarly tendency to abandon the discussion at this point in favor of further examination of resistance for men in gangs. Rather, this chapter moves away from the father to scrutinize what lies within the mother's two solitary lines, within her marginality in the book's opening poem. For answers, I turn this initial page of *My Father Was a Toltec* to encounter the mother's and daughter's shared experiences of gang life, which transpire behind the closed doors of the private sphere.

The Absent Father as Colonial Apparatus

In studying the Toltec chapter of Castillo's poetry collection, Adriana Estill contends that "the father about whom this daughter-speaker writes represents not authority but rather rebellion."[46] While the father may represent "rebellion," the early poems of the Toltec chapter suggest that the father does not *entirely* represent revolt for the daughter-speaker, because his gang life hinges on the elision of his wife and daughter. Beginning with "Electra Currents"—the poem that follows "The Toltec"—the daughter indicates that she and her mother experience the father's gang lifestyle as an absent fatherism/husbandism that exacerbates a nexus of oppression where the family, domesticity, heteropatriarchy, and effects of capitalist inequality coagulate. "Electra Currents" reads:

> Llegué a tu mundo
> sin invitación,
> sin esperanza
> me nombraste por
> una canción.
>
> Te fuiste
> A emborrachar.[47]
>
> [I arrived to your world
> without invitation,
> without hope
> you named me after
> a song.
>
> You went
> to get drunk.]

The daughter-speaker notes that detachment has permeated her relations with her father since her birth. Like "The Toltec," the poem's form underscores the distance between the father and daughter, and what each represents, by bracketing off the characters in separate stanzas. Although the first stanza discloses the daughter's birth as unplanned (at least, from her perspective), the stanza also suggests promising relations between the two. Unlike the mother and father in "The Toltec," not only do these two characters inhabit a stanza together, but the father naming his daughter after a song expresses an emotional investment in her.[48] Despite these early indications that portend auspicious kinship ties between the two, the father quickly abandons his daughter in favor of alcohol, which the poem also emphasizes in the father's desertion of his daughter in form, the father leaving the communal first stanza for his own, where his bottle awaits.

Furthermore, the contrast between these two stanzas and characters indicates a dissonance between the distinct life chances that each stanza and character represent. According to Rosa Linda Fregoso, "the private realm is more than the home, for the private encompasses both the official economy of paid employment (the private system of market relations) as well as the family (the private lifeworld sphere)."[49] While Fregoso departs from many separate spheres theorists in reading paid employment as private (a point I return to shortly), she adheres to traditional theorizations of the public and private spheres in conceiving of the family as private. Thus, whereas the daughter and the first stanza imply a life committed to the private sphere and attached to the nuclear family, the second stanza connotes a life free of private responsibility. Instead, the second stanza evokes the recreational liberty to travel as one pleases throughout drinking spaces in the public sphere—the sphere where the father mobilizes material, ontological, and psychological (de)colonial projects through gang life. The daughter's presence, then, represents not only a threat to the resistance that the Toltecs accord the father, but also the "threat" of the private sphere regulating and policing his life. While the fame and admiration the father receives from his barrio combat the belittled, abject status that the US nation-state often imposes on many people of color, the intersubjective recognition and esteem the father might receive from his wife and daughter do not appear to satisfy him. Instead, he continually forsakes their potential appreciation of him for the abstract and physical rewards of gang life in the public sphere.

This theme of the absent father manifests throughout "Red Wagons" and "Saturdays" as well. In contrast to "Electra Currents," however, these two poems focus on the mother's and daughter's lives in the private sphere, divulging the effects of absent fathers for the female socialities of men in gangs who do not envision these women alongside them. In particular, "Red Wagons" attends to the daughter's experience of her gangbanging, absent father:

> In grammar school primers
> the red wagon
> was for children
> pulled along
> past lawns on a sunny day.
> Father drove into
> the driveway. "Look,
> Father, look!"
> Silly Sally pulled Tim
> on the red wagon.
>
> Out of school,
> the red wagon carried
> kerosene cans
> to heat the flat.
> Father pulled it to the gas
> station
> when he was home
> and if there was money.
>
> If not, children went to bed
> in silly coats
> silly socks; in the morning
> were already dressed
> for school.[50]

Whereas the father receives adulation from his barrio for his reputation for violence and fashion, the daughter of this poem, whom, as a working-class Chicana, the US nation-state relegates to a miniscule social standing, also yearns for intersubjective recognition. But where the father renounces the nuclear family in favor of a gang life that provides him adoration and a heightened social status, the Chicana daughter aspires to jettison her social invisibility in the US nation-state, and potentially in her barrio, through kinship bonds within her nuclear family. She cries out for her father to recognize her existence ("Look, / Father, look!") on the scarce occasions that he returns home. Yet, as "Red Wagons" later insinuates, the father rarely grants his daughter this desire, because he maintains an infrequent and arbitrary presence in the home, instead preferring the company of his camaradas and other (possibly white) women. "Red Wagons" thus intimates that fathers whose gang lives require a rejection of the nuclear family force the women of their families to experience these men's gang membership as an absent fatherism that exacerbates their social invisibility.

Additionally, as much as "Red Wagons" underscores the intersubjective and abstract consequences of absent fathers for these men's socialities, the poem also spotlights the material effects of absent fatherism on the families. Inundated by poverty, the young children who likely cannot physically haul kerosene cans in their wagon "to heat the flat" must rely on their father to do so, "when he was home / and if there was money." But because the father maintains an unpredictable presence in the home, the children often "went to bed / in silly coats / silly socks." Incapable of heating their flat, the children must wear their school clothes to sleep, to keep warm. As a result, when they wake in the morning, they are "already dressed for school" but must attend appearing "silly" in their sleep-wrinkled clothing. As mentioned earlier, fashion in the opening chapter of *My Father Was a Toltec* has an integral and omnipresent role: the father weaponizes style to participate in ideological warfare, signifying a politics of (de)colonial gang life. But whereas, for the father, fashion connotes resistance, power, and acclaim, for the children of "Red Wagons," clothing signals and heightens their marginality, poverty, and abjection. These connotations specifically arise as a result of the father not lighting the kerosene because his gang life requires a repudiation of the nuclear family. They materialize not only in the father's unavailability to haul the kerosene, but also in the family's penury ("when he was home / and if there was money"), which, as I soon show, the father's gang life contributes to as well. In short, the father's psychologically and materially liberating membership in the Toltecs depends on aggravating the hardship of the women of his nuclear family.

In "Red Wagons," the mother's absence resonates conspicuously, as does the financial juxtaposition between the father's lavish, customized clothing and his children's poverty. Addressing these preponderances,

"Saturdays" advances Castillo's chronological narrative to reveal how women's internalization of—or adherence to—the ideologies of the coloniality of gender helps enable material and psychological resistance for men in gangs. "Saturdays" also discloses how absent fatherism systemically produces absent motherism for many working-class Latina/o/x families, igniting a cyclical pattern where gang members' female socialities experience gang life, as well as the family, as their burden to bear. "Saturdays" begins with the lines, "she worked all week / away from home, gone from 5 to 5."[51] Besieged by poverty, the mother works from 5 am to 5 pm, to house and feed her children, and to supplement the household income that her absent husband does not sufficiently contribute to because he prefers a life of drinking, philandering, and gang wars. Consequently, the family's financial destitution that the father's gang life augments also engenders absent motherism, escalating the children's feelings of invisibility as the mother's and father's infrequent presences impede both parents from regularly recognizing their children's subjectivity.

Since the father's (de)colonial gang life transpires primarily outside the realm of family and domesticity, the mother's continual absence from, and paid employment outside, the home may (for some) suggest access to the public sphere and its liberating freedoms. As Nancy Fraser says, the term "public sphere" "has been used by many feminists to refer to everything that is outside of the domestic or familial sphere. Thus the 'public sphere' in this usage conflates at least three analytically distinct things: the state, the official-economy of paid employment, and arenas of public discourse."[52] Following Jürgen Habermas's theoretical model of the "public sphere," Fraser rejects the tendency to homogenize the public sphere as subsuming every facet of the world outside of the home, domesticity, and "private" life. Rather, for Fraser and Habermas, the public sphere refers to "a theater in modern societies in which political participation is enacted through the medium of talk. It is the space in which citizens deliberate about their common affairs, hence, an institutionalized arena of discursive action."[53] Understanding the public sphere as an arena of public discourse that (ideally) epitomizes democracy, Habermas and Fraser view the official-economy of paid employment as disparate from the public sphere, because the public sphere "is not an arena of market relations but rather one of discursive relations."[54] Thus, as Fregoso observes, Habermas and Fraser consider the "(official) capitalist economy" as instead endemic to the "'private' system of market relations."[55]

While I do not reduce the public sphere solely to a theater of public discourse—instead regarding various aspects of public life and space discrete from family and domesticity as also comprising the public—I adhere to Habermas's and Fraser's re-conceptualization of the official-economy of paid employment as private. As Fregoso explains, for working-class Chicanas, deeming employment private "is important ... because in order to support their families, Chicana working-class women are allowed to work outside the home in the 'private' official economy of paid employment."[56] Although many working-class Chicanas and Latinas access employment outside the home and, thus for some, the public sphere, the official-economy of paid employment does not necessarily lead to the typical benefits that citizens of a non-subaltern status amass in the economic market, such as power, freedom, capital, and extravagant materialism. Despite the mother of the "Toltec poems" working, not only do her children and she remain impoverished, but her employment instead *limits* her freedom, as her employer's time clock imprisons her, requiring her to work twelve-hour shifts five (and possibly six) days a week so that her family can barely subsist. Moreover, the patriarchal rule of the father still regulates her meager wages. The father pilfers his wife's income to finance his dandyish clothing that signifies his (de)colonial ideologies, the daughter-speaker of "Saturdays" commenting that her father "donned the tailor-made silk suit / bought on her credit."[57]

Although the mother spends most of her time toiling in the official-capitalist-economy, her workweeks do not conclude on Friday evenings, but continue as domestic labor in the unofficial-economy of the home. Just as the father purloins his wife's labor in the official-economy to finance the tailored and customized clothing essential to his gang life, so, too, does he inundate the mother and daughter with domestic labor to help enable his (de)colonial projects. As the daughter-speaker explains:

> Saturdays she [the mother] did the laundry,
> pulled the wringer machine
> to the kitchen sink, and hung
> the clothes out on the line.
> At night, we took it down and ironed.
> Mine were his handkerchiefs and
> Boxer shorts.[58]

After working at least a sixty-hour week, the mother joins the daughter in domestic labor, washing the laundry and ironing her husband's clothing, the daughter "his handkerchiefs and / boxer shorts" and the mother his "shirts / press[ing] the collars / and cuffs, just so."[59] The profits that the father extracts from his sociality's domestic and official-economic labor differ vastly from the rare theorizations of the dynamic between male gang members and their female partners not in gangs, given that these accounts often read women as impeding their male partners' gang membership. For instance, José Navarro analyzes the gang-exploitation film *Boulevard Nights* (1979) to uncover how male gang members' girlfriends inhibit the carnalismo and community gangs often accord men.[60] *My Father Was a Toltec*, on the other hand, divulges how even though gang members' female socialities may view gangs antagonistically, their actions do not always disrupt gang life for the men in their lives. Rather, as with the father's daughter and wife, their subjugation and the exploitation of their domestic and official-economic labor may instead enable gang life for male gang members. The father retains the freedom to enact (de)colonial projects in the public sphere because he circumvents parental responsibility and relegates this duty—including its financial elements—to the mother, and he exploits the domestic and official-economic labor of his wife and daughter to obtain and perform the fashion style integral to his 1950s Chicago gang life.

In part, the father's ability to benefit from his wife and daughter's labor relies on the ideologies of the coloniality of gender permeating the home, with the father's Chicano patriarchy creating a cyclical, gendered pattern of domestic labor. The final stanza of "Saturdays" reads:

"How do I look?"
"Bien," went on ironing.
That's why he married her, a Mexican
woman, like his mother, not like
they were in Chicago, not like
the one he was going out to meet.[61]

After donning a tailored silk suit, the father has the mother adjust his tie and asks her opinion of his appearance before he visits his paramour. Though the daughter-speaker discerns the father's unfaithful intentions, the mother's submissive and dutiful reaction suggests cognizance on her part as well. But rather than vocalize objections at her husband spending a night out with another woman while she and their daughter remain steeped in domestic work, she only acknowledges her husband's fashionable image and continues ironing his clothing, like a servile and subordinate "Mexican" wife—the reason the father has married her.

Although the mother trashing the father's gang jacket in "The Toltec" might indicate resistance and a denunciation of her husband's alienation of her, this stanza begins to show how the Toltec poems reject a binary passive/resistance portrayal of her, instead insinuating her conflicted emotions and thoughts about her husband and his treatment of her. In this stanza, the mother's passivity to her husband's brazen infidelity nods toward an internalization of (or adherence to) heteropatriarchal expectations of Mexican and Chicana women—at least at this stage in the chronology of the Toltec chapter's narrative. In *Borderlands/La Frontera*, Gloria Anzaldúa writes, "The culture expects women to show greater acceptance of, and commitment to, the value system than men. The culture and the Church insist that women are subservient to males. If a woman rebels she is a *mujer mala*. If a woman doesn't renounce herself in favor of the male, she is selfish."[62] Referring to Chicana/o/x and Mexican "culture," Anzaldúa insists that if women are not subservient to men, their cultures and communities ostracize them, casting them as "*mujer*[*es*] *mala*[*s*]." In the mother of "Saturdays," the reader not only observes how this adherence to, or possible internalization of, gendered subordination renders her stagnant in the coloniality of gender whereby the father, gang life, and Chicano patriarchy function as oppressors. The poem also discloses how the mother's refusal to defend her daughter from domestic exploitation contributes to a generational cycle of gendered labor for girls and women. The daughter-speaker having to iron her father's "handkerchiefs and / Boxer shorts" is an act that symbolically insinuates the daughter's possible learning of the salacious elements of Toltec gang life—and of her father's infidelity.[63] In its representations, "Saturdays" and later poems in the Toltec chapter that I soon address illuminate how, as Méndez says, "gender works to entice a series of complicities to and with colonial logics."[64] These poems show how both racialized men and women, either consciously or unconsciously, become complicit with the ideologies of the coloniality of gender, helping to maintain hierarchical systems of gendered subordination that continue to exploit Chicanas.

A Note on Racializing Sexism

For some readers, these poems may cast a disturbing picture of the Chicana/o/x family and Chicana/o/x culture, potentially informing the pathologization of Chicana/o/x people.[65] In part, this reading may arise because the Toltec poems subsume coloniality's/colonialism's role in creating financial and emotional trauma for Chicanas, and in manufacturing and maintaining Chicano patriarchy. As Raymund A. Paredes remarks, scholars analyzing Chicana/o/x literature and culture "must engage a complex of cultural traditions often described as among the most patriarchal in the world. Inevitably, directly or indirectly, the writer must come to terms with machismo, that distinctive Latin American code of masculinity so widely misunderstood in the United States."[66] Indeed, many inside and outside academia alike perceive Chicana/o/x, Latina/o/x, and Latin American cultures as inherently and excessively patriarchal, and men of these ethnicities as obsessed with performing whatever racist reduction of machismo these people envision.[67] As Alma García writes in her critique of white feminism, "Machismo, some Chicana feminists proposed, had been highly exaggerated, especially by white feminists, as it pertained to Chicano men, and this constituted an example of white feminists racializing sexism."[68] For many Latina/o/x studies scholars, the exaggeration of machismo racializes sexism to "justify" white colonial intervention under the mask of saviorism. By invoking and pathologizing machismo, "the structural dimensions of sexism," in Lionel Cantú's words, "are displaced under the racist subterfuge."[69]

For this reason, this chapter hopes to help stymie the recuperation of *My Father Was a Toltec* as a tool for racializing sexism, by noting "the structural dimensions" of the Chicano patriarchy that Castillo's book explores. According to Fregoso, the patriarchal subjugation of women stems more from the foundations of modern capitalist societies than from ethnic cultural values.[70] The gendered division of labor that deems the home, family, and child-rearing as women's societal obligations simultaneously privileges the "public (masculine) citizen-subject in the formation of the nation-state," creating an "institutional arrangement" that forms the "linchpin of modern women's subordination."[71] Moreover, the economic inequality afflicting many racialized persons cultivates the absent fatherism that *My Father Was a Toltec* critiques. For example, in her memoir *Men We Reaped*, Jesmyn Ward deliberates about her father abandoning his family when she was a child, leaving her mother, sisters, and her to struggle in penury: "This tradition of men leaving their families... seems systemic, fostered by endemic poverty.... Like many of the young Black men in my community across generations, the role of being a father and a husband was difficult for my father to assume. He saw a world of possibility outside the confines of family, and he could not resist the romance of that."[72] Overcome by the challenge of sufficiently providing for a family while suffering from underemployment and undereducation, Ward's father absconds to attain "a world of possibility" devoid of the financial burden of family. Likewise, "outside the confines of family," the daughter-speaker's father can enact (de)colonial projects in gang life in a way not possible if he fulfilled his financial and fatherly/husbandly duties to his family. The pattern of absent fathers—and the hardships it produces for women—thus prevails not because of an inherent pathology but, in part, because of the racialized, economic inequality that propagates patriarchal, male selfishness.

Cultural inheritances from Spanish colonialism also figure in Chicano patriarchy and its attempted subjugation of Chicanas. Octavio Paz notes that the Spanish were notorious for their maltreatment and demonization of women, as they claimed that a "woman's place is in the home, with a broken leg" and that a woman "is a domesticated wild animal, lecherous and sinful from birth, who must be subdued with a stick and guided by the reigns of religion."[73] As the latter statement insinuates, the Catholic church influenced Spanish misogyny and the regulation of women's autonomy. According to Paredes,

> Traditionally in Spanish culture, women have carried the primary responsibility of preserving and conveying church doctrine. And as loyal Catholics, they have also been expected to obey church fathers as diligently as they would their natural ones. The profoundly patriarchal structure and vocabulary of Catholicism instilled in Spanish women an intense reverence and humility before their various father figures. The church promoted patriarchy... as a social [principle], considering it to be the cornerstone of orderly community life.[74]

In other words, the Catholic church regarded women as subordinate to father figures (religious and biological) and deemed women's adherence to patriarchy and men necessary for "community life."

Although the Spanish Catholic church regarded patriarchy as a prerequisite for social order, the confinement of women to the home also managed the Spanish anxiety about miscegenation and men's inability to "protect" women. Jean Franco observes that "the virtual confinement of women to the home had not only been required by the Church but was also intended to ensure the purity of blood that Spanish society had imposed after the war against the Moors."[75] Despite Spanish concerns about racial mixing, which "excused" policing women's sexuality and reducing them to sexual property, these fears would later materialize in the Spanish colonization of the Aztec empire, and in the birth of the mestizo. As during any colonial project, cultural violence and conversion (a.k.a. the cultural bomb) eventuate as much as, if not more than, physical violence, and the lasting hegemony and inheritance of Spanish Catholicism still shape contemporary Chicana/o/x and Mexican communities.

This brief overview of the roles of the legacy of conquest, capitalist economies, and systemic racism in influencing both Chicano patriarchy and absent fatherism does not attempt to vindicate the daughter-speaker's father or the Chicano maltreatment of Chicanas. But in tracing the structural dimensions of Chicano patriarchy, I aim to resist the pathologization of Chicana/o/x culture as inherently and extraordinarily sexist without recognizing that European and US colonialism/coloniality influence Chicano patriarchy and its attempted subjugation of Chicanas. Because *My Father Was a Toltec* does not specifically address these influences, some may try to co-opt the book to racialize sexism as a strategy for reifying white supremacy and racism. Nonetheless, scholars and critics should not dismiss Castillo's poetry collection. The book remains invaluable for theorizing how gang life extends to gang members' socialities, as well as how gang members' (de)colonial projects often hinge on exacerbating the effects of the coloniality of gender for Chicanas. Even so, for all the toxicity between the father and his wife and daughter in *My Father Was a Toltec*, the public sphere, gang life, and the father are not *entirely* dichotomous with or absent from the private sphere or the daughter's life. Rather, the father's rare entrances into the home and the way his public life and gang persona "hybridize" the private sphere have liberating—as opposed to *only* oppressive—ramifications for the daughter. Simply put, despite the complex and contradictory relations between the father and his daughter, the introduction of gang culture and public life into the home facilitates raced, classed, sexual, and gendered (de)colonial projects for the daughter in her emergence as la Heredera.

Enter la Heredera

Chicana/o/x and Mexican cultures often expect women to conform to patriarchal expectations that govern their autonomy, sexuality, and life chances. Part of this conformity entails abiding by marianismo, an ideology that emerges in Spanish colonialism. Marianismo idealizes the Virgin Mary, demands women's subordination to men, and criminalizes their sexuality—stipulating that women should never find pleasure in sexual intercourse, but still must submit to their husbands' sexual desires out of their marital and reproductive "duty." It has also promoted the gendering of the separate spheres by impelling fathers to sequester their daughters from the public sphere to try to ensure their sexual and moral "purity" and their dependence on men.

The private and public spheres, however, are not so dichotomous. Prior scholarship on Chicana gang members and the public sphere has focused on Chicanas escaping the home/private sphere to enter public life through gangs, such as Fregoso's analysis of the film *Mi Vida Loca* or Miranda's ethnography of Northern California girl gangs, *Homegirls in the Public Sphere*. These two works present fruitful accounts of how Chicana gang members mobilize counterhegemonic projects in the public sphere, but these and many other theorizations of the separate spheres focus primarily on the private infiltrating the public, rarely considering how the public penetrates the private.

In contrast, I view the public and private spheres similarly to how Homi Bhabha reads the colonizer/colonized relationship. In *The Location of Culture*, Bhabha regards colonizer/colonized relations as porous, featuring cross-pollination that produces cultural hybridization. For Bhabha, this hybridity leads to what he terms "mimicry"—a phenomenon where the colonized adopt the colonizer's culture, such as language, government, clothing, or religion. This hybridity spans multiple directions, entailing colonizers mimicking the colonized historically and contemporarily, such as white persons dressing up as the racial Other for holidays and parties. Similar to the racial mimicry of the colonizer/colonized relationship, the private and public spheres also "hybridize" and are not exclusive. Castillo's "The Suede Coat," "Dirty

Mexican," and "Daddy with Chesterfields in a Rolled Up Sleeve" help visualize this porousness. These later poems of the Toltec chapter expose how the entrance of public and gang life in the home may "hybridize" the private sphere and facilitate (de)colonial projects for working-class Chicanas.

In "The Suede Coat," the father's arbitrary presence visibly brings gang/public life into the home for the first time in the sequence of the poems, providing the avenue for his daughter to resist economic inequality and the regulation of her gender and sexuality. The poem reads:

> Although
> Mother would never allow
> a girl of fourteen to wear
> the things you brought
> from where you wouldn't say—
> the narrow skirts with high slits
> glimpsed the thigh—
> they fit your daughter of delicate
> hips.
> And she wore them on the sly.
>
> To whom did the suede coat with
> fur collar belong?
> The women in my family
> have always been polite
> or too ashamed to ask.
> You never told, of course,
> what we of course knew.[76]

As "The Toltec" first conveys, style is crucial to the father's gang and public persona, often broadcasting his (de)colonial ideologies. By contrast, in "Red Wagon," unfashionable, wrinkled, and "silly" clothing for the father's young children evokes neglect, poverty, and the private sphere. But despite the mother's past attempts to trash the clothes (emblemed jacket) so paramount to the father's gang culture, the mother cannot conceal from her daughter's gaze all the clothing that the father amasses in public life. No longer the child of "Red Wagon," the teenage daughter of "The Suede Coat" swaps her "silly" attire for "narrow skirts with high slits" that the father "brought / from where [he] wouldn't say."

Although the origins of these revealing skirts and "the suede coat with / fur collar" remain a mystery, the women of the daughter's family's silence and shame at these clothes' presence in the home imply that this attire arises from the father's relations with other women, belonging to (or gifts he plans for) the women he forsakes his wife for.

These clothing items, however, do not evoke a universal signification for all the women in this home. Whereas, for the mother, the skirts and coat heighten subordination in invoking both the father's brazen rejection of her and the Chicano patriarchy that demands her silence at this offense, these clothes enable the daughter to undermine and circumvent economic inequality and Chicano patriarchy in abstract and material ways. The mother may remain the dutiful Chicana wife who attempts to police her daughter's sexuality in "never allow[ing] / a girl of fourteen to wear / the things [the father] brought / from where [he] wouldn't say," but the appearance of immodest fashion "hybridizes" the daughter's life in the private sphere to allow her to circumvent the regulation of her gender and sexuality. Though the daughter still remains in the private sphere and subject to patriarchal rule—indicated by her need to wear these clothes "on the sly"—she no longer fully adheres to the ideologies of marianismo that regard women's sexuality as deplorable, and sexual intercourse as a marital and reproductive duty. Rather, she breaches the confines of Chicano patriarchy—even if still in its domain (the home)—to reject "proper" Chicana decorum and embrace her sexuality and womanhood through sexualizing clothing that "glimpsed the thigh." Moreover, the suede coat, in particular, contains further emancipating consequences for this working-class Chicana. Whereas, as a young girl, "silly" and wrinkled coats magnified her indigence, this elaborate coat with its "fur collar" permits her, if temporarily, to live and fantasize about the luxurious materialism of an upper-class status and to psychologically migrate away from the penury that structures her life.

These skirts and the suede coat that arise from the father's infrequent presence in the home help facilitate a new ontology for the daughter, what Fanon might call the veritable creation of a new woman. She identifies the (de)colonial projects available to working-class Chicanas in gangs that allow her to circumvent and contest the coloniality of gender. As a result, the daughter emerges as la Heredera in "Dirty Mexican" and "Daddy with Chesterfields in a Rolled Up Sleeve" to commit fully to gang life, broadening her capacity to resist the US white supremacy, racism, and heteropatriarchy that regulate Chicana lives.

"Dirty Mexican" opens with the daughter, now a fully-fledged gang member, mirroring her father's prior gang behavior, both in style and violence:

> "Dirty Mexican, dirty, dirty Mexican!"
> And i said: "i'll kick your ass, Dago bitch!"
> tall for my race, strutted right past
> black projects,
> leather jacket, something sharp
> in my pocket
> to Pompeii School.
> *Get those Dago girls with teased-up hair*[77]

Akin to her father who in his emblemed jacket heads into Bridgeport to war with Irish gangs, the daughter-speaker exchanges her suede coat for the leather jacket that typifies the greaser aesthetics adopted by many Chicago Latina/o/x gangs, and she ventures into Italian territory to attack "Dago" (an epithet for Italians) girls. Unlike her father, however, the daughter need not travel to the South Side to battle racist Italians, but only a few blocks north of Taylor Street of the Near West Side—the street where Castillo lived as a teenager and an "area with a strong Italian identity," despite growing Latina/o/x settlement.[78] During the 1950s, 60s, and 70s, Taylor Street, as O'Connor and Corrado say, "was an epicenter of gang activity," running through territories of several Latina/o/x or Italian gangs, including the Popes, the Majestics, the Vicounts, the Jousters, the Bishops, the Deuces, and famed Taylor Street Dukes.[79] Though the Taylor Street areas were predominantly Italian and Latina/o/x (until becoming primarily Mexican American in the mid-1970s), a smaller black population also resided in a nearby public housing section.[80] When pursuing *"Dago girls with teased-up hair,"* the daughter-speaker "strut[s] right past" these "black projects" to hit up "Pompeii School," a reference to the Shrine of Our Lady of Pompeii—an Italian Catholic school and church built in the early 1900s and located a couple blocks north of Taylor Street, on Racine and Lexington. Established as an official national Italian parish in 1911, the Pompeii church and school mark this block as Italian territory, a vicinity the daughter-speaker infringes on after Italians label her a "Dirty Mexican, dirty, dirty Mexican." Similar to the "Dirty nigger" hailing that Fanon discusses, these words attempt to racialize the daughter and render her inferior in support of white supremacy.[81] But unlike her mother, who often accepts the degradation that her husband casts upon her, the daughter has developed a new consciousness, refusing the sub-ontological difference that the Italians attempt to impose on her. She rejects the Italians' power over her and their racial contract discourse that attempts to dehumanize her. Instead, as a gang member, the daughter-speaker replies with the equivalent of Fanon's famous "'Fuck you,' madame"—"i'll kick your ass, Dago bitch!"—to threaten these Italians with violence, advancing with "something sharp / in [her] pocket" to "Pompeii School" to "*Get those Dago girls with teased-up hair.*"[82]

Not guilty of only vocalizing racist epithets, the Italians in "Dirty Mexican" also deploy racialized sexualized violence against a likely Chicana woman in Sheridan Park, located only one block north of Taylor Street and two east of "Pompeii School." The daughter-speaker notes:

> Boys with Sicilian curls got high
> at Sheridan Park, mutilated a prostitute one night.
> i scrawled in chalk all over sidewalks
> MEXICAN POWER CON/SAFOS
> crashed their dances,
> *get them broads, corner 'em in the bathroom*[83]

These boys who murder this prostitute sport "Sicilian curls," indicating that they, too, descend from or are Italian immigrants. The ethnic identity of the prostitute remains anonymous, but the daughter's immediate responsive tag in the succeeding lines and her declaration of "MEXICAN POWER" suggest that the Italians kill a Mexican/Chicana prostitute, which provokes the daughter's retribution. The daughter also tags "CON/SAFOS" after her proclamation—a colloquial phrase in Chicana/o/x barrios that, according to George Lipsitz, "serves to 'protect' the writing on the walls by warning 'don't touch,' . . . or 'anything negative that you say or do about this graffiti will happen to you.'"[84] Scrawling "MEXICAN POWER CON/SAFOS" "all over sidewalks" in (presumably) Sheridan Park proclaims the area as Mexican/Chicana/o/x territory and "protects" this space and its denizens with a "don't touch" warning. In doing so, the daughter-speaker, like her father, expands her gang's territory by claiming Sheridan Park—and possibly Pompeii School. By "winning space" in public life, the daughter-speaker in part counteracts the material capitalist imbalances she suffered as a child, and she does so against racist Italians perpetuating the coloniality of gender against Chicanas. As I am insinuating, the con safos admonition in Sheridan Park has several meanings in this case: "don't touch" this tag, territory, *or* Chicanas. Con safos promises violent punishment to anyone who violates the protection its tagger offers, and the daughter fulfills this threat by responding to the Sicilian boys' racialized violence against Chicanas with (de)colonial violence against Italian women. She "crashe[s] their dances" in search of Italian "*broads*" whom she and her gang surround in the bathroom.

In this instance, the daughter-speaker incorporates white women into her (de)colonial projects much differently than does her father. Whereas the father may philander with potentially white women to aggrandize his own masculinity, symbolically challenging his "feminized" and "fundamentally penetrable" status as the racial Other, his daughter plans to satisfy the con safos contract by treating Italian women—who are not civilians in this war, as they term the daughter a "dirty Mexican bitch"—in the same manner that the Italians acted toward the prostitute: violently.[85] While her father's womanizing may represent an act of figurative "violence" that defies the "white-male-colonizer father" by "seizing" white women, the daughter-speaker's actions manifest as literal gendered violence. In her violence, she appropriates heteropatriarchal ideologies similar to those that Las Casas discusses when Spanish colonizers harm native women before the eyes of native men. In jumping Italian women, the daughter-speaker proclaims to a larger Italian heteropatriarchal apparatus that Italian men cannot protect "their" women, and she symbolically emasculates the Sicilian boys who mutilate the prostitute in Sheridan Park. In this way, the daughter-speaker does not necessarily fully delink from the ideologies of the coloniality of gender, even if her gang life accords her a range of strategies for resisting oppressions that intersect at class, race, gender, and sexuality.

The abstract and physical violence the daughter-speaker fights against through gang life, however, does not stem only from racist white actors in public space. For this Chicana, gangs provide an avenue for bypassing the violent and heteropatriarchal life chances Chicanas are subject to in some Chicana/o/x homes. In "Daddy with Chesterfields in a Rolled Up Sleeve," the daughter-speaker explains how her father's mother encounters violence similar to the prostitute in Sheridan Park:

The curandera from Guanajuato—
with jars of herbs

grown in coffee cans—
had raised the Toltec long
after her sons had grown,
her only daughter murdered by her husband.[86]

This curandera—the father's (Toltec's) alleged mother who supposedly gives "birth to him at 60"—raises and cares for him as her only child, her past sons grown and "her only daughter murdered by her husband."[87] In this poem, Chicano patriarchy possibly reaches its acme in the ambiguity of the death of the curandera's daughter. Why does this husband kill her daughter? Are the husband's actions a byproduct of emotional instability and/or alcoholism, which culminates in a fatal outburst directed at his wife's daughter? Or does this murder arise from a larger misogynist ideology that sanctions the Chicano patriarch to penalize women's transgressions, in this instance, with death? Did the daughter skirt marianismo and exert sexual agency with white men, and does the father rationalize murdering the daughter with the need to defend his fragile masculinity from any emasculation that this potential transgression might represent?

Though the poem never addresses why the husband murders the daughter, this death has several consequences for the Chicanas in the Toltec's family. On the one hand, this murder conjures the longstanding Mexican/Chicana/o/x folktale of the young woman "Delgadina" that helps to illuminate the daughter-speaker's mother's subservience both to her husband and to the policing of her daughter's gender and sexuality. In the story, Delgadina's father develops a sexual interest in her and demands that she sleep with him. When Delgadina refuses, he imprisons her in a tower and denies her food and water, promising to free her only if she will become his lover. Although Delgadina beseeches her mother, sister, and brother for food, water, and freedom, they remain loyal to her father and reject her wishes, leaving Delgadina to starve to death after she refuses to capitulate to her father. In theorizing the women of Delgadina's family and their refusal to help her, Emma Pérez writes,

> Each one fears violating the father's order, his sexual laws, so they each ostracize Delgadina. Her mother and sister, who are 'an integral part of a phallic masculine economy,' betray her. And yet, what is their alternative?[88]

For Pérez, Delgadina's mother's and sister's allegiance to her father stems from fear of his violence and retribution, from the possibility that they, too, might find themselves imprisoned in this tower for disobeying him. They have no alternative but to adhere to the law of the father, or three women may die instead of one.

Likewise, the death of the curandera's daughter at the hands of her own father may insinuate that the Toltec's wife rarely challenges him out of a sense of preservation for herself and her daughter. Whether she is aware of this death on her husband's side of the family or not, she knows her husband is, after all, a violent man, even if readers only see him direct this violence at Irish gang members. Is the mother's passivity and policing of the daughter-speaker solely a result of internalizing the ideologies of the coloniality of gender? Or is her (in)action a symptom of her precarity and her desire to ensure her and her daughter's lives? Perhaps the mother "would never allow / a girl of fourteen to wear" "narrow skirts with high slits" that "glimpsed the thigh" out of concern for what her patriarchal husband might do (to both her and their daughter) if their daughter violates the gender and sexual decorum that marianismo stipulates. Although the Toltec poems often strike a combative relationship between the mother and daughter, responsibility and fear for her daughter may shape how and why the mother acts in such a patriarchal manner toward her daughter.

On the other hand, the daughter-speaker pursues an alternative form of self-preservation than the type her mother opts for. Realizing the life chances afforded working-class Chicanas after witnessing the maltreatment of her mother, experiencing patriarchal oppression from her mother and father, and—as the speaker of the poem—knowing of this murder in her family, the daughter-speaker eludes this limiting future through gang life. Her gang membership also grants her a violent means of self-defense, indicated by her previous willingness to fight back against Italians with "something sharp / in [her] pocket."[89] As the mother says to the daughter-speaker:

> You're like your father,
> don't like to work,
> a daydreamer,
> think someday you'll be rich and famous,
> an artist, who wastes her time
> travelling,

wearing finery she can't afford,
neglecting her children and her home!⁹⁰

The daughter-speaker mimics the recreational and opulent characteristics of her father's gang life ("travelling, / wearing finery she can't afford") that contrast with the poverty of her childhood. In doing so, she daydreams of and pursues life chances beyond the Chicano patriarchal expectations that she remain in the private sphere and within the confines of heteronormative familia, engaging in reproductive futurism and caring for her children and house. Instead, in gang life, she repudiates "appropriate" Chicana decorum and "say[s] 'man,' smoke[s] cigarettes, / drink[s] tequila" and adorns "the silk dress accentuating breasts" to "try and catch those evasive eyes."⁹¹ In embracing her sexuality and stepping outside the boundaries of patriarchal rule, the daughter-speaker opposes herself to marianismo's idealization of the Virgin Mary. As a result, she says here, for the first time in the Toltec chapter, "And so, i exist," revealing how gang life has precipitated an alternative ontology, the veritable creation of a new woman.⁹² Through her entrance into gangs, the daughter-speaker has mobilized (de)colonial projects to contest and circumvent the oppressive effects of the coloniality of gender that she encounters from white persons in public life, as well as from her Chicana/o/x family in the private sphere.

The Sociality of a Gang Girl

Despite these (de)colonial consequences of gang life, the daughter-speaker's membership in a gang means that she, like her father, maintains a sociality of gang life. This chapter's previous postulations about male gang members' female socialities implicate female gang members' socialities as well. In theory, for many female gang members, several of this chapter's contentions about the shared experience of gang life for female socialities of the private sphere still apply. Gang life that requires absence from the home carries classed and gendered consequences for working-class Latinas in white capitalist, heteropatriarchal societies that privilege a gendered division of labor. In many working-class homes, ideologies of "keeping house" materialize through a generational cycle that assigns domestic responsibility to girls and women. Even when fathers are not absent from working-class households, financial austerity typically requires the employment of both parents, creating a gendered succession of labor where young girls must take up the "duty" of domesticity while their mothers work in the official-economy of paid employment. If the gangbanging daughter/mother/sister abandons the home, then her absence may also intensify gendered burdens for the women of her family who depend on her domestic aid.

In Castillo's Toltec poems, the reader can infer that the daughter-speaker's (de)colonial gang life worsens gendered and classed hardship for the mother in much the same way that the father's behavior does so. This absent daughter, who neglects "her home," no longer remains to assist her mother with domestic labor, nor do the Toltec poems indicate where the daughter attains the funding to finance the "finery she can't afford." Does the daughter-speaker attain wealth through black market economies, or has she, so like her father, learned to also purchase this "finery" on her mother's credit? At the same time, although the daughter-speaker's gang life implicitly hinges on intensifying the exploitation of her mother, her experience with the coloniality of gender in the Chicana/o/x home also provokes an alternative gang member ontology that simultaneously departs from her father's. Like her father's, the daughter-speaker's gang life entails a version of "philandering" with women. However, differing from her father's infidelity toward his wife, the daughter-speaker's queer homoerotic engagements with Chicanas help ameliorate the marginalized status of these women.

The daughter-speaker's interactions with Chicanas also depart from her incorporation of Italian women's bodies into her (de)colonial projects. In her attack on Italian women, the daughter appropriates heteropatriarchal colonial ideologies that rely on gendered violence—a type of violence that, whether enacted by male or female colonizers or *de*-colonizers, always results (at least, in part) in the reification of *a* heteropatriarchal hegemony. In the daughter-speaker's circumstance, her retributive hit on Italian women acts as a (de)colonial project for Chicanas that rebels against Italians' use of racialized gendered violence. The daughter-speaker's (de)colonial violence, however, paradoxically struggles to delink from the ideologies of the coloniality of gender, even as her actions arise in response to this coloniality. Her violence against Italian women concomitantly perpetuates, for them, Italian heteropatriarchy in rendering their bodies ammunition against Sicilian boys who attack Chicana sex workers. But when enacting (de)colonial projects with and through Chicana bodies, the daughter-speaker's "philandering" enables psychological liberation from heteropatriarchal rule for these women of her sociality.

In the final few stanzas to "Daddy with Chesterfields in a Rolled Up Sleeve," the speaker says:

> Men try to catch my eye. i talk to them
> of politics, religion, the ghosts i've seen,
> the king of timbales, México and Chicago.
> And they go away.
> But women stay. Women like stories.
> They like the thin arms around their shoulders,
> the smell of perfumed hair,
> a flamboyant scarf around the neck
> the reassuring voice that confirms their
> cynicism about politics, religion and the glorious
> history that slaughtered thousands of slaves.
>
> Because of the seductive aroma of mole
> in my kitchen, and the mysterious preparation
> of herbs, women tolerate *my* cigarette
> and cognac breath, unmade bed,
> and my inability to keep a budget—
> in exchange for a promise,
> an exotic trip,
> a tango lesson,
> an anecdote of the gypsy who stole
> me away in Madrid.[93]

The disinterest that men have in a Chicana who rejects her proper "place" in the heteropatriarchal family—and instead develops an epistemology aware and critical of the violent politics, religion, and colonialism that "slaughtered thousands of slaves"—emphasizes the queer homoeroticism of the daughter-speaker's engagement with women. She wraps her "thin arms around their shoulders," allowing the "smell of perfumed hair" to linger, while she whispers reassurances. In these titillating lines, the daughter-speaker and the Chicanas she flirts with approximate L. H. Stallings's idea of "sexual guerillas"—a term that references black women's instrumentalization of the erotic and imagination as a form of "epistemic self-defense," producing "a countermeasure to structural and epistemic sexual violence" and "a simultaneous creation of new knowledge and an acquisition of knowledge through the body."[94] Similarly, through their queer homoerotics, these Chicana "sexual guerillas" begin to cultivate a vicarious "countermeasure" to heteropatriarchal rule, fostering a (de)colonial epistemology and psychological preservation between women that the latter of these two stanzas exemplifies. The daughter-speaker's interactions with Chicanas flirt with the boundaries of the marianismo and Chicano patriarchy that regulate their sexualities—demanding heterosexuality, reproductive futurism, and maternal care for children. Moreover, for these women, the daughter-speaker functions as an epistemologically (de)colonial figure who confirms their skepticism about ideological apparatuses (politics, religion, and colonial histories) that suppress and govern their lives at the intersections of race, class, gender, and sexuality. Her meetings with these Chicanas in the private sphere also allow the women to migrate psychologically away from the heteropatriarchal rule that denies them the agency and freedom to pursue the exhilarating life the daughter-speaker lives. The women may thus also vicariously escape from the economic inequalities that, in these poems, Chicanas bear the brunt of. These Chicanas psychologically circumvent patriarchal rule and capitalist imbalances through the anecdotes of a life beyond domesticity and beyond a working-class status ("exotic trips," "tango lessons," excursions with gypsies in Madrid) that the daughter-speaker disseminates. In this way, the daughter-speaker's relationship with her female sociality does not *entirely* mirror her father's, in that she does not completely forsake Chicanas to pursue gang and public life. Rather, in her return to the private sphere to help these Chicanas persist vicariously, these women remain at the center of her (de)colonial project.

In *Homegirls in the Public Sphere*, Miranda writes, "Since politics and power are defined as public displays, the study of alternative politics and forms of empowerment produced in the private realm by women and children, sibling and kinship relations, and community networks are demeaned and insufficiently analyzed."[95] In studying the (de)colonial projects that the daughter-speaker launches in the public sphere, this chapter does not attempt to reify false dichotomies that, as Miranda observes, essentialize the public as the realm of political action, and the private as devoid of empowerment. Rather, I interpret the daughter-speaker's erotic engagements with these women in the private sphere similarly to how Pérez reads the ways that slain Tejana singer Selena Quintanilla navigated her patriarchal, controlling father. Pérez writes,

> She is still trapped within the confines of patriarchal conditions ... but we cannot forget how she manipulates that control for her own benefit, for her own agency. And that is the power of the seduction fantasy. A woman can be a desiring subject; she is not just an object whose life is determined by a patriarch.[96]

Selena's capacity to manipulate patriarchal authority to exercise her own agency and sexual desire, despite remaining entrenched in patriarchal confines, resembles how these Chicanas in Castillo's poem use the site of their "proper" domestic place (the kitchen) to enact a liberating, queer politics and desire, circumventing patriarchal, working-class life chances through the vicarious living the daughter-speaker provides. The daughter-speaker may exit private life and join gangs to enact (de)colonial projects in public space, but the conversations she has with these women in the kitchen, as the "seductive aroma of mole" permeates the air, showcase how, just like the public sphere, the private sphere can operate as a site of political discourse and action that manipulates and challenges patriarchal rule. In "Daddy with Chesterfields in a Rolled Up Sleeve," these women's agency, desire, and empowerment in the home materialize through the medium of "private" talk where the gang girl and her female sociality create "alternative politics" to precipitate psychological resistance against Chicano patriarchy and the economic inequality of the US capitalist colonial structure.

"That's right, honey, I'm Mexican!"

My Father Was a Toltec's portrayal of gang membership helps Castillo's book depart from the common literary/cultural trope that associates Latina feminism with assimilation, class privilege, and/or whiteness. The book contests this notion through coinciding with previous scholarship on Latina/o/x gangs that reads these subcultures as anti-assimilationist, imagining how Latina gang members may practice a (de)colonial feminism that affirms ethnic/cultural heritage.

In "Dirty Mexican," the daughter-speaker exemplifies the anti-assimilationist ideologies of Latina/o/x gang subcultures. This working-class Chicana not only embraces her Mexican/Chicana background but also wars with whiteness, as opposed to attempting to approximate white culture. Recall the daughter-speaker's tag in "Dirty Mexican"—"MEXICAN POWER CON/SAFOS"—that declares her protection of her newly claimed territory and of Chicana women from Italians. As much as this tag defends her space and people, the statement also avouches her affinity for her heritage—a point she reiterates when racist Italians label her a "Dirty Mexican." Refusing to read "Mexican" as a marker of shame and an ethnicity to distance herself from, the daughter responds in affirmation: *"That's right, honey, I'm Mexican! / Watchu gonna do about it?"*[97] Through gang life, the daughter-speaker circumvents and contests the effects of the coloniality of gender in abstract and physical ways, but contrary to literary and cultural tropes, her (de)colonial feminist projects are not linked to an approximation of whiteness and white culture. Instead of Simone de Beauvoir galvanizing the daughter-speaker's feminist stance, Chicana/o/x gang culture catalyzes her resistant mindset.

Although *My Father Was a Toltec* has not amassed the same amount of scholarly recognition as some of Castillo's other work, Adriana Estill is one of the few academics to examine the Toltec chapter. Her reading, however, conflicts with my understanding of the father, the daughter-speaker, and gang life as signifying anti-assimilationist cultural ethics. Estill interprets the father as white (culturally and biologically), rather than Chicano or Mexican, making the daughter's identification with the father an investment in and identification with whiteness. In "Daddy with Chesterfields in a Rolled Up Sleeve," the daughter relays a memory of her father arriving at her school:

> The school principal was a white lady
> who came to class one day
> to say a man claiming to be
> my father
> was in her office.[98]

For Estill, the principal's apprehension about the validity of the father's claim to fatherhood implies a difference in skin gradation—the daughter brown and the father white. As Estill says, "The principal's doubts about his claim to parentage suggest his possible visual and *therefore* racial difference from his daughter."[99] Estill corroborates her reading of the father as not Mexican or Chicano in his response to his wife's accusations:

—No creo que fue tu mamá,—your wife whispers.
"I don't care!" you reply.
—Que ni eres mexicano,—
"I don't care!" you say for
doña Jovita,
la madre sagrada
su comal y molcajete
la revolución de Benito Juárez y Pancho Villa,
Guanajuato, paper cuts, onyx, papier-mâché,
bullfighters' pictures, and Aztec calendars.[100]

[—I do not believe that she was your mother,—your wife
   whispers.
"I don't care!" you reply.
—nor that you are Mexican,—
"I don't care!" you say for
doña Jovita,
the holy mother
her griddle and pestle and mortar
the revolution of Benito Juárez and Pancho Villa,
Guanajuato, paper cuts, onyx, papier-mâché,
bullfighters' pictures, and Aztec calendars.]

In these lines, the mother impugns the father's Mexican lineage and questions that the curandera could possibly birth him at sixty years old. When accounting for the principal's hesitation and the father's English (rather than Spanish) rejoinders, Estill concludes that the father "does not have the same cultural background (or at least as 'authentic' or 'pure' a heritage) as she [his wife] does, a point she underscores by speaking to him in a language in which he obviously cannot answer."[101]

When Estill reads the father as white or not Chicano/Mexican "enough," she predicates her contention on a rationale that is, for multiple reasons, erroneous. Firstly, Estill deduces that, because the principal perceives a "visible" difference between the daughter and father (read: skin tone), the daughter and father "therefore" must differ racially. This presumption about skin tone negating ethnic lineage disregards the entire history of mestizaje by essentializing all Mexicans and Chicana/o/xs as brown-skinned, whereas the blood of the Spanish colonizer has resulted in many light-skinned Mexicans and Chicana/o/xs.

Secondly, Estill sutures language to ethnic and cultural authenticity. Because she believes that the father cannot speak Spanish (answering "I don't know" instead of "no sé"), she argues that he does not have an "authentic" or "pure" Mexican/Chicana/o/x heritage, thus making him culturally—in addition to phenotypically—white. But the father's ability to respond in Spanish matters not for his Mexican/Chicana/o/x cultural authenticity. As Anzaldúa has famously said of language and authenticity,

> Often with *mexicanas y latinas* we'll speak English as a neutral language. Even among Chicanas we tend to speak English at parties or conferences. Yet, at the same time, we're afraid the other will think we're *agringadas* because we don't speak Chicano Spanish. We oppress each other trying to out-Chicano each other, vying to be the 'real' Chicanas, to speak like Chicanos. There is no one Chicano language just as there is no one Chicano experience. A monolingual Chicana whose first language is English or Spanish is just as much a Chicana as one who speaks several variants of Spanish.[102]

As Anzaldúa adroitly points out, Chicana/o/xs speak a range of different dialects of Spanish and/or English, and no single version can measure one's authenticity or "purity." In fact, attempting to evaluate or gauge "authenticity" only leads to Chicana/o/xs and Latina/o/xs "oppress[ing] each other trying to out-Chicano [and Latina/o/x] each other." It serves to victim-blame through faulting the subaltern subject (Latin American migrants and their descendants) for the "linguistic terrorism" of the US nation-state, and uses the same ideology as nativists who equate American authenticity with language through statements such as "English only" or "if you are in America, you need to learn English."[103] In short, for Estill, skin color and language proficiency constitute Mexican/Chicana/o/x authenticity, which, even if this logic were not misguided, the Toltec poems also contradict.

Regardless of the father's language proficiency and his skin tone, he and his Toltec gang are still anti-assimilationist symbols that connote and affirm Mexican/Chicana/o/x culture. In her analysis, Estill carefully does not address that Doña Jovita—the curandera and father's alleged mother—"had raised the Toltec long."[104] Moreover, as the daughter-speaker expresses, even if Doña Jovita were not the father's biological mother, she nonetheless exemplifies Mexican cultural "authenticity" as "la madre sagrada" with "su comal y molcajete." The daughter-speaker associates her with "la revolución de Benito Juárez y Pancho Villa," Mexican cities (Guanajuato), Mexican cultural practices (bullfighting), and indigenous heritage ("Aztec calendars"). Designating the father as culturally inauthentic after this woman raises him thereby reads as an inaccurate and a selective analysis. The accusation of whiteness and cultural inauthenticity also ignores the father's participation in the Toltec gang, which embraces indigenous, pre-conquest ancestry in the appropriation of the Toltec name and wars against—rather than alongside—whites. For these reasons, the daughter's identification with the father and gang life still enables her to achieve an anti-assimilationist (de)colonial politics that avows Mexican/Chicana/o/x identity.

Ultimately, this chapter has shown that *My Father Was a Toltec* discloses how gang life is always a shared experience between members and their socialities, which sometimes exacerbates the hardship of female socialities and, in other instances, precipitates their own entrance into gang subcultures. In the case of Castillo's poetry collection, gang life enables Chicanas to materially, ontologically, and psychologically circumvent Chicano patriarchy and the imbalances of the US capitalist colonial structure. But throughout my explication of Castillo's book, a purposely unaddressed aporia has haunted this chapter: the internal politics of gangs. If, as an array of scholars in critical gang studies documents, many gangs often venerate maleness, hypermasculinity, and heterosexuality, how, then, does this queer Chicana heiress of *My Father Was a Toltec* become a citizen-subject of her gang to mobilize (de)colonial projects? Perhaps inadvertently, *My Father Was a Toltec* sidesteps this concern, covering only the daughter-speaker's reign as a full citizen-subject of her gang. For this reason, I now turn to another Latina gang narrative, to wrestle with the vital question of the heteropatriarchal politics of heterosexual male-dominated gangs and their ramifications for their women members: Yxta Maya Murray's *Locas*.

3 | THE TOXIFIED FEMALE MASCULINITIES OF (DE)COLONIAL GANG GIRLS

IN THE 2005 FILM *HAVOC*, ANNE HATHAWAY AND BIJOU PHILLIPS play two white upper-class teenagers named Allison (Hathaway) and Emily (Phillips) from the Pacific Palisades, an affluent coastal neighborhood in West Los Angeles. The young girls are part of an opulent white high school gang called the "PLC," though this gang does not replicate the racial hatred of white supremacist groups. Instead, the PLC fetishizes and arrogates African American gangster rap culture. The majority of the PLC members' days consist of rapping and dancing to Tupac Shakur, speaking African American Vernacular English, pontificating about their penchant for violence and the peril of "the streets," and wearing 2000s hip-hop aesthetic clothing, like oversized Ecko and Enyce hoodies, and diamond chains. Although the PLC views itself as a dangerous, aggressive, and "from the bottom to the top" gang, its participants have all grown up in lavish, two-parent homes and drive luxury vehicles.

Cognizant of the PLC's facade and wishing to experience "real" gang life, Allison and Emily travel to the barrios of East Los Angeles to purchase cocaine and meet Latino gang members. After spending weeks cultivating relations with a gang member named Hector, the two young women approach him about admission into his 16th Street gang, an allusion to the actual 18th Street Latina/o/x gang of Los Angeles. Eventually, Hector and other male members of 16th Street relent and offer the two membership, but these men claim that Allison and Emily must first fulfill a requirement before they can join the gang: roll a die and have sex with the number of male gang members that their die rolls. The two ladies agree—Allison rolling a one and Emily a three—and begin to have sex with gang members for their initiation into the gang. But midway through the process, the two have second thoughts and run out of the room, leaving the gang and gang culture for good after deducing that the lives of authentic gang girls consist only of serving as sexual objects for the pleasure of male gang members.

This assumption about women as nominal gang members whom their male counterparts exchange as sexual cattle permeates much of the representation of female gang members in popular culture and academia.[1] Recently, however, some scholars have begun to contest this belief about female gang members—such as T. W. Ward, who argues that "very few gangs allow its [sic] female members to get sexed in," because doing so "denigrates women and makes their gangs look weak."[2] Additionally, Daniel Enrique Pérez contends that though some women may encounter oppression in male-dominated gangs, they "sometimes still attain leadership roles and assume positions within a gang where they have authority over the others."[3] Pérez's assertion coincides with many female gang members' claims. In her ethnography of the Chicana/o/x gangs White Fence and El Hoyo Maravilla, Joan W. Moore asks former and current female gang members about the assumption that their male colleagues mistreat them. According to Moore, "Most of the women—almost two thirds, older and younger—vehemently denied the truth of such assertions. A White Fence woman said, 'No, I think my homeboys treated us good, the way we should be treated.'"[4] Likewise, Sonia Rodriguez's memoir *Lady Q: The Rise and Fall of a Latin Queen* attests that women gang members achieve positions of leadership and power in the Latin Kings, one the largest Latina/o/x gangs in the United States, which has since renamed itself the Almighty Latin King and Queen Nation.[5]

While these studies and narratives challenge the presumption that female gang members are sex objects ineligible for citizenship in male-dominated gang life, the notion that women occupy marginal statuses in these subcultures, admittedly, holds some truth at times. After all, in Moore's study, two-thirds of former and current female gang members may have denied that men in gangs treated them improperly, but one-third of women agreed with the allegation. In some cases, these gangs are not always—or entirely—generative for all women. Many male-dominated gangs subscribe to the patriarchal logics of the coloniality of gender, and reproduce and exacerbate the abstract and material oppressions Latinas experience in the United States and in their families and barrios. But this possibility does not mean that Latinas never successfully navigate patriarchal gangs, transform them, and/or find material and psychological rewards in them. For this reason, any analysis of female gang members still should attend to the internal politics of male-dominated, heteropatriarchal gangs—considering *how* women negotiate these subcultures and the effects that their methods have on themselves and other women.

Released in 1997, Yxta Maya Murray's *Locas* represents how women experience and subvert patriarchal hierarchies in male-dominated gangs to enact (de)colonial projects in, through, and against these subcultures. Murray, who graduated with a JD from Stanford in 1993, wrote the novel after clerking for judges Harry Hupp and Ferdinand Fernandez in the Central District of California and Ninth Circuit Court of Appeals in Pasadena. During this time, she met many clients who were gang members and heard their stories about gang life through courtroom proceedings, as well as learning about "what 'really' goes on in the judicial process."[6] For Murray, this period provided the knowledge and testimonies she needed to inform *Locas*: the lived experiences of gang members and how the United States and its judicial system view and treat working-class Latina/o/xs.

Murray sets *Locas* in Echo Park, Los Angeles and in three eras: 1980–1985, 1985–1990, and 1997. The story centers on two young Latinas in this neighborhood in these time periods: Cecilia, a birthright citizen of the United States whose undocumented mother immigrated from Mexico, and Lucía, an undocumented immigrant who accompanied her mother in her own migration from Mexico. The two Latinas struggle in poverty for most of their young lives, until Cecilia's brother Manny—whom Lucía dates—forms the Echo Park Lobos, a gang that ameliorates his family's and Lucía's penury.[7] Initially, Cecilia and Lucía join Manny in the Lobos. But after Cecilia is consistently subjected to domestic violence at the hands of her boyfriend (also a Lobo) to a point where she miscarries, she drops out of the gang, and briefly pursues a lesbian romance with a rival gang girl. Ultimately, though, Cecilia comes to reject her lesbian relationship and former gang life entirely (both of which she reads as criminal and immoral), to join the Catholic Church and adhere to marianismo. Lucía, on the other hand, perseveres against the emotional and physical abuse she faces in the Lobos to eventually seize power and a "patrón" status, to create a girl gang called the Fire Girls, and to rule the Lobos, Fire Girls, and Echo Park by the end of the novel.

In depicting these women who circumvent and succumb to the coloniality of gender in male-dominated gang life, Murray's novel imagines potential connections between the manipulation of masculinity and femininity and women who become full-citizen subjects of male-dominated gangs. In doing so, the book reveals: many unaddressed avenues for theorizing racialized female masculinity; femininity as an empowering performance in male-dominated, hypermasculine gangs; and the role of the coloniality of gender in toxifying female masculinity. In *Locas*, racialized female masculinity operates as a (de)colonial strategy that grants Latinas citizenship and power in male-dominated gangs, helping them to circumvent white capitalism, domestic and maternal labor, gendered violence, and a second-class status. But this masculinity ironically hinges upon the contradictory reproduction of the coloniality of gender, resulting in the women of the Lobos violently abusing and devaluing other working-class Latinas. This paradoxical representation, however, enables Murray's novel to unravel how the psychological, material, and ontological effects of patriarchal and capitalist colonial structures might toxify the female masculinities and (de)colonial projects of Latina gang members.

Reconsidering Female Masculinity and Femininity

In 1998, Jack Halberstam resisted the tendency to read masculinity as "a synonym for men or maleness" in *Female Masculinity*, the influential study of butches in film, literature, and culture.[8] In this book, Halberstam defines masculinity not as limited to men, but as a cultural performance available to any gender.[9] Taking this premise as an organizing principle, Halberstam analyzes "the topic of female masculinity to explore a queer subject position that can successfully challenge hegemonic models of gender conformity."[10] Scrutinizing how female masculinity challenges both the modern gender system and hegemonic masculinity valuably advances understandings of gender and sexuality, and of the ideologies that regulate and construct these models. Still, many have critiqued Halberstam for idealizing female masculinity as a bastion of resistance, and for not accounting for how female masculinity may replicate structures of oppression for women and gender nonconforming persons.

Halberstam defines "dominant masculinity" as "conjur[ing] up notions of power and legitimacy and privilege; it often symbolically refers to the power of the state and to uneven distributions of wealth."[11] This masculinity, for Halberstam, "seems to extend outward into patriarchy and inward into the home; masculinity represents the power of inheritance, the consequences of the traffic in women, and the promise of social privilege."[12] Halberstam commendably illuminates how female masculinity deconstructs the logic and rule of heteropatriarchy/normativity. But, if women as well as men can perform masculinity, then how might female performances also reproduce masculine hegemony and its "notions of power and legitimacy and privilege" that suppress those neither desiring nor performing a masculine identity? What are the consequences of female masculinity when women perform masculinity in a manner that also relies on "the traffic in women"? In what circumstances would women perform versions of masculinity troubling for other women and gender nonconforming persons, and why? These are questions that Halberstam's book does not attend to, but that *Locas* directly engages—specifically at the intersection of gender, race, and class, which remains another dynamic that Halberstam's book does not sufficiently tease out when theorizing female masculinity.

Though incredibly nuanced, Halberstam's analysis of butches and female masculinity favors class-privileged white persons, scarcely accounting for masculine performances by working-class women of color, and for how and why female masculinity may change in various racial and class contexts. In fact, when addressing the visibility of female masculinity, Halberstam rationalizes the need to *not* analyze race. Halberstam writes, "lesbians of color tend to be stereotyped along racial, as well as sexual, lines: the black lesbian, for example, is often stereotyped as the butch bulldagger or as sexually voracious, and so it makes no sense to talk about such a construction in terms of visibility and spectrality."[13] Because the gender performances, sexualities, and sexual practices of lesbians of color are "often stereotyped"—or, in other words, exoticized and fetishized, such as in BDSM pornography or prison television shows—Halberstam deems racialized female masculinities and lesbians of color's sexualities visible in a way that the "sexual scenes and sexual practices and pleasurable identifications" of white lesbians are not, leading to an "inarticulateness of white lesbian sexuality."[14] In this reasoning, Halberstam overlooks how fetishization and stereotypes also function as a form of invisibility, as much as they make visible racialized masculinity and sexuality. This stereotyping and fetishization also operate as disciplinary control. They mask the violent and criminal "sexual scenes and sexual practices" women of color experience—such as the high frequency of rape and sexual assault, and the low prosecution rates of the abusers. As Halberstam's logic ironically discloses, stereotypes and fetishization often enable persons to *not* discuss, hear, or view the trauma, voice, and gender and sexual performances of the stereotyped person, because they believe they already have.

One of the few instances where Halberstam attempts to analyze racialized female masculinity transpires in the discussion of Queen Latifah's butch, bank robber character Cleo, in the film *Set It Off* (1996). Halberstam writes, "the black female masculinity that Latifah portrays is convincing precisely because it is infused with racial and class dynamics that render the masculinity part and parcel of a particular form of abjected female identity.... Cleo's masculinity is as much a product of her life in the hood as it is about her lesbianism; it is a masculinity learned in poverty."[15] Despite recognizing that Cleo's masculinity arises in part from her life in a working-class, racialized space, Halberstam never grapples with this thread to examine how Cleo's masculinity differs from the surplus of white, class-privileged masculinities *Female Masculinity* discusses. Because Halberstam does not allocate more than two paragraphs to Cleo, readers never learn why—beyond a blanket "poverty"—Cleo's masculinity differs, what the performance affords and denies her, its effects on other women, how Cleo's masculinity may model itself after subaltern (as opposed to dominant) masculinities, or how or if her masculinity that relies on lethal violence and crime becomes toxified.

On the other hand, recent Latina/o/x studies scholars like Ellie Hernández and T. Jackie Cuevas have begun to theorize racialized female masculinities in Latina/o/x culture. In studying the representation of butchas, mariconas, and machas in the television shows *Vida* and *Madam Secretary*, as well as in Gloria Anzaldúa's "La historia de una marimacha," Hernández reveals how "Latinx female masculinity, however enigmatic, delivers a complexity that rewrites queer abjection," acting as a "lesbian agent and sexual subject whose aesthetic presence commands power."[16] Cuevas has likewise examined racialized female masculinity in *Bruising for Besos* (2016), arguing that this film delinks Chicana lesbians' masculinity from "violence and the imperative to use it to enforce dominance, opening up boundaries of what masculinity can mean."[17] Cuevas extends her theorization of racialized female masculinity in her book *Post-Borderlandia*, a study that reveals how "butchness for some Chicana lesbians is not about riding a stylistic, aesthetic, or political trend," but acts as a pedagogical orientation to gender identity and spatial belonging in many working-class Chicana/o/x communities.[18]

The work of Hernández, Cuevas, and others in Latina/o/x studies, like Francisco J. Galarte, has unveiled what prior queer feminist theory has too often elided: that race and class intersect in, and often reshape, female masculinity. *Clicas* builds from the avenues these scholars have laid by considering a racialized female masculinity that may also dabble in "the traffic in women" and manifest in toxified ways. Theorizing this possibility in Latina/o/x culture means accounting for the nuances of machismo—a subaltern masculinity that emerges in reaction to the legacy and effects of colonization/coloniality. In "La Chicana: Her Role in the Past and Her Search for a New Role in the Future," Bernice Rincón delineates the manifold characteristics of machismo:

> Positive: 1) Bravery, loyalty; 2) Pride in self as an individual; 3) Responsibility of leadership in the family; 4) Sacredness of the family (La Raza); 5) Human values: Love of fellows: compassion, suffering, liberty for all; 6) Lack of concern for money; 7) Love of music, dancing (joy of life); 8) Love of children; 9) Respect for religion; 10) Respect for elders; 11) Modesty and reserve; 12) Liberal political orientation; 13) Good manners; 14) Willingness to fight when needed.
>
> Negative: 1) Absolute power: a) Exploitation, b) Self centeredness, c) Violence used to maintain power through fear, d) Closed aloofness; 2) Women seen as a subordinate creature created to make man's lot more comfortable and pleasurable; 3) Too much pride; 4) Absolute power-inclination to strong man politics; Hero-worship-dictatorships; 5) There is sharing of the joys of life only as man sees fit. Woman's place is home; 6) Large families (here the church has also contributed); 7) Too much responsibility placed on the male to maintain his "position"; 8) Drinking, wenching, etc. seen as a sign of manhood; 9) Fighting seen as proof of masculinity; 10) Too modest and reserved for survival in today's society.[19]

Whether reading the positive or the negative aspects of machismo, many have categorized the performance as a subaltern masculinity that arises in response to the aftershocks of colonization/coloniality. As Micael Tapia insists, "*Machismo* is not in itself a cultural ethic for Latinos, but more so a product of imperialism and colonialism."[20] Tapia regards machismo as "an act of overt power over Latinas and less *macho* or effeminate men, but it is power coming from the powerlessness."[21] If machismo constitutes a subaltern masculinity that arises from and responds to colonization/coloniality, then racialized female masculinities are also subaltern masculinities, because men and whiteness always hold some type of hegemonic position in the United States. But even if resistant and representative of "power coming from the powerlessness," subaltern masculinities may also have detrimental effects on other subaltern persons. In this case, if any gender can perform masculinity—and, by extent, machismo—then these negative components of machismo that Rincón outlines are available for women to perform as much as are the positive ones.

I pursue these possibilities by considering how the racialized female masculinities in *Locas* epitomize the (de)colonial, how the gang girls of the novel use masculine performances as a strategy for navigating patriarchal male gangs, but in a way that hinges on the suppression of other multiply marginalized persons. Rather than dismiss these masculinities as toxified, however, I theorize how and why negative components of machismo materialize in the racialized female masculinities in *Locas*. Reading these masculinities as contradictory—as (de)colonial—also means that this chapter's exegesis of *Locas* shows that negative traits of machismo might accord competing possibilities when performed by working-class Latinas. The Latina gang members of *Locas* often perform these negative qualities in a way that enables them to circumvent the subordination that the coloniality of gender imposes on them personally, while simultaneously reifying coloniality's harm of other women.

Insofar as this chapter theorizes *Locas*'s representation of female masculinity, it also considers the novel's portrayal of femininity in hypermasculine, male-dominated gangs. Because many humanist and social science studies of gangs and gang culture take hypermasculine, heterosexual men as their subjects of analysis, femininity in these subcultures rarely receives serious attention. The few scholars who concentrate on women and/or femininity in gangs usually view femininity as a frailty that female and male gang members must shed to attain citizenship in gangs. Mark Totten, for instance, argues that, in gangs, masculinity signifies "power" and "aggression, dominance, independence, and violence," and femininity conveys "powerlessness" and "passivity, dependence, nurturance, and non-violence."[22] Similarly, T. W. Ward writes that in "gang ideology, femininity is seen as a weakness," and "[t]o be accepted within the gang, homegirls must act like one of the guys."[23] Justin Gifford, in contrast, is one of the few who depart from this presumption, contending that woman-authored, African American street fiction—such as novels by Teri Woods, Sister Souljah, Vickie Stringer, and Nikki Turner—divulges femininity's agential capacity in male-dominated subcultures such as underground drug markets and pimping rings.[24] Gifford writes that in this genre the working-class black woman's "expression of sexuality illustrates her agency within the very limiting confines of society defined by patriarchal capitalism."[25] For Gifford, femininity and sexuality allow women to "subvert the aims of would-be pimps, hustlers, and gangsters and reverse the power dynamics in those misogynist relationships."[26]

Likewise, Catherine S. Ramírez and Nadiah Rivera Fellah have both contributed similar observations about pachuca and chola femininity. Ramírez notes that insofar as pachucas embodied a "competing masculinity," they also practiced an "aberrant femininity" that did not compromise their capacity to "invad[e] the masculine public sphere" and "encroac[h] upon the male and masculine realm of resistance."[27] Rather, pachuca femininity was seen as integral for signifying the anti-assimilationist politics of the Latina/o/x gang tradition. As Ramírez explains, pachucas' "attire, hairstyles, and use of cosmetics" signaled "a declaration of insubordination. By exaggerating the accoutrements of ladyhood, pachucas . . . claimed and thereby threatened a powerful (however attenuated) cultural category from which they had been excluded."[28] Rivera Fellah develops an analogous argument about the insurgent capacity of contemporary chola femininity, contending that Graciela Iturbide's photographs of cholas of White Fence visualize how the aberrant femininity of the chola aesthetic enables these gang girls to claim "as their own" "White Fence gang culture," and contest "the patriarchy of US culture."[29]

In this chapter, I build from Gifford's, Ramírez's, and Rivera Fellah's observations about femininity to place their findings in conversation with Latina/o/x gang literature. When studying *Locas*, *Clicas* interprets the gang girls of the novel who preserve (at least some aspect of) conventional femininity—as well as aberrant chola femininity—to consider a range of questions. In what ways may Latina gang members politicize femininity, making use of its ostensible weaknesses, to subvert their male-dominated, hypermasculine gangs? How might femininity facilitate not passivity and subordination, but instead agency and power? What connections does femininity share with abstract and material (de)colonial projects in, through, and against male-dominated, hypermasculine gangs?

"What It Is to Become a Man"

To understand how Latina gang members in *Locas* perform racialized female masculinity and femininity to circumvent the patriarchal power dynamics of their gang, we must first understand the subaltern masculinity that the male Lobos idealize. As the founder and initial leader of the Lobos, Manny, whom most of the gang's male members model themselves after, exemplifies Lobos masculinity. Manny forms the Lobos to amass power, aggrandize his social status, and circumvent the poverty that afflicts him and his fellow Latina/o/xs in Echo Park. To prepare himself to accomplish these goals, Manny begins enlarging and strengthening his body, symbolically signifying the veritable creation of a new man. Cecilia says,

> I saw with my brother what it is to become a man. And I wanted to be a man like that. He got stronger, his skinny body moving up and curves coming out of his arms. His belly hardened into muscle and even the points of his eyes got sharper and sparked like black diamonds.[30]

Not only does Manny's transformation signal to Cecilia that physical strength and power are requisites for masculinity and citizenship in the Lobos, but Cecilia also identifies this masculinity as a pathway toward economic upward mobility. In perceiving "black diamonds" in Manny's emerging masculinity, Cecilia sutures Lobos masculinity to the amelioration of the poverty that structures the lives of the Latina/o/xs in *Locas*.

Indeed, this masculinity contributes to altering the penury that afflicts Manny by requiring participation in robberies and black-market economies, which Manny's new, chiseled body equips him for. Cecilia continues,

> He starts moving from picking pockets to stealing cars, and then sees how that money can *fly* in specials. Locals with a little rainy-weather cash start coming to him looking for a piece, and he'd reach into the back seat of his chopshop car and pull it out.... He'd

charge a hundred even, and I know he'd grin when he'd slip the bills in his pocket.[31]

After committing robberies, Manny organizes his own black-market enterprise to earn money and improve his own and his family's quality of life. As Cecilia says, Manny begins "leaving five hundred dollars on the table and he's not even seventeen," so that his mother will not have to wash "up after rich *rubia* ladies with smooth blond helmet hair who'd call her Maria even though her real name's Corazón."[32] In helping his mother and sister, Manny's masculinity features the responsibility for family that Rincón identifies as a positive trait of machismo. Manny does not just alleviate his mother's indigence, either. His actions also mitigate her exploitation and social invisibility by freeing her from having to perform menial labor for white bourgeois women who refuse to call Corazón by her name.

Though Manny's subaltern masculinity may feature a few positive aspects of machismo, he must rely almost entirely on its negative characteristics to eradicate his family's poverty, many of which harm other members of his barrio. First, although Manny later has the Lobos sell drugs to white people not of Echo Park, his victims are mostly his fellow neighborhood Latina/o/xs—including, ironically, his own family. He batters other Latino men who participate in the black-market and jeopardize the Lobos' income, such as "Gato," whom "Manny chopped . . . up into raw meat with those fast fists of his," and he even insinuates violence against his mother when she orders him around.[33] Since "[n]o boss man listens to an old lady, and no patrón lets his mama tell him what to do," Manny cautions his mother not to infringe on his authority, with "his left hand quivering down by his hip like a wild animal" to show her that "he would hit her just like she was just any other woman."[34] Because the patriarchal logics of the coloniality of gender inform the subaltern masculinity that Manny and the male Lobos perform, any woman who oversteps her position in the sexist social stratum threatens these men's masculinity, which these men must police and uphold through violence against women.

This subaltern masculinity also encompasses creating and regulating heteropatriarchal gender dynamics not only in relations between mothers and their gangbanging sons, but within the Lobos, as well. In his gang, Manny and his Lobos treat female gang members similarly to how Manny treats his mother—an obstacle that the daughter-speaker of *My Father Was a Toltec* does not have to overcome in her gang life.

The male Lobos subordinate the women of the gang by relegating them to inferior statuses, and granting them only nominal membership. According to Lucía, women in the Lobos hold a "sheep" ranking. This means that "girls wasn't doing shit in the clika" because men reduce them to reproductive hosts, domestic servants, and second-class citizens.[35] Invoking common stereotypes about women in gangs, *Locas* initially portrays male gang members as envisioning female gang members as only "good for fucking" and "squeezing out kiddies."[36] As Lucía remarks after pondering how a fellow Lobo named Paco views her, "He just saw some girl, a *chavala* good-for-nothing, a piece of ass."[37]

Part of the reason that male Lobos reduce women to "piece[s] of ass" that are only around for "squeezing out kiddies" stems from how having children (specifically boys) supposedly increases men's masculinity in the gang and barrio. As Manny says to Lucía after haranguing her for not getting pregnant, "I'm looking bad being the only one with a vieja who can't squeeze out no little doggies."[38] Without a woman to birth his "seed," Manny appears sterile and effeminate. This obsession with impregnating female gang members also has other patriarchal agendas. As T. W. Ward explains, pregnant women lose

> status within their gangs because of the expectation that they should curb their participation in order to protect the baby. This is especially true if the father of the child is an active member of the gang. He is likely to put pressure on his pregnant wife or girlfriend to "chill out." . . . In addition, pregnant homegirls are seen as a liability in gang warfare because of the perception of pregnancy as a physical handicap.[39]

While pregnant, women cannot reasonably participate in gang violence and the gang's social bonding activities, like rumbles and parties where drinking, smoking, and huffing consistently occur in Murray's novel. For this reason, pregnancy becomes a strategy for men to excommunicate Lobos women, who are already denied full citizenship in the gang, once the women have served their "purpose."

Additionally, Lobos men charge the women with fulfilling the gang's domestic needs. Lucía comments that, at home, Manny aggressively forces her into domestic labor, saying to her, "Chingada, I'm only gonna tell you once, hear? Clean up this fucking floor, I ain't living like a pig just cause you're lazy."[40] This behavior continues in gang meetups as well, as Manny and the Lobos men mandate that Lucía and all

Lobos women continue the domestic work they perform in the home. Lucía says:

> Sometimes we'd all get together and have a barbecue at the park. There's me and the other girlfriends running around making sure the food's good, the tacos and chicken all steamy and spicy just perfect. And then the men standing around swigging beer and talking business.... I didn't always wanna be doing the food, though, all that stirring and wrapping and putting out the plates. I wanted to be over there on the vatos' side of the line and listen to them talk about clika deals. But any time I tried to cross over, when I walked up to Manny and his homeboys and listened in to what they're saying, Manny would slam me. "Hey, chavala. This is man business now, go on over there." He'd put his hand up and then look at me, giving me his stop sign, and I didn't press it.[41]

While the gang holds social outings or conducts meetings to deliberate about their black-market business, Lucía and other women must wait on the men, preparing their food and the table. When the women are not serving, the men segregate them. The Lobos men force women to the sidelines, because the men's masculinity requires that women not learn of the gang's business operations, so that the men may remain the empowered "breadwinners" and in independent and superior positions in the Lobos. This ideology recurrently manifests itself when the Lobos men also bar women from joining them in gang fights and hits on rivals. Because Lobos women cannot access the black-market economy of the gang, and must rely on the men to care for them financially, they are almost powerless to amend their subordinate "sheep" statuses in the Lobos. In performing a subaltern heterosexual masculinity that predominantly incorporates the negative characteristics of machismo and reduces women to their bodies and to domesticity, the men of the Lobos reproduce the oppressive power of the coloniality of gender. They thus reinforce the heteropatriarchal hegemony, compulsory heterosexuality, and reproductive futurism that women like the daughter-speaker of *My Father Was a Toltec* might seek out gangs to escape.

Despite the troubling effects this subaltern masculinity has on women, many of the female gang members in *Locas* desire the power it precipitates in the Lobos and their barrio. Cecilia, for instance, mentions that, after witnessing her brother grow stronger and seeing diamonds in his eyes, she saw "what it is to become a man" and "wanted to be a man like that."[42] Though Manny's masculinity requires misogyny, violence, crime, and the subordination of women, his masculinity facilitates (de)colonial projects for him and his male Lobos, helping them circumvent the sub-ontological difference and capitalist imbalances that structure their lives in coloniality. Cecilia realizes that this masculinity helps accord these privileges in and through Lobos gang life, but she also knows that "woman" means "sheep." At this point in the novel, therefore, these (de)colonial rewards are attainable only for men, leaving Latinas to rely on men's "charity." Regardless of her initial desires, Cecilia elects to remain in this subordinate position throughout most of the novel, replacing the heteropatriarchal hegemony of the Lobos with the Catholic church's. Lucía, in contrast, appropriates this subaltern masculinity to earn citizenship and power in the gang, transforming the Lobos into a space where she may access the paradoxical benefits that gangs might offer.

And So the Sheep Donned Her Pendleton

To perform the racialized female masculinity necessary for her to acquire full citizenship and power in the Lobos, Lucía sheds her "spiky heels" and "slut dresses" of conventional femininity in favor of the primarily masculine chola aesthetic popular in 1980s and 90s California, often featuring baggy Dickies khakis and Ben Davis jeans, Pendleton flannels, Nike Cortez and Chuck Taylor sneakers, bandanas, dark sunglasses, and aberrantly feminine hoop earrings, teased and dyed long hair (red for Northsiders and black for Southsiders), and dark makeup and eyeliner (either brown for Southsiders or red and burgundy for Northsiders).[43] As Lucía says, "I'd dress chola with my girls, button up my Pendleton, wear them black jeans, tough jacket, put on a dark mean mouth.... I knew that no sheep could look like I did right then."[44] In adopting this chola aesthetic, Lucía's appearance conveys masculine intimidation and de-emphasizes her prior sexualized, conventionally feminine style that leaves her "melons" "sticking out."[45] When Lucía dons this chola aesthetic, her buttoned, baggy Pendleton covers up her breasts that her previous "slut dresses" revealed, while her billowing pants mask her legs and rear that these dresses may accentuate.[46] Her new aesthetic occludes body parts that signal for her undesired connotations of a conventional feminine embodiment—either frailty (small arms, tiny frame, etc.) or sex object and reproductive host (breasts, legs, rear)—to instead connote terrifying aggression.[47] Although Lucía preserves the aberrant femininity of the chola aesthetic in wearing dark lipstick ("put[ting] on a dark mean mouth"), the dark color synchronizes with her de-sexualized and menacing, masculine appearance—similar to how the aberrantly feminine "comb, teased hair, and long red fingernails" of the 1940s pachuca "allude[d] to violence" and to "the ostensibly masculine."[48] Furthermore, Lucía not only undertakes measures that outwardly resist the maternal and sexual evocations of her body; she also begins taking birth control pills "nice and quick and didn't tell a soul."[49] In taking birth control, Lucía further distances herself from a "woman/sheep" status in the gang by nullifying biological capacities that mark her as a nominal gang member whose primary purpose centers on birthing male children to aggrandize Manny's masculinity. Instead, she bypasses the requirements of reproductive futurism in the Lobos, and ensures that pregnancy cannot expel her from the gang she desires to earn citizenship in.

In elaborating on the male version of this gang aesthetic, Richard T. Rodríguez notes that the cholo style has performative and linguistic components as well, entailing a "bold stance" and "distinct language (think caló mixed with hip-hop parlance)."[50] When adopting the chola aesthetic to masculinize herself, Lucía mirrors the linguistic and performative aspects of this male version, consistently skirting the grammar of standard English, frequently cussing, and speaking Caló words like esá, vato, chola, and órale. Caló, in particular, has a crucial part in the masculinization of the chola and cholo aesthetics. Ramírez argues that pachuco slang—a colloquially interchangeable term for Caló—connotes masculinity and men: "Like black jive, pachuco slang's origins are in activities and realms generally associated with men and masculinity, such as the criminal underworld, androcentric jazz subculture, and the working class, which, in and of itself, is often configured as male and masculine. Consequently, it has been widely regarded as a 'male-dominated, intragroup form of communication.'"[51] Chiefly appearing in male-dominated spaces, Caló exemplifies talking "manly." Thus, by speaking Caló like the rest of the male Lobos, Lucía rejects gendered expectations of linguistic propriety, such as speaking meekly, modestly, and without curse words.

Moreover, many Latina gang members note that the style and "bold stance" of the chola aesthetic empower their capacity to move through space, to "win space" from men in ways previously inaccessible to them. As a Latina gang member of Mendoza-Denton's ethnography explains, in the chola aesthetic "[n]obody could fuck with you. You got power. People look at you, but nobody fucks with you. So when you walk down the street, you got that special walk.... [Y]ou walk all slow, just checking it out" and thinking "I look like a dude, ¿que no?"[52] When Lucía adopts the chola aesthetic, she also performs its masculine bold stance and saunter in a way that enables her to win space, just "like a dude." She says that she "started walking straight like a man does, taking them long-legged roomy steps so people start getting out of my way. Watch it, esé, that's the look I had on my face."[53] When Lucía would wear a conventionally feminine aesthetic in the past, Manny and the other Lobos would dictate her ability to move through space with a straightened palm, halting her from crossing domestic boundaries that segregate women in Lobos meetups. In her masculine chola aesthetic, however, Lucía stands tall and confident, taking "long-legged roomy steps" to navigate and win space. She sheds the passive ideology of a "sheep" that mandates women yield to men as they walk throughout the world. Instead, she claims that her strut and face demand that men defer to her, as she uses the Caló word esé that refers to men—rather than the feminine esá. By declaring that her face and stance force men to "watch it" so that they move out of her path, she demonstrates how the racialized female masculinity of the chola aesthetic has begun to grant her power over men, and the capacity to contest the patriarchal barriers of the Lobos and her barrio. In this way, Lucía showcases how the chola aesthetic helps her circumvent the limitations the coloniality of gender imposes on her, for, as Mendoza-Denton explains, this aesthetic "not only confounds wider community notions of how girls should act, dress, and talk, but throws into question the very gendered category that girls are expected to inhabit."[54]

Having assumed a new identity and ontology through adopting this aesthetic, Lucía further breaches the "sheep" "category that girls are expected to inhabit" by becoming more active in the Lobos, its territories, and the public sphere. During her sheep days, Lucía implores Manny to teach her how to drive, so that she "wouldn't have to take no RTD every place I go."[55] But since "[s]heep don't drive" and instead "walk or bus or wait for their men to get behind the wheel," Manny tells her to "sit your ass down" because "[y]ou don't see no other woman driving round here."[56] Manny and the male Lobos' rationale for keeping women from driving centers on attempting to imprison them in the private sphere, furthering their financial and social dependence, and excluding women from gang life. Accessing the public sphere only through public transportation, walking, or their male partners' "generosity" limits women's ability to earn economic independence, purchase food and clothing, or attend gang meetings and activities without male Lobos' approval. It also helps ensure that women remain in the home to raise the children of Lobos gang members and perform domestic duties. But once Lucía begins dressing, talking, and walking like a man, she also refuses to remain in the private sphere like sheep. Rather, like a man, she starts driving to enter the streets and public sphere more easily. Lucía says,

> I even got myself driving. You can't be a real grouper if you ain't behind your own wheel. . . . I learned how to drive out in empty parking lots after dark, squealing around and pumping up the gas like some crazy-ass. Park, Neutral, Drive, Reverse. But once I got out on that road, *wacha* out! The wind coming through the rolled-down window playing my hair and the AM radio blasting some good song, my wheels driving me where I wanna go.[57]

Refusing to wait for a Lobo to teach her to drive, Lucía collects enough money to purchase her own "banged-out old Ford Maverick" so that she may go wherever she pleases.[58] By taking birth control, Lucía circumvents the maternal expectations of the private sphere for women, but by learning to drive, she rejects the realm of the gendered category of "sheep" entirely in forgoing the private sphere.

In fact, once Lucía owns her own vehicle and can drive, she spends the majority of her time on the streets, an area that also contributes to her racialized female masculinity. Miranda defines the streets as "a particular kind of space—urban space—through which the citizen navigates to reach other institutions and places of production."[59] While the streets facilitate re-entrance into the private sphere (the home) after leaving, they are also necessary for persons to access the various "institutions and places of production" that compose public life. For this reason, and because the private sphere traditionally codes as feminine and the public as masculine, many scholars understand the streets as a marker of masculinity. As Raewyn Connell says, "[T]he street then is a zone of occupation by men."[60] Lucía's presence in the streets, thus, becomes an integral component to her racialized female masculinity. Additionally, because the majority of Lobos gang life transpires in the streets or in other sites of the public sphere, the streets also facilitate Lucía's entrance into the Lobos gang in a way not available to other

Lobos women, who must rely on men to bring them to gang events. The streets are therefore paramount to Lucía becoming a full citizen-subject in the Lobos—especially because of the behavior she displays on the streets once she finally accesses them.

When in the streets, Lucía performs the violent (negative) aspects of the masculinity/machismo that she learns from Manny. Like Manny committing robberies in public spaces, Lucía, too, organizes robberies on the streets, hunting white people in public. She says,

> You've got to go to the whitefolks for the real money. Before I got my hands on drug deals, the best jobs was stealing them sweet credit cards.... Órale, all them richie folks, you can spot them from a mile away. They wear clean-pressed suits and fancy shoes, silk ties, and you know they've got a square of pretty VISA plastic in their wallets.[61]

By orchestrating crimes against middle- and upper-class whites to obtain money, Lucía ameliorates the economic inequality she experiences in her Echo Park barrio, escapes the dehumanizing mistreatment she may face if working menial labor for rich rubias like Cecilia's mother Corazón, and partially severs her financial dependence on male Lobos. In doing so, Lucía also augments her racialized female masculinity in the Lobos, as the masculinity the gang idealizes depends on violence, power, money, and crime. Although Lucía's reasons for performing this masculinity are more complicated than the male Lobos'—since Lucía experiences multiple marginality along racial, class, and gendered lines—she, nonetheless (like Manny) relies on the negative characteristics of machismo. This is especially so because she does not limit her violent attacks to bourgeois whites, but targets working-class Latinas as well—a complex topic this chapter later tackles.

Because the Lobos valorize violent hypermasculinity, Lucía's racialized female masculinity partly enables her to alter her standing in the Lobos: from a sheep to a ruler who exerts power over all Lobos members, and who controls the gang's operations. Although some male Lobos still resist Lucía's presence in the gang, most come to view her as their equal and, for many others, their superior. After Lucía earns full citizenship in the Lobos, Manny now invites her to come along with him in attacks against rival gang members, and Lucía also participates in gang meetings. As she says, "The sheep are supposed to stay put during the meeting.... But not this chica. Those days were over. I was dressed just like a gangster... and I walked right into the Big Room like I belong."[62] Taking bold steps into the "Big Room," Lucía deliberates with the other gang members about how to handle their current gang war. Though one Lobo protests to Manny, "No bitches in the Big Room," Manny responds, "Shut the FUCK up! Shut up!" to defend Lucía's right to remain, which she does.[63]

Eventually, Lucía attains so much power in the gang that she announces to Manny, "I gotta cock on me now, Manny. I'm the one making the money go round and round. I'm the one making sure we're not getting fucked by these lowlifes and mama's boys."[64] Because Lucía has obtained control of the gang's drug and gun economy, and no longer behaves like a sheep, even rival gang members recognize her as the Lobos' true leader. For instance, during the Lobos' war with the C-4, a gang that a defecting Lobos member establishes, the C-4 leader, Chico, visits Lucía—not Manny or other male Lobos competing for leadership of the gang—to discuss terms. This leads Lucía to remark, "I was feeling loca high cause the main C-4 boss man comes looking to *me*."[65] By the end of the novel, Lucía has evolved from a sheep to the monarch of the Lobos, Fire Girls, and streets of Echo Park. As she says in the final chapter of *Locas*,

> See that street? Alvarado Street, the straight black road lined with the bodega stores and the little cholas hanging by the corner? It belongs to me. And Elsinor, Benton, Reservoir streets with the old peel-paint houses and the rusted chain-link and the pickups by the curb? All mine. If you say my name out loud there every Mexican walking by is gonna stop and look at you careful. They all know who I am.[66]

As is the case with the Toltec of Castillo's poetry collection, the entire barrio knows of Lucía. She has shed her prior social invisibility and abject and impoverished status. While she remains a second-class citizen in the eyes of the US nation-state, through gang life, this veritably created new woman materially and psychologically offsets her alterity by participating in and ruling the Lobos and Fire Girls, and by claiming and holding Echo Park as her property. This is a meaningful achievement, given that she manages to hold Echo Park even while this neighborhood begins to gentrify toward the end of the novel.[67] These (de)colonial rewards materialize in part because Lucía's racialized female masculinity grants her full citizenship in the Lobos, creating the avenue for her to appropriate, transform, and rule the gang. In this way, Lucía strategically works within the confines of the coloniality of gender that regulate her life, and thus circumvents the restrictions its heteropatriarchal ideologies impose on her. By co-opting and performing the negative characteristics of machismo, Lucía escapes male Lobos' ability to relegate her to domesticity, motherhood, and the private sphere. As the current chapter soon argues, however, her capacity to evade these effects of the coloniality of gender hinges on exacerbating its power over other working-class Latinas.

Admittedly, part of the reason why Lucía can become a gang leader in the Lobos stems from her position as the male leader's girlfriend. At times, this arrangement means dating Manny, but at other times, Lucía must orchestrate a mutiny and install another man whom she can manipulate. Nevertheless, while Lucía must stand alongside a man as the Lobos queen, she refashions the sheep/man dynamic in the Lobos to demote male leaders to nominal ruling statuses. A man may remain the face of the gang, but Echo Park, the Lobos, and gang rivals realize that Lucía controls and oversees the gang. This is indicated by "every Mexican walking by" who stops once he or she hears Lucía's name, and by Chico visiting Lucía to negotiate a gang war. But this "behind-the-scenes" power that requires a man initiates my next point.

Most criticism on *Locas* concludes at realizing that Lucía's female masculinity facilitates her capacity to obtain citizenship and power in the Lobos. Monica Brown, for example, observes that by the end of the novel, "Lucía and her Fire Girls transform the sexual economy of the Lobos gang; where they once had value as 'good for fucking,' they now have more choices and agency."[68] For Brown, this agency and choice that some women now have emerge from their female masculinity. Similarly, Daniel Enrique Pérez writes that some of the female Lobos "decide to transform their identities from docile young women to powerful entities that do not only participate fully in a gang but also control other gang members. To do this, they are required to not only gain power (i.e., a phallus) but also to exert it over others, including male gang members."[69] According to Pérez, Lucía's transformation in the gang requires a symbolic metamorphosis where she adopts a phallus and deploys its power over other gang members and civilians in the barrio.[70]

I do not disagree with any of these readings, and, as this chapter has shown in tracing out Lucía's masculinity, I also contend that racialized female masculinity enables Lucía to obtain full citizenship and power in the Lobos. But I also work from the insights of many of these scholars by extending the criticism on *Locas* in multiple ways. I consider how Lucia's masculinity manifests as a toxified racialized female masculinity and theorize what this toxicity reveals about the effects of the coloniality of gender on masculinity, Lucía, and other gang girls and women. Furthermore, I also part ways with those that deem Lucía's rise to power solely a result of her masculinity. I elect also to center the critical role of her femininity in her ascendance in a hypermasculine, male-dominated subculture. As mentioned earlier, though Lucía rises to the status of a monarch by the end of the novel, she must always position herself alongside a man to do so, even if she thoroughly dictates and manipulates him. When achieving this elevated status in the Lobos, Lucía does not always perform masculinity. She sometimes reverts to a conventional feminine embodiment, though not necessarily to a sheep status, because of the subversive capacity femininity has in the gang and in her relations with Lobos leaders.

Gang Girl Femininity

Although Gifford, Ramírez, and Rivera Fellah break from the norm, many others typically understand femininity, either in a woman or man, as antithetical to—or, at best, subordinate in—hypermasculine, male-dominated gangs and other subcultures.[71] Even in revisionist gang narratives that feature women as full citizen-subjects, or in studies that identify women's agency in gangs, scholars often view women gang members as only able to participate in gangs—beyond maternalism and as sexual objects—through jettisoning their femininity to become "men." This is because femininity ostensibly only impedes, rather than facilitates, gang citizenship.[72] *Locas*, however, clashes with many of these presumptions about femininity, and coincides with the findings of Gifford, Ramírez, and Rivera Fellah. Though preferring the primarily masculine chola style, Lucía selectively performs a conventional femininity (as opposed to the aberrant femininity of the chola aesthetic) to manage her indigent life chances in the United States, and to generate opportunities for earning citizenship in the Lobos, thereby creating the avenue to transform the gang into her own (de)colonial subculture.

Prior to Lucía entering the Lobos, conventional femininity enables her to combat the economic inequality she experiences as an undocumented woman in a low-income barrio. In the beginning of the novel, Lucía is sitting on the porch outside the house that her mother cleans for work. Manny, who at this point has already established the Lobos and started their participation in the black market, drives by in a luxury vehicle and introduces himself. During this encounter, Lucía says to herself, "He was the ticket. . . . I didn't even stop to think. I ran right into them arms of his like they was gonna save my life."[73] In Manny, Lucía—whose undocumented status limits her options for employment and upward mobility—identifies an opportunity for evading the perils she watches her mother succumb to. Rather than resigning herself to cleaning bourgeois people's homes on her hands and knees, or "hooking from the gutter" to persist financially, Lucía recognizes that Manny can rescue her from such a fate.[74] To pursue a somewhat better future, Lucía instrumentalizes her sexuality while performing an eroticized femininity to manipulate Manny and his heterosexual masculinity. She says, "I spent all my time putting on lip gloss, pumping up my hair so I'm looking like Charo, squeezing into skin-tights and five-inch heels. I knew I had to flirt and swing and show off my best parts to keep my man happy."[75] Whereas in adopting Pendleton flannels and baggy pants Lucía obscures her "best parts," here she wears clothing that sexualizes her body, because letting Manny pull "on [her] bow like he was opening up a birthday present" accords her economic upward mobility.[76] As Manny's girlfriend, Lucía no longer toils in penury, but improves her class status. She explains that Manny "set me up in my own apartment, got me food, everything, a rabbit-fur jacket so I was strutting around the park."[77] Not only does she garner food and housing through a sexualized, feminine performance, but Lucía also temporarily approximates feelings of a lavish life by wearing a "rabbit-fur jacket" and "strutting around the park," allowing her barrio to, she believes, gawk in envy of her. In doing so, Lucía aggrandizes her self-esteem and sense of status, rejecting the social invisibility and abjection that her exploited mother and Corazón—whose name her white employers cannot remember—face.

Admittedly, Manny may only crave Lucía because she augments his masculinity and patrón status. Although Manny handles her like a sexual possession whom he flaunts amongst his male friends, Lucía claims that she "didn't care," because "I thought I'd won the sheep lotto."[78] Lucía profits from performing a sexualized feminine aesthetic in a way that economically improves her life chances compared to the limited ones she believes available to her that entail menial labor or "hooking from the gutter." Thus, in the early pages of its narrative, *Locas* begins to disclose the agential capacity of a conventional femininity, its power to dictate and exploit heterosexual masculinity, and its connections to Lucía's psychological and material circumvention of coloniality.

Eventually, Lucía grows dissatisfied with the treatment her sexualized feminine aesthetic invites, and she transitions to the primarily masculine chola style to help herself achieve citizenship in the gang. Her later preference for the chola aesthetic, however, does not mean Lucía views conventional femininity as purposeless in her rise to power. Before Lucía can profit from the subversive effects of the chola aesthetic, she must first acquire a power in the gang that, in the novel, only conventional femininity's invisibility and ability to manipulate heterosexual masculinity can grant. Lucía first establishes an avenue for attaining citizenship and power in the Lobos by exploiting her position as Manny's sexual possession. After the police arrest Manny for selling guns and drugs, he spends seven months in prison, and the Lobos' income stalls. As a result, Lucía, cognizant that Manny struggles to have sexual intercourse with women in prison, instrumentalizes a sexualized, conventionally feminine aesthetic to manipulate his heterosexual masculinity. When visiting Manny in prison, Lucía dresses "*linda* looking" with her "hair all done up, curled and sprayed," and wears "purple eyeshadow and a pink dress."[79] Lucía's feminine appearance has an advantageous effect on Manny, as it beguiles him into disclosing where he stashes the weapons that the Lobos sell. Because Lobos men regard conventionally feminine women as incompetent, Manny trusts Lucía with the location of the guns. He does not believe she has the intellect to supplant his leadership by stealing these weapons to head the Lobos' black-market economy. Instead, Manny charges Lucía with acting as a mule, ordering her to deliver the guns to his fellow Lobo Paco, whom he surmises will not betray him. But when Lucía uncovers the guns, she realizes that she has the means for ending her sheep status in the Lobos. Observing Lucía in this moment, Cecilia says, "I could see how her brain started going tick-tock and working overtime" because "she got an idea of how she could earn it [money] for herself."[80] With access to the Lobos' weapons, Lucía begins to formulate strategies for ending her economic dependence on Manny. Lobos men's perception of feminine women as stupid, when joined with

112 | *Clicas*

conventional femininity's ability to manipulate heterosexual masculinity, has created the opportunity for her to do so.

Lucía, however, does not pilfer the guns. She instead delivers them to Paco and deploys similar manipulative tactics to gain information about how the Lobos run their gun and drug trade, and about which Lobo snitched on Manny to send him to prison. She reasons that, with the knowledge of the culprit's identity, she can increase Manny's confidence in her, in the process learning and gaining greater access to more of the Lobos' weapon-and-drug enterprise. After Paco smokes marijuana, Lucía instrumentalizes her sexualized feminine aesthetic to seduce him:

> He'd taken a couple of hits already and the boy opened like a door as soon as I cuddles up to him.... I get braver and start to blink and coo and even paw him a little, stroking his shoulder with my finger just once, like a light tickle on top of his thin white t-shirt.... Paco talked on, his mouth moving just cause I touched him like that.... and he's bragging now. He's got a load of front-page news stuffed in his head and why not tell the sexy thing with the tickle finger a thing or two?[81]

Successfully captivating Paco, Lucía entices him to talk so that she can alter her power dynamic with Manny. After obtaining the information she seeks, she says, "I knew enough so that it's Manny who's gonna have to come to *me* with questions."[82] In enabling her to learn about the operations of the Lobos' black-market economy and which Lobo sent Manny to prison, Lucía's weaponized femininity allows her to—for the first time in their relationship—relegate Manny to a dependent state in forcing him to come to her to satisfy his wants.

Moreover, through profiting from feminine women's invisibility in the Lobos, Lucía continues to amplify Manny's dependency to the point where he must relinquish control of the Lobos to her. Lucía claims that sheep are "invisible to men. If a chica stands round quiet long enough, a man just forgets her."[83] Though the men usually forget about conventionally feminine women because they deem them incompetent, domestic maids, or sexual objects, this invisibility does not necessarily always render them powerless. Rather, as Ralph Ellison's narrator in *Invisible Man* claims, "It is sometimes advantageous to be unseen."[84] In *Locas*, conventional femininity's invisibility enables Lucía to challenge the patriarchal hierarchy that limits her status in the

Lobos. For example, although, with Paco and Manny, Lucía performs a conventional feminine aesthetic to manipulate these men into releasing crucial information, at other times Lucía achieves knowledge of the Lobos' black-market operations through going unnoticed. She says that once a man forgets about a woman's presence, "He'll let forty cats out of their bags before he turns around and sees her watching him, her ears as big as jugs."[85] Lucía uses these "ears as big as jugs" multiple times to learn of the gang's operations and politics, primarily in gang meetings where women must serve men food and beer. As she says, "They'd all hang around in a bunch getting drunker and drunker, eating our food with their big mouths chewing open and sloppy, and pretty soon they're grinning and hollering.... I got eyes and ears."[86] Because of the Lobos' drunkenness and their misogyny that regards women as incompetent servants, the men unwittingly contribute to their own demise.

Eventually, Lucía's feminine aesthetic enables her to overthrow Manny when she cajoles him into ceding to her the financial management of the Lobos' underground economy, which she now understands well enough to run on her own. Unnoticed while serving Manny breakfast, Lucía observes that Manny has trouble with math and can no longer balance the Lobos' accounts after the Lobos' black-market business has flourished. She says,

> I'm feeding him breakfast but his face is just hanging like a drape. He's drumming his fingers on the table, tapping his pencil. I see there's nothing but scribbles on the page, doodles, cuss words, a couple numbers jumbled together. And I move like a hungry bird.[87]

Upon realizing his confusion, Lucía begins coaxing Manny and taking advantage of his perception of feminine women as too stupid to threaten his rule. She inquires about Manny's scribbles while talking "nice and sweet" and "putting fat rolls of *pan dulce* on his plate."[88] Lucía sits beside him and says, "Honey, I can do the maths for you. I just do it for a minute, while you eat up."[89] As opposed to the aggressive, masculine Caló she talks when performing the chola aesthetic, Lucía, in this exchange, speaks meekly and incorrectly pluralizes "math," fostering Manny's belief that a feminine woman cannot subvert him because of her supposed ineptitude and frailty. Manny acquiesces to Lucía's request, allowing her to continue to manage the gang's finances, but he "didn't let any of his vatos find out that a woman's doing Lobos money business."[90] If the gang were to discover that Manny has permitted a woman to handle the Lobos' funds, then his masculinity and patrón status would both dissipate because of the Lobos' patriarchal foundation. Therefore, he must keep his reliance on Lucía secret, a dilemma that Lucía uses to blackmail Manny and obtain control of the gang.

Only after Lucía alters the power dynamic in her relationship with Manny does she begin performing the racialized female masculinity of the chola aesthetic to obtain full citizenship in, and eventually rule, the Lobos. Because Manny remains the nominal patrón, Lucía not only demands that he recognize and endorse her leadership in the gang, which will cause the Lobos to accept and treat her as a full citizen-subject, but also that he finance her Fire Girls gang. If he does not, Lucía threatens to leave and run the gun and drug business on her own, saying, "ain't nobody gonna help you like I can. So think about it hard, honey, cause I'll walk right out that door and leave you all alone."[91] Because Manny now depends on Lucía to keep the Lobos' gun and drug trade operating (and must keep this arrangement quiet), and because Lucía now understands how to appropriate and reproduce black-market operations, Manny has no choice but to grant whatever Lucía asks.

Lucía also uses a sexualized, conventionally feminine aesthetic to reproduce this same arrangement with another male leader she installs after recognizing that Manny's weakening masculinity will lead to a mutiny and compromise her new position in the gang. Because Manny cannot murder a rival gang leader who shot a Lobo, many Lobos begin questioning Manny's capability to lead them. Foreseeing how an alternate and more capable leader may cause her to return to sheep standing, Lucía replaces Manny with another Lobo whom she can order and manipulate. Momentarily shedding her predominantly masculine chola aesthetic, Lucía reverts to a conventional feminine appearance and deploys the same machinations against another Lobo, Beto, that she did with Manny, to convince him to supplant Manny. Lucía says that after Manny "blows that hit on Chico"—the rival gang member who shot a Lobo—she visited Beto "fancied up in my best pink skirt, the one they like grabbing under, and my hair teased high, my lips as red and glossy as ripe cherries."[92] Unlike the dark lipstick she wears when dressed chola, Lucía dons red lipstick and a short skirt to profit from the sexualization of her feminine body. As a conventionally feminine woman in this encounter with Beto, she "makes doe eyes" at him and whispers in his ear like a honeydripper. "Beto, you're the special man, ése. . . . Manny's getting soft, right? He's a loser, honey, and the Lobos need a leader now. They need a tough-guy patrón just like you."[93]

After manipulating Beto's heterosexual masculinity, Lucía has him "eating out of my hand like a bird" so much that he acts on Lucía's desires, overthrows Manny, and maintains a nominal patrón standing that Lucía exploits because, as she says, "men are too easy."[94]

For these reasons, although in the Lobos, conventional femininity invites oppression, sexualization, and domesticity, this femininity in women also has profitable potential. This is because of the effects the performance has on heterosexual masculinity, and of male gang members' sexist perception of feminine women. While racialized female masculinity may solidify Lucía's citizenship and power in the gang, femininity also has a formative role in generating the avenue for Lucía to co-opt and circumvent the patriarchal structure of the Lobos. In this way, although *Locas* features the exploitational gang girl stereotypes found in films like *Havoc*, the novel appropriates these stereotypes to refashion them, and to present alternative representations of Latinas who gangbang. In these disparate depictions, Murray's novel becomes one of the few cultural products available that enables readers to conceive of Latina gang members as citizen-subjects who use crime and violence to resist the alterity that arises from the coloniality of gender.

Toxified Female Masculinities

Lucía's Fire Girls operate as a queer girl gang that compensates for the second-class status its female members experience in the Lobos and in their Echo Park barrio. Although none of the Fire Girls ever disclose themselves as non-heterosexual (though this possibility exists), I interpret the Fire Girls as queer in Lee Edelman's conception. Edelman defines queer as "the side of those *not* 'fighting for the children,'" persons who do not participate in conventional modes of reproductive futurism and thus do not further heteronormativity and the idealization of the child as the future.[95] Under this model, the Fire Girls are queer in that the gang outlaws heterosexual sex and pregnancy, and they are, thus, antithetical to heteronormativity and the cult of the child.

In forming the Fire Girls, Lucía requires that her "girls didn't have no babies"—either as a result of rape or consensual sex—by having them take birth control.[96] While no men participate in the Fire Girls, Lucía understands that pregnant women in *Locas* represent "sheep" because of how men use pregnancy to aggrandize their own hypermasculinity and exclude women from gang life. Because Lucía, in part, forges the Fire Girls to help Latinas shed their sheep statuses in the barrio, she requires that her gang members never revert to behaving as sheep when with men. This dictum means banning pregnancy and heterosexual sex altogether. For example, when Star Girl, a member of the Fire Girls, flirts with a man named Chavez to sell him drugs, Chavez says, "I'll buy some if I get a taste of you" and "mov[es] his hand" to "give her a little pinch on the ass."[97] Witnessing this event and how, in her mind, Chavez attempts to make Star Girl "beg him like she's some whore," Lucía interjects and "pushed him rough so he ain't touching my Girl no more."[98] Though Star Girl uses the same tactics as Lucía to manipulate heterosexual masculinity for financial gains, Lucía demands that her Fire Girls not replicate this behavior because only "sheep" allow men to use their bodies for sexual pleasure and treat them like "some whore." Of course, Lucía participates in both the Lobos and the Fire Girls and, though she bans heterosexual sex in her girl gang, she continues to have sex with men in the Lobos to maintain her authoritative position. In this way, Lucía views herself as an ironic, sacrificial savior for her girl gang members, whom she considers "a new family" and protects as their matriarch.[99]

In many ways, transforming the Fire Girls into a non-heteronormative/non-reproductive space means Lucía mimics—even as she queers—the Lobos' heterosexual masculinity. She does so by policing women's sexualities, similarly to how the Lobos men regulate women's sexualities by pressuring them to bear their children—even if, in Lucía's mind, her actions protect gang girls and resist heteropatriarchy. But Lucía's disciplinary actions illustrate how, just as racialized female masculinities may co-opt the negative qualities of machismo to challenge its heteropatriarchal logics, so, too, can positive traits of machismo (defending family and loved ones) reproduce a patriarchal hegemony that regulates women's bodies and sexualities. Ergo, this sexual dynamic suggests how Lucía's racialized female masculinity, even if (de)colonial for her, begins to materialize as oppressive for other working-class Latinas.

The toxicity of this racialized female masculinity reaches its acme when the Fire Girls orchestrate violent attacks on unsuspecting, possibly undocumented (though definitely immigrant) "sheep" in the streets and rob them. After Lucía jumps in Chique (another member of the Fire Girls) and Star Girl, the three prowl the neighborhood for easy victims. Before graduating to robbing middle- and upper-class white people, Lucía says,

> At first we was doing mamas, them poor-ass Salvadoran and Oaxaca mamas who dig around here, doing their little shopping and carrying all them babies on the hips. These women are weak as lambs but they always got a couple dollars on them.... We'd run up to a lady, circle her like Indian fighters, and I'd poke her some and laugh.... We'd push down and get us the bitty cash they had, sweep it up and run down the street smoking like a train.[100]

Like the Lobos, Lucía dubs women who were pregnant at one point "sheep" (calling them "lambs"), and she and her Fire Girls prey on these ladies because sheep are passive targets who do not stand up for themselves to resist violent robbery and battery. Although racialized female masculinity enables the Fire Girls to reject sheep statuses and amass economic independence through violent robberies, their attacks on other women epitomize the contradictory dynamics of the (de)colonial. The Fire Girls contest the subordination that the coloniality of gender imposes on them. Their subversion of this oppressive structure, however, does not entail delinking from the modern/gender system, but only appropriating it for their own empowerment in the Lobos and in their low-income barrio. In mimicking male Lobos' patriarchal rule and misogynist masculinity, the Fire Girls paradoxically circumvent, as well as affirm, the coloniality of gender. They thus insinuate that they may not necessarily have a problem with this gender system, as much as with their positionality in it. Their actions, even if (de)colonial, are not abolitionist.

Many critics of *Locas* have romanticized the novel's representation of female masculinity because Lucía uses the performance to circumvent the patriarchal rule of the Lobos and to claim citizenship in the gang, though some still acknowledge this masculinity as unsettling. Amaia Ibarraran-Bigalondo, for instance, recognizes that Lucía's "shift towards criminality is clearly vengeful and full of hatred" and "reproduces the most violent and vicious features" of the Lobos.[101] Likewise, even though Brown views the Fire Girls as "about belonging, community, and a sense of personal agency," she notes that these women "mirror abusive practices by men."[102] Emma Pérez, however, urges scholars to venture beyond merely recognizing that some women reproduce the coloniality of gender. Speaking on the relationship between Chicanas and the white-male-colonizer father, with the patriarchal system he imposes, Pérez says, "it is necessary to understand why we [Chicanas] are so addicted to the perpetrator of destruction. Why do we uphold the law of the white-colonizer-European father, knowing the extent of damage and pain for Chicanas and Chicanos?"[103] Following Pérez in attempting to understand the underlying causes of paradoxical addictions to the "perpetrator of destruction," this chapter unravels the reasoning behind Lucía's and the Fire Girls' toxified masculinities and contradictory behavior—considering why, despite the Lobos men treating them so horribly, these women might become "addicted to the perpetrator of destruction" and reproduce the misogynist elements of the Lobos masculinity they mimic.

Violability and Vulnerability

In envisioning alternative subaltern masculinities, Richard T. Rodríguez asks, "Do reconfigurations of masculinity in nonheterosexual contexts (say by gay men) necessarily entail a break from heterosexual contexts? If so, in what ways are these reconfigured masculinities useful?"[104] While *Locas* does not feature the emancipating queer masculinities Rodríguez hopes for in that the Fire Girls do not fully break from Lobos masculinities, its depiction of female masculinities in a non-heterosexual/non-reproductive girl gang is useful in that the novel's troubling representation of these women reveals how the abstract and material effects of the coloniality of gender might toxify racialized female masculinities. In this way, *Locas* helps visualize the structural conditions that require attention before these masculinities often present in gang subcultures and are able to decolonize.

The novel unravels the links between the coloniality of gender and the toxification of the Fire Girls' masculinities by making vulnerability and violability constant in most of its Latina characters' lives, beginning with Cecilia's mother Corazón in the book's opening pages. An undocumented immigrant from Oaxaca, Corazón never visits the hospital while pregnant with Cecilia (until she must deliver her) because she fears deportation. As Cecilia says, "Mama was so afraid of what the INS would do when they caught her without her green card that she wouldn't go to the doctor until she was screaming with those labor pains and I was pushing out of her, small and wet and trying to be alive."[105] Although monthly visits to a doctor are crucial for pregnant women, Corazón never seeks out medical care, and risks jeopardizing her and Cecilia's lives, because she fears that the government will deport her.[106] Corazón's anxiety underscores the omnipresent fear that undocumented immigrants in the United States suffer, and its effects on their well-being. Because of their criminalized status, undocumented persons remain in a constant state of vulnerability and violability. These persons often cannot pursue the State's protection (such as by contacting the police) should they be a victim of violent crime, and they fear seeking out medical care because many believe—sometimes correctly—that doing so will result in deportation.[107] Even when undocumented persons seek the State's protection, the State often does not adequately (if at all) enforce laws to safeguard them from violent crimes, such as in the poor/under prosecution rates of those who commit vigilante violence against undocumented people.[108]

This violability, vulnerability, and lack of confidence in the State to protect undocumented Latinas, as well as those who are US citizens, repeatedly manifests in *Locas*'s theme of domestic violence. Several main and minor female characters in *Locas* suffer from domestic violence, including women in the Lobos. Lucía, for instance, encounters domestic violence in her home as a young child, noting that her father frequently beat her mother in front of her. Reminiscing about one of the more vicious attacks, Lucía says, "He slammed down on my mami like she was a punching bag and he's Roberto Duran, giving her an uppercut so that she's bleeding from the mouth, and he wouldn't stop for Dios or the devil. She got broke up so that she can't even open up her eyes and I can't breathe there in the corner, where I stayed quiet and learned my lesson."[109] Lucía's father assaults her mother so viciously that Lucía compares his punches' damage to those of former Panamanian boxing champion Roberto Durán. Furthermore, Lucía divulges the traumatic effects this abuse has on her. Though she was not the direct recipient of her father's punches, his fists nevertheless harm her emotionally, psychologically, and physically, as she panics to the point where she struggles to breathe. She also remarks that, at this moment, she "learned my lesson." While she never discloses the content of this lesson, this incident—as well as the numerous other instances of domestic violence she witnesses in her house—portend to Lucía what her future life as an undocumented Latina might entail. These moments reveal to her how low-income Latinas in the barrio are subject to men's violence, and how little assistance and resources these battered women receive toward halting these attacks, especially undocumented women. Just as Cecilia's undocumented mother must accept Manny's insinuations of domestic violence and can only squeeze "back into her skin like she wants to hide" because she depends on Manny's financial contributions, Lucía's mother faces economic pressure to endure this battery because of the limited opportunities for upward mobility available to undocumented immigrants, and the consequential need for multiple income providers in the home.[110] Moreover, as with Corazón's refusal to visit a doctor while pregnant, the fear of deportation implicates battered undocumented women's ability to stop domestic violence, as well.

This refusal to pursue aid when suffering from domestic violence also occurs with every other victim in the story, even the US citizens. In the Lobos, for example, a woman named Laurita dates Chevy and has his son. Even though Laurita meets Lobos men's expectations of birthing and raising a Lobo's child, Cecilia says that, when Laurita did not obey Chevy, the "[v]ato put her in line, maybe slapping her around a little and giving her a piece of his mind."[111] Likewise, Cecilia suffers from domestic violence while a Lobo and pregnant. After her Lobos boyfriend beats her for the first time, domestic violence becomes a daily routine in their relationship. Cecilia says, "Men, they get that taste for beating on their lady. It's like whiskey, worse maybe, they take a drink then they get more thirsty so it doesn't ever stop. It only gets harder."[112] Cecilia claims that domestic violence resembles an addiction that provides men sadistic pleasure, leading them to batter women more harshly to satisfy themselves. Indeed, the severity of Cecilia's beatings increases, and she eventually miscarries her baby because of her boyfriend's violence.

Like Corazón and like Lucía's mother, neither Laurita nor Cecilia ever attempts to end this violence by calling the police or seeking out a battered women's shelter, even though they are both citizens. In part, as for the two mothers, economic factors influence their decisions not to abandon their partners by pursuing a shelter. Cecilia additionally reveals a sense of hopelessness and lack of confidence in others' willingness to protect Latinas. While Lucía claims that battered women "don't win a prize if you just hang on and take it," Cecilia says that battered women "hang on and take it" because "they'll say it's her fault. That she doesn't deserve a man and that's why she gets hit."[113] Though seemingly defeatist, Cecilia's comments are not without reason. For instance, in her autobiographical gang narrative that explains her transition from gang member to police officer, Mona Ruiz, a Chicana from Santa Ana, CA, admits that she frequently suffered from domestic violence before she became a cop. But when she calls the police, the cops rationalize her abuse, saying to her, "[T]here is no crime here. So your husband had a few drinks and got mad because you burned dinner or said the wrong thing, whatever. So he hit you. Get over it."[114] Likewise, sociologist Sudhir Venkatesh explains that many battered women of color refuse to call the police not out of hopelessness, but from fear of police violence or faulty charges that would lead to their own—rather than their abusers'—arrests.[115] In this way, Cecilia's defeatism and lack of faith in the State to protect Latinas from domestic violence are a realistic reflection of how the police are often not an option for people whom, as Lisa Marie Cacho says, the State "mark[s] as disposable and violable, as legitimate targets of state and vigilante violence."[116]

To Slaughter the Sheep

Miranda contends that the tough exterior of masculine gang girls functions as a form of self-defense, arguing that toughness acts as "an enabling ethos—a disposition, character, or fundamental value. Toughness displays that one is not accessible; it may project impenetrability."[117] According to Miranda, toughness connotes "impenetrability"—a statement that has sexual connotations as well, as "impenetrability" implies a defense against multiple forms of violence against women, including rape. For Lucía and the Fire Girls, relying on the intimidating toughness of their toxified masculinities is one of the few options available that enable them to defend themselves from the gendered violence that haunts them in their Echo Park barrio. After adopting the chola aesthetic, mirroring Manny's subaltern masculinity, and ascending in the Lobos, Lucía says, "take a hard look at me. You see any bruises? You see any shitty diamond ring? No. I don't need no one. This chica knows qué pasa. No man touches me like that now."[118] Upon developing her new persona, Lucía declares that no man beats her anymore, and by mentioning her lack of a wedding ring, she alludes to the potential threat of sexual assault that she may encounter from men as well, suggesting that no man touches her sexually anymore without her consent. In this way, Lucía's masculinity enables her to achieve a gang life where she can resist the violence plaguing her and the other women in her Fire Girls. While these women's membership in gangs might open them to other types of violence, their new masculine identities reject the passive ideologies of "sheep," and instead provide them with a method for fighting back and defending against violence in a way not available to the feminine and non-gangbanging women in the novel.

Although *Locas* portrays these racialized female masculinities as paradoxically empowering and harmful to women, the novel also works to unravel the structural causes of this toxicity, suggesting that the psychological and physical trauma that the coloniality of gender induces helps to "entice a series of complicities from racialized folks to and within colonial logics."[119] In reflecting on witnessing her father beat her mother, Lucía says,

> My mami and papi would scream at each other in our little house, the sounds bouncing hard off the walls so that you couldn't get away from it no matter where you ran, he's hitting on her like she's a punching bag, making blood-red and dark blue marks over her little eyes and wet mouth, and there was those *rancheras* on the radio over his yelling making me crazy.[120]

Lucía admits that these attacks on her mother, which Lucía could not escape "no matter where you ran," harm her mental well-being, making her "crazy." These violent encounters that damage Lucía's psyche—and which she cannot stop recalling throughout her adult life—shame and embarrass her, and she consistently attempts to forget them. For instance, when Lucía's father later abandons her mother, Lucía says she would deny her mother's existence and refuse to visit her because of the traumatic history she recalls for Lucía. As Lucía says about her mother,

> I used to tell people lies about her, to help me forget. "She's dead," I'd say, and I wouldn't even blink. "Died when I was a baby." It wasn't true, though. She didn't even live that far.[121]

Even though her mother only resides a few streets away from her, Lucía avoids visiting her or revealing to people that she is alive, because recognizing her mother's existence also means acknowledging her own past experience with domestic violence, and the possibility of replicating her mother's life.

For these reasons, both Lucía's violence against Latinas and her denial of her mother suggest a psychological repression that arises from her traumatic history and the omnipresent violability and vulnerability that threaten her. Freud writes that "*the essence of repression lies simply in the function of rejecting and keeping something out of consciousness.*"[122] In using a metaphor to explain how repression removes "something out of consciousness," Freud compares repression to a process where "an external stimulus becomes internal . . . by eating into and destroying a bodily organ."[123] For Freud, the ingestion of this "external stimulus" causes "*physical pain*" and "the only things which can subdue it are the effect of some toxic agent in removing it and the influence of mental distraction."[124] In applying this metaphor to Lucía, her violability, vulnerability, and history with domestic violence represent consumed external stimuli that cause her psychological, emotional, and physical pain. Toxified female masculinity, as the "toxic agent," attempts to subdue the pain and her trauma by "removing" this "external stimulus." The women Lucía attacks in the streets represent, for her, "sheep" who meekly accept domestic violence and submit to heteropatriarchal expectations. The "poor-ass Salvadoran and Oaxaca mamas" she jumps have children whom they will raise and care for in the private sphere, a space where, in Locas, domestic violence is ever-present.[125] Consequently, these women might signify her mother who, to use Lucía's words once more, "just hang[s] on and take[s] it," and thus represent the harmful effects of the coloniality of gender that perennially haunt Lucía's life.[126] In moving to repress this history and possibility of becoming a "sheep," Lucía attempts, psychologically and physically, to "kill off" sheep and the trauma and life they symbolize by ridding the barrio of them. To accomplish this agenda, she either recruits women who suffer from domestic violence into the Fire Girls as a method for defending themselves and shedding their "sheep" statuses, or she physically beats "sheep" out of the streets and out of her view. In this way, Lucía represents an alternative possibility to Emma Pérez's claim that "men of color experience racial oppression and displace their frustration onto women of color."[127] Lucía experiences the racialized oppression of the coloniality of gender, and this oppression cultivates psychological and physical trauma that leads to her and her Fire Girls displacing their frustration, anger, precarity, and trauma onto other women.

Cecilia further suggests this connection between attacking "sheep" and the repression and displacement of the violence, trauma, and dismal life chances they signify in the novel. While trying to integrate Cecilia into the Fire Girls after discovering that Cecilia's boyfriend beats her, Lucía urges Cecilia to batter and rob a "Lincoln mamacita" walking with her daughter.[128] Cecilia initially refuses, but after admiring how the Fire Girls are "acting so tough, wearing their man-looking clothes" and reminiscing about her partner "beating on me and my mama yelling," she says, "I wanted to break off loose the same as Lucía and her cholas. I wanted to scream and sing and run away and fight dirty, steal money, hit somebody else real hard."[129] Not only does Cecilia desire the (de)colonial potentiality of the Fire Girls' masculinity when thinking about her status as a domestic violence victim, but she also reveals that, when Lucía presents her with "sheep," these traumatic memories re-surface, leading her to want to "hit somebody else real hard." Whether Cecilia attacks her boyfriend, "sheep," or "somebody else" does not matter to her, so long as she can repress and find an outlet for her trauma and precarity through violence. Thus, Cecilia's and Lucía's histories with domestic violence and their desire to assault others like them disclose the connection across the toxicity of certain racialized female masculinities and the psychological, emotional, and material trauma that the coloniality of gender induces in women like those in Murray's novel. The State's disregard for Latinas in the barrio propagates and excuses patriarchal violence against them, contributing to the toxification of Latina gang girls' masculinities in ways that lead to the victimization of other multiply marginalized persons.

By studying how *Locas* appropriates and refashions exploitative stereotypes about women in gangs, this chapter has revealed potential ways that gang life—and the impetus for gang membership—can operate at the intersection of race, class, gender, and sexuality. In *Locas*, female gang members' masculinities entail violence and crime as a way of circumventing the material, ontological, and psychological effects of the coloniality of gender. Yet in recognizing that these masculinities are contradictory, this chapter advances the theorization of female masculinity by considering how the coloniality of gender can both toxify racialized female masculinities and cultivate complicities to colonial logics from subaltern persons. The chapter has also helped reconceptualize how scholarship regards femininity in hypermasculine, heterosexual, and male-dominated gangs. Rejecting the tendency to dismiss femininity as a deficiency in these subcultures, this book has disclosed femininity's agential potential in its ability to manipulate heterosexual masculinity. Taken together, Chapters 2 and 3 have shown the means by which Latina literature envisions how male-dominated gang subcultures might accord (de)colonial possibilities to women, albeit in a paradoxical manner. Now, I shift to Dino Dinco's *Homeboy* to consider other multiply marginalized people often thought not to exist in hypermasculine, heterosexual, male-dominated gangs, but who frequently find strategies for transforming these subcultures into (de)colonial spaces: gay *locos*.

4 | (DE)COLONIAL GAY LOCOS, DISIDENTIFICATIONS, AND COUNTERPUBLICS

IN DINO DINCO'S 2012 DOCUMENTARY *HOMEBOY*, WHICH DETAILS the presence of gay Latino men in gangs, Richard Avila, a former gang member from Bell Gardens, Los Angeles, says gay men "are disgusting, and they ought to be shot and killed"; we should "beat the fuck out of them." Similarly, Cisco Rios, also a former gang member, says, "All the gays and lesbians should be in San Francisco with the gate and be shot." Despite the ease with which Avila and Rios speak these threats, neither of the two is the original author of these bigoted statements. Rather, Avila and Rios are gay men who formerly participated in heterosexual gangs and are underscoring the violent, homophobic intimidation they encountered in gang life. Because of this intolerance, neither Avila nor Rios ever came out to their gangs. In fact, homophobia caused the two to recede further into the closet and reproduce this bigotry to safeguard their lives. As Avila says, "I think I even said it—[gay men] ought to be shot and killed—and then just hearing shit like that, it was like okay, I'm going way deeper into the closet. I'm hiding under all the dirty clothes down there, and I'm never coming out." Rios, on the other hand, says that at one point he considered coming out to his "homeboys," but on hearing their rigid stances that demanded death for gay men, said, "Fuck that. Shit, I'm straight.... Coming out at that time? No, no, can't do it."

Attempting to intervene in the violently homophobic gang space that Avila and Rios detail, *Homeboy* features several gay current and former gang members who voice their stories of how and why they initially joined heterosexual gangs, regardless of an environment that refuses to tolerate gay men openly: Larry Apodaca, Sergio Romero, Robert Jaramillo, Cisco Rios, Richard Avila, Juan Verdi, and Phillip

Garcia. Upon meeting these men onscreen, the viewer notices that, in spite of the deluge of mainstream cultural representations that associate gay men with femininity and frailty, these men are equally as intimidating and hypermasculine as are heterosexual male gang members.

In presenting these hypermasculine gay gang members, *Homeboy* participates in a recent cinematic trend that has migrated away from the steadfast heterosexuality and homophobia in numerous gang-exploitation films of the late 1980s and early 1990s, such as *Colors* (1988), *American Me* (1992), and *Blood In, Blood Out* (1993). Instead, recent movies, like *On the Downlow* (2004), *Quinceañera* (2006), and *La Mission* (2009), have insinuated the presence of gay gang members while critiquing homophobia in gangs, barrios, and the United States. Yet none of these contemporary films approaches the harshness of gang homophobia, the existence of gay gang members, or gay men's capacity to attain citizenship in heterosexual, homophobic gangs with the severity of Dinco's documentary. As one of the only films to feature actual former or current gang members, *Homeboy* provides a rare avenue for theorizing hypermasculinity and homophobia in Latina/o/x gangs; why and how some subaltern heterosexual masculinities target gay men; how gay gang members appropriate and transform hypermasculinity and violence in gangs to enact (de)colonial projects; and the ways that gay men physically and psychologically survive in gangs that penalize gay sexuality with supreme brutality.

In pursuing *Homeboy*'s engagements with these subjects, this book responds to Vanessa R. Panfil's observation that "there is virtually no research that has documented the lived experiences of gay gang members."[1] While Panfil has recently attended to this shortcoming with the first book-length study of gay gang members, *The Gang's All Queer*, her ethnography focuses primarily on gay men in gay gangs, and the trauma gay men encounter in straight gangs.[2] Her work does not theorize gay men's agential presence in heterosexual gangs, the possibility of them succeeding in these subcultures, or why subaltern heterosexual hypermasculinities in gangs often entail violence against gay men.

In addressing these topics in my interpretation of *Homeboy*, I draw from José Esteban Muñoz's theory of disidentification, which he defines as "descriptive of the survival strategies the minority subject practices in order to negotiate a phobic majoritarian public sphere that continuously elides or punishes the existence of subjects who do not conform to the phantasm of normative citizenship."[3] In this same vein, Muñoz also contends that "disidentification is a strategy that works on and against the dominant ideology.... [T]his 'working on and against' is a strategy that tries to transform cultural logics from within."[4] The gay gang members in *Homeboy* identify with their homophobic heterosexual gangs for various familial, psychological, or socioeconomic reasons, and their actions and consciousness of their contradictory positions constitute disidentifications. These disidentifications act as agential survival strategies that enable the men to succeed at their gangs' idealization of violent hypermasculinity, and attain subcultural citizenship in their clicas. In doing so, the men develop (de)colonial epistemologies and ontologies that reject certain ideologies of the coloniality of gender and its modern gender/sexual system. Instead, they employ gang life, culture, and aesthetics as ironic means of challenging the homophobia, hate crimes, and social and familial ostracism they encounter *outside* their gangs.

Moreover, although *Homeboy* subscribes to troubling gang-exploitation and documentary conventions that can invite viewers to interpret the film in racist ways, its publication of these men's disidentifications also enables the dissemination of the movie to function as a (de)colonial performance that rearticulates gay sexuality into a signifier for hypermasculinity (rather than connoting common stereotypes of femininity). The film thus destabilizes the logic of the coloniality of gender that organizes heterosexual gang life and potentially alters gang culture to create a space for gay men in heterosexual gangs. The film's exhibition generates a counterpublic aimed at ameliorating the unforgiving politics to which gay men who gangbang may find themselves subjected.

The Poetics of Gang-Exploitation Film

Despite the abundance of gang-exploitation films in American cinema, the genre has seldom received critical attention in Latina/o/x and American film studies, with B. V. Olguín remaining one of the relative few to produce an incisive history of the formation of gang-exploitation film. Olguín locates "the gratuitously violent gangxploitation genre" in the origins of blaxploitation filmmaking.[5] Blaxploitation film arose in the 1970s from the rising social consciousness that the Civil Rights and Black Arts Movements engendered in the 1960s. According to Ed Guerrero, these social movements left "a large black audience thirsting to see their full humanity depicted on the commercial cinema screen.

This surge in African American identity politics led also to an outspoken, critical dissatisfaction with Hollywood's persistent degradation of African Americans in films among black leaders, entertainers, and intellectuals."[6] In addition to black audiences desiring a cinema that broke with the stereotypical images of black people in Hollywood film, the political consciousness of the civil rights era led many black viewers to reject black actors who achieved mainstream success in the Hollywood film industry, such as Sidney Poitier. As Donald Bogle notes, Poitier transcended racial barriers in Hollywood and in the United States because he was "the model integrationist hero.... When insulted or badgered, the Poitier character stood by and took it. He differed from the old servants only in that he was governed by a code of decency, duty, and moral intelligence."[7] While Bogle recognizes Poitier's acting talent, he also contends that Poitier's success in Hollywood largely arises from him playing versions of "Uncle Tom" characters.

On the other hand, blaxploitation film departed from Hollywood's erasure of blackness and its demand for black actors to play "Uncle Tom" derivations. Instead, blaxploitation film, directed by both black and white people, featured a predominantly black cast and a socially conscious and resistant black (anti) hero or heroine. In these films, black actors were not limited to hackneyed roles as servants or plantation hands. Rather, blaxploitation film housed a range of black characters, such as vigilantes, police, or pimps. Although blaxploitation movies like Melvin Van Peebles's *Sweet Sweetback's Baadasssss Song* (1971) or Jack Hill's *Foxy Brown* (1974) often depicted crime and violence in black urban neighborhoods, Novotny Lawrence observes that "the motive [for violence and crime] is always justified by the protagonists' standard of living."[8] Because blaxploitation films normatively cast whites as villains perpetuating and profiting from capitalist colonial systems, this cinema depicts black violence as righteous in its resistance to white supremacy, structural racism, and US empire. As Lawrence elaborates, whites' "defeat at the hands of the African American protagonists is symbolic of blacks overcoming racism perpetuated by the machine."[9]

Despite the anti-racist, pro-black countercultural movement generated in blaxploitation film, Hollywood eventually co-opted this cinema. This change resulted in the now almost ubiquitous gang-exploitation movies, which remove the representation of the impetus for violence, and instead regurgitate and transform past cops-and-robbers, Mafia, and bandido paradigms into narratives that homogenize black and Latina/o/x people as pathologically violent, overly salacious, and vastly homophobic and misogynist gang members. In Olguín's view, even potentially anti-gang-exploitation films that explain the systemic causes of crime and violence in black and Latina/o/x communities, such as *Boyz n the Hood* (1991) or *Menace II Society* (1993), "have been eclipsed by the Hollywood fetish for the presumed minority predisposition to pathological conduct."[10] According to Colin Gunckel, eliding coloniality's role in creating and perpetuating gang violence and barrio crime remains the central characteristic of the gang-exploitation genre, which includes major Hollywood motion pictures as well as low-budget, straight-to-DVD films. As Gunckel explains, Hollywood and independent cinemas that produce gang-exploitation film rely on "sensationalistic imagery and emphasiz[e] intensified enforcement rather than structural causes or proposing a broader range of solutions."[11] Because gang-exploitation films pathologize working-class communities of color, these films can seem to corroborate the need for over-policing in black and Latina/o/x neighborhoods, and for harsher, mandatory prison sentences that disproportionately target racial minorities.

As blaxploitation films demonstrate, however, images of violent, criminal gang members and racial minorities are not always or intrinsically sensationalist. However, the refusal to couch this violence and crime as a response to, and cultivated by, coloniality renders these images exploitative. This qualification to violence and crime separates barrio, "hood," and/or gang films like *LA 92* (2017) from others like *End of Watch* (2012). The former features footage of the 1992 Los Angeles Riots but clarifies this violence as a reaction to the acquittal of four white police officers who beat Rodney King at a traffic stop, as well as a response to Soon Ja Du murdering Latasha Harlins and judge Joyce Karlin refusing to sentence Du to prison, despite the jury finding her guilty of voluntary manslaughter (a felony that carries a maximum prison sentence of 16 years). The latter film represents black and Latina/o/x people as unrepentant gang members and delinquents committing crime and murder for no reason other than ostensible cultural deficiencies.

Of the many films that compose the gang-exploitation genre, Edward James Olmos's *American Me* persists as the one Latina/o/x movie to receive a large amount of scholarly recognition. Several scholars have adopted divergent positions on *American Me*, with many critiquing the film for its barbaric, unvaried depiction of Chicana/o/xs and its male-centric narrative. Olmos claims that the film attempts to represent Chicanas as the barrio's "glimmer of hope," and the character "Julie" (the love interest of the film's gangster protagonist) as "the only hero of the film." Rosa Linda Fregoso, however, criticizes the film's elision of its alleged savior: "Who is this new subject, this Chicana whom Olmos claims is the heroine of *American Me*, the hope in our barrios? His story [Olmos's film] ends before hers can begin."[12] Along with this gendered omission, Fregoso argues that *American Me*'s gang-exploitation portrayal of Chicana/o/xs affirms racist discourses, as "the film's focus normalizes dominant culture's view of Chicanos as poverty-infested 'gangs.'"[13] At the other end of this discussion, Olguín, while acknowledging the film's male-centrism, offers an insightful reading grounded in alternative spectatorship. As Olguín contends, *American Me* "begins by undoing its apparent filiation with one of Hollywood's most racist genres through perspective shots that enable us to recast the gaze at the cultural, historical, and material arenas in which Chicana/os are figured and treated as one of America's abject populations."[14] In incorporating Chicana/o/x aesthetics—specifically the film's representation of Chicana/o/x tattoos, Caló, and pinto gait—Olguín submits that "underclass minority spectators" may identify with the film and read its portrayals as affirmations of "barrio-rooted agency," rather than with the usual "conditioned resistant spectatorship" that they adopt when viewing Hollywood stereotypes of Chicana/o/x culture.[15]

Despite their opposing positions, Fregoso and Olguín agree that *American Me* epitomizes the gang-exploitation trait of refusing to pursue "the root causes of gang membership," instead pathologizing Chicana/o/x culture and people.[16] Fregoso writes that during a screening in San Francisco, "the major objection . . . had to do with the film's simplistic account of the gang phenomenon in the barrios. Eliding the economic roots of youth violence, *American Me* emphasizes instead the dysfunctional relationship between Santana and his father."[17] In its neglect of the impetus for gang membership, *American Me* potentially reifies culture-of-poverty hypotheses that stigmatize Latina/o/x communities as epicenters of family dysfunction and pathology. This "ideological closure," as Olguín terms it, renders the film derivative of the gang-exploitation genre.[18]

Homophobic Latina/o/x "Culture"

Though *Homeboy* deviates from the heteropatriarchal conventions of gang-exploitation film in revealing how gangs are not solely the domains of heterosexual men, the documentary adheres to genre conventions in representing past and current gang members as participants in violent crime, while remaining silent about coloniality's role in cultivating criminality, hypermasculinity, and homophobia in gangs. For this reason, and in keeping with this book's overarching theorization of a (de)colonial gang life that hinges on the suppression of other multiply marginalized persons, I follow Teresa Córdova's call for scholars to engage the "economic and political dynamics that cause unnecessary suffering in Latino communities."[19] In this spirit, I preface *Homeboy* here by scrutinizing the interwoven relations among the performance of gender and sexuality, the homophobia in many male-dominated, heterosexual gangs, and the effects of coloniality on many Latino men in the United States.

Many working-class and low-income Latino men struggle to perform American hegemonic masculinity (the most dominant, idealized, and romanticized masculinity in the US), in part because "the masculinity that they deploy cannot be exchanged for the most dominant forms of power and capital."[20] As Pancho McFarland explains, since American hegemonic masculinity equates to "dominance and power over others," "[e]conomic status often determines the means by which we perform our masculinity. Financial power is reserved for the wealthy, and wealthy men can prove their masculinity through their bank accounts and their positions."[21] For this reason, men must first obtain nationally valued forms of wealth, power, and capital (high-ranking employment positions, a substantial six figure salary, home ownership, luxury vehicles, etc.) before they can perform American hegemonic masculinity. Such requirements restrict this masculinity only to those in privileged socioeconomic positions—normatively white men—and help render working-class and low-income Latino men "feminized," "penetrable subjects" who are "castrated" in "relation to the white-male colonizer father."[22]

Because of the coloniality that reduces working-class and low-income Latino men to these statuses, such men may often rebound with hypermasculine performances as a means of protecting their unstable masculinities, masking their socioeconomic emasculation, attempting to mimic hegemonic masculinity, or—as detailed throughout this book—mobilizing a subaltern masculinity as a method for enacting (de)colonial projects. For instance, in his study on machismo, Alfredo Mirandé finds "the cult of virility and the Mexican male's obsession with power and domination as futile attempts to mask feelings of inferiority, powerlessness, and failure."[23] Additionally, Richard

Mora argues that "some young men of color, especially those who are working class or poor," choose to adopt a "masculinity that often emphasizes toughness, male superiority, heterosexuality, physical dominance, and both the ability and willingness to use violence."[24] Mora credits this masculinity not to cultural deficiency, but to the second-class status to which the United States relegates these men and to, as Judith Kegan Gardiner says, the "dominant U.S. masculinity [that] invites men to attack weakness in others and ridicule those already shamed."[25] In short, coloniality's denial of working-class and low-income Latinos' access to capital and power may partially lead these men to overly perform derivations of an American hegemonic masculinity that already depends upon violence, dominance, and power.

Heterosexual versions of this subaltern masculinity also routinely entail a homophobia that in part stems from American hegemonic masculinity's basis in sexuality, as much as in wealth and power. Judith Butler draws from Sigmund Freud's conception of melancholia, which he defines as a process where "an object which was lost has been set up again inside the ego—that is, that an object-cathexis has been replaced by an identification," to rethink Freud's hypothesis on the human's choice of an initial love object, which, he contends, occurs during the oedipal stage.[26] Butler, in turn, posits that "the prohibition on incest [in the oedipal conflict] presupposes the prohibition on sexuality."[27] In this Freudian approach to melancholy, Butler suggests that because the preemption of a same-sex love object transpires at a young age—and continues to persist in the dominant culture throughout adulthood—the dominant heterosexual culture enters a state of melancholia where persons grieve for, and identify with, the homosexual love object that heterosexual society has denied them since their childhoods. In this rationale, heterosexuals produce their sexuality and gender through rejecting homosexual love. As Butler says, "Becoming a 'man' within this logic requires not only a repudiation of femininity, but also a repudiation that becomes a precondition for the heterosexualization of sexual desire."[28] As a consequence of this repudiation, gender and heterosexuality remain haunted by their melancholic identifications with their homosexual love objects, allowing threats to heterosexuality to compromise gender. For, as Butler argues, "in a man, the terror over homosexual desire may well lead to terror over being constructed as feminine, feminized, of no longer being properly a man or of being a 'failed' man."[29]

Yet while Butler supplies a valuable contribution to helping to understand how heterosexuality is "compulsory" and "permeates the whole of the coloniality of gender," she focuses her analysis on a single, dominant culture that forecloses the possibility of attaining a homosexual love object.[30] If we were to limit similarly our theoretical scope to the boundaries of one authoritative culture, we would logically deduce that an emerging space for homosexual mourning in the United States offers opportunities for mourning for all homosexual persons, regardless of class, race, or ethnicity. On the contrary, although the United States may have loosened its heterosexual and heteronormative social standards to enable this space for mourning to develop, the nation's growing acceptance of LGBTQ+ people hinges on whiteness and homonormativity, a politics that Lisa Duggan contends "does not contest dominant heteronormative assumptions and institutions, but upholds and sustains them, while promising the possibility of a demobilized gay constituency and a privatized, depoliticized gay culture anchored in domesticity and consumption."[31] This burgeoning, homonormative tolerance of the LGBTQ+ population often does not apply to persons of color of non-normative sexualities and lifestyles, nor to persons occupying criminalized spaces. Therefore, because working-class and low-income Latino men struggle to procure the power, wealth, and capital required to perform American hegemonic masculinity—and because the favorable reception of white homonormativity has not sufficiently produced spaces for homosexual mourning in many of these men's communities—Butler's contentions that men must foreclose the possibility of homosexuality to establish their gender and that homosexuality threatens and feminizes masculinity remain relevant to working-class and low-income Latino men whose masculinity US coloniality already reduces to a precarious state. This argument does not conflate class and LGBTQ+ issues but, rather, suggests that Butler's postulation on gay sexuality's threats to heterosexual gender identities has important implications for working-class and low-income Latino men. Establishing oneself as a hegemonic, masculine man under the coloniality of gender relies on possessing power, wealth, and capital. Working-class and low-income Latino men may therefore see themselves in emasculated positions and find their masculine male gender identities in a perilous state. As a result, heterosexual working-class and low-income Latino men may exhibit homophobia and thus distance themselves from homosexuality to protect their insecure masculine male genders, since, as Butler says, homosexuality for many heterosexual men leads to "terror over being constructed as feminine."[32]

In *Homeboy*, Juan Verdi's and Phillip Garcia's comments on sexuality's relation to gender identity demonstrate the pertinence of Butler's argument. Verdi says that in many heterosexual, male-dominated gangs, gay means "that you're less than a man. That's why you'll see a boy tell another boy, 'Oh man, you're acting like a faggot.' What he's telling him is that you're acting less than a man." Likewise, Garcia argues that in these subcultures, "being a homosexual is a sissy." As these two men show, certain working-class/low-income Latino men in gangs who cannot perform American hegemonic masculinity may refuse to tolerate gay sexuality, may perform hypermasculinity, and may spew homophobia because of the ways that gay sexuality threatens their unstable masculinities and gender identities.

Certain scholars have contested forms of this theory on the connections between a low socioeconomic status and the performance of gender and sexuality. Lionel Cantú, for example, has critiqued arguments that insinuate that "macho performances of masculinity are a response to feelings of inferiority," since "such arguments are deterministic and maintain a static conception of Latino culture."[33] Despite this claim, Cantú, in theorizing a more optimal method for analyzing subaltern masculinities among working-class/low-income Latino men, later cites Matthew Gutmann, whom Cantú paraphrases as saying, "gender identities must be understood as historical constructs . . . that are shaped by changing political, social, cultural, and economic conditions."[34] Later, Cantú draws from Pierrette Hondagneu-Sotelo and Michael A. Messner, who, according to Cantù, claim that "varying displays of masculinity are shaped by . . . the power relationships of some men over other men, so that 'marginalized and subordinated men tend to overtly display exaggerated embodiments and verbalizations of masculinity that can be read as a desire to express power over others within a context of relative powerlessness.'"[35] Despite Cantú's denunciation that explaining violent, homophobic hypermasculinities as byproducts of feelings of inferiority only maintains a static conception of Latina/o/x culture, Hondagneu-Sotelo and Messner's assertions speak to the intersection of the political, social, cultural, and economic conditions that Gutmann argues scholars should account for when theorizing Latino masculinity. Because this theorization depends on certain conditions of coloniality (low socioeconomic and sociopolitical statuses), readings of violent, homophobic Latino hypermasculinities as responses to "feelings of inferiority" are not "static conceptions of Latino culture" but, rather, conditional on the social, cultural, political, and economic positions of working-class/low-income Latinos in the United States. As such, they maintain the possibility for commensurate change, should dominant idealizations of American hegemonic masculinity—or working-class/low-income Latinos' statuses within coloniality—alter.

In unraveling the connections across violent hypermasculinity, homophobia, race, gender, sexuality, and class, I am not attempting to justify or explain away Latino gang homophobia and hate crimes. I do, however, aim to resist passive neglect of the pitfalls of cultural production that may inadvertently contribute to, or reinforce, conceptions of gang and Latina/o/x culture as intrinsically homophobic and bigoted. In studying *Homeboy*, I acknowledge the film's troublesome conventions in its partial commitments to the gang-exploitation genre, but I do so to impede the pathologizing of Latina/o/x culture and gang life. The documentary's apertures are opportunities to reveal how the effects of coloniality on Latino men in the barrio systemically contribute to the production of an environment that persecutes gay men.

If violent and homophobic hypermasculinities among Latino gang members partly arise from the coloniality that organizes contemporary life—rather than exclusively from congenital cultural bigotry—answering questions such as the following becomes increasingly challenging: why would gay men continue to participate in heterosexual, homophobic gangs, or even join these gangs, if their sexual orientations jeopardize their well-being? How could these bigoted subcultures facilitate (de)colonial projects for gay men? How could gay gang members manage the psychological trauma of navigating their sexual identities in one of the more violently homophobic spaces a gay man can find himself? If homophobic gang environments partly arise from coloniality, then altering bigotry in primarily heterosexual, male-dominated gangs does not seem feasible without substantial transformation of the epistemological, institutional, and structural fabric of life in the United States. Consequently, gay men's presences in these gangs logically generate connotations of psychological, emotional, and physical trauma devoid of any possibility of alleviation (short of abandoning the gang), rendering attempts to comprehend gay men's willing participation in these spaces incredibly difficult.

However, I suggest that, ironically, it is precisely because these Latino men *do* find themselves suffering from the abstract and material effects of coloniality that they choose to join these gangs—in spite of the gangs' bigotry. Gang life enables these gay men to circumvent the classed, racialized, gendered, and sexual elements of the coloniality of gender that they face *outside* their gangs. Of course, hypermasculine, heterosexual, male-dominated gangs are often spaces where homophobia flourishes, potentially leading to psychological trauma for their gay members. But the gang members of *Homeboy* also allow viewers to understand how gay men in heterosexual, homophobic gangs may disidentify with these subcultures as an agential survival strategy to initiate (de)colonial projects in and through gang life.

From Familia to Gay Chingasos

When asked why he joined a gang, Juan Verdi says, "It comes from dysfunctional families. My mother and father didn't have enough time to spend with me, so I found somebody who did." Similarly, Luis J. Rodriguez, who, though heterosexual, also appears in *Homeboy*, attributes gang activity to "something inadequate in their [gang members'] life the gang fills." Phillip Garcia adds: "[The gang's] more like a family, a close-knit family.... I seen it as a bunch of outsiders, you know, knit together, and trying to become as one." Verdi's, Rodriguez's, and Garcia's comments on the impetus for, and communal benefits of, gang membership might appear to tread close toward affirming regurgitative culture-of-poverty hypotheses that stigmatize families of color as pathologically dysfunctional. But readers should note how the psychological and material trauma of coloniality affects many of the nuclear families of people who join gangs. In *Always Running*, Rodriguez writes, "'[F]amily' is a farce among the propertyless and disenfranchised. Too many families are wrenched apart, as even children are forced to supplement meager incomes. Family can only really exist among those who can afford one."[36] Rodriguez credits the economic inequalities afflicting working-class and low-income populations as partly responsible for the destruction of nuclear families. Often, children must take on jobs, or parents must take on additional employment—such as the mother of *My Father Was a Toltec* does—to house, clothe, and feed their families. This positions parenting and familial bonding as secondary to survival.

Similar to how the socioeconomic emasculation of working-class/low-income Latino men can cultivate violent and homophobic hypermasculinities that compensate for the inability to perform American hegemonic masculinity, the abstract and material conditions of coloniality also foment a hostile atmosphere that contributes to the dismantling of family. Because many parents of at-risk gang youth may encounter feelings of inferiority or stress affiliated with working menial labor, or an inability to provide for their families financially—in addition to being subjected to racism, discrimination, and prejudice on a daily basis—parents may abuse their children as an outlet for their own anger and frustration. For instance, in *Going Down to the Barrio*, Joan W. Moore interviews several gang members on abuse in their homes, finding that "[m]ost of the descriptions of 'grouchy' fathers (and even some 'happy' ones) reflect ... the pressures and insecurities of hard manual labor."[37] More specifically, a young gang member in Moore's study notes the pattern connecting financial instability and her father beating her mother: "If things were going all right, they'd get along good. If things were bad financially, there was problems."[38] Ultimately, the emotional and psychological trauma that the effects of coloniality produce may precipitate family abuse, a ramification that often compels persons—such as Verdi, Garcia, or Rodriguez—to seek gang membership in order to find community and belonging.

In his comments above, Rodriguez suggests that, like Verdi and Garcia, he joined a gang partially because of the community and belonging his family could not provide. For Verdi, Garcia, and the other gay men of *Homeboy*, however, their sexualities amplify the ostracism and alienation they experience from their families and in society, potentially resulting in them feeling a greater need for communal support than heterosexual gang members have. Cisco Rios, for example, hints at the homophobia in his family when discussing his response to family members who may learn of him publicizing his sexuality in *Homeboy*, saying that he "doesn't give a fuck if his cousin hears this shit." Rios's hostility toward his cousin and his need to not "give a fuck" implies that his cousin behaves antagonistically toward Rios because of Rios's sexual orientation. As such, gang life ironically provides an avenue that enables him to compensate for the social and familial ostracism he encounters *outside* of his gang because of his sexuality—even if he must closet himself in his gang because of his gang's homophobia.

In many gangs, violent hypermasculinity and crime are crucial for generating the aggrandized status, community, and sense of belonging that the men of *Homeboy* cite. In her study of gay men in gangs, Panfil asks her participants why they engage in violence. One man named Casper responds, "Respect too, because a lot of 'em would try to disrespect. Like I said, we would be on the bus or somewhere, anywhere, and someone would disrespect us, and all it take is for one (snaps fingers), and then we're all up, stuff like that."[39] Similarly, Panfil writes that another gay gang member named Aga says that "[w]e don't be playin' about our brothers and sisters and my gay kids" and that a man named Jeremy "added that his group was 'real close' and they 'take up for each other,' especially 'if somebody was to disrespect one of us in public.'"[40] For these gang members, violence strengthens the gang's communal support system and internal bonds by protecting the social dignity and honor of fellow gang members whom they refer to in familial terms: "brothers," "sisters," and "kids." Although Panfil focuses on the dynamics in gay gangs, violence as a tool for generating community and support operates in heterosexual, mixed-gender, and girl gangs as well. In his study of gangs in North America, for instance, Steven Dudley notes that gang violence "appears to be a way to build group cohesion."[41] Likewise, in Murray's *Locas*, Lucía and her Fire Girls' attacks against "poor-ass Salvadoran and Oaxaca mamas" help form a familial subculture that, albeit in a toxic manner, compensates for their initial alienation in the Lobos and the psychological and material trauma they experience from their second-class statuses in the United States.[42] Conversely, women's absence from violence in the Lobos (participating in rumbles or jumping rivals) preempts their citizenship in the gang.

In addition to the men in *Homeboy* noting the community and belonging they obtain in gangs that, for men like Rios, rectify the alienation they feel from their homophobic families, many also idealize their histories of gang violence: stabbing rival gang members, having these rivals pull guns on them, and participating in fistfights with them. Because their gang violence is a precursor to the community in gang life that offsets the homophobic ostracism they experience outside their gangs, the gay gang members of *Homeboy* queer a (de)colonial gang violence that hinges on the harm of other multiply marginalized persons. They attain the community-building rewards of gang life through attacking rivals, and the possibility remains of them also harming innocent persons uninvolved in gangs—since (unlike Lucía) the men never reveal whether they harm civilians.

Beyond these assaults on rival gang members that help create group cohesion, the men in *Homeboy* explain that gang life enables them to resist the violent homophobia and hate crimes they encounter outside their gangs. In one of the opening scenes of the documentary, for example, Sergio Romero says he joined a gang because of those who questioned his sexuality, labeled him a maricón (a derogatory epithet for

Figure 4.1 *Sergio Romero explains how gang membership provided a defense against those who physically and verbally attacked him for his sexuality. Video image supplied by the author.*

gay men), and physically assaulted him (Figure 4.1). As Romero remarks, "I was raised as a kid to defend myself, and the only group of kids that I knew that fight to defend themselves are gangbangers." Oddly enough, despite the homophobia pervading his gang, Romero joined—though he remained closeted—because the gang provided him with protection from those who considered his sexual orientation justification for verbal and physical assault. Romero's conception of the gang as a vehicle for self-defense intimates how gang life precipitated the veritable creation of a new man who embodies the resistant ideology of many gang members. As former gang member and now university professor Robert J. Durán explains, "Joining a gang means shifting one's image from that of a victim who weakly tolerates affronts to that of a strong and courageous warrior who reacts quickly to perceived disrespect."[43] Along with having to live in a country imbued with racism, and State attempts to police and regulate their bodies, the men of *Homeboy* face disparaging epithets and physical violence from people outside their gangs because of their sexuality. As a result, this "strong and courageous" ideology in gang life provides the avenue for these men to use violence to demonstrate symbolically "that they are not inferior or controlled by others," to combat bigotry and hate crime outside their gangs, and to attain feelings of, and prove, power and personal sovereignty—even if these gang members closet their sexualities in their gangs.[44] Indeed, as Rios says of his experience stabbing someone, "It felt *weird*.... Blood just flowing, stabbing that person, and seeing the expression on their damn face 'cause *you have the power* for their ass."[45] For Rios, the appeal in committing violence stems from altering a dynamic from one where he, a gay, working-class, and socioeconomically emasculated man, succumbs to bigotry and State disempowerment to one where he may achieve a violent hypermasculinity and resist gay sexuality's "subservience" in a heterocentric, homophobic society, by attaining power over another, possibly heterosexual, person.

To Disidentify with la Vida Loca

In *Homeboy*, many of the gay men who delineate their reasons for joining gangs outline, whether they are cognizant of the process or not, an agential survival strategy that facilitates their capacity to develop alternative epistemologies and ontologies that circumvent the ideological power of the coloniality of gender. Muñoz's theory of disidentification supplies a way for understanding why gay men participate in homophobic heterosexual gangs, and how they manage a subculture intolerant of their sexuality. To reiterate, Muñoz defines disidentification as "a mode of dealing with a dominant ideology, one that neither opts to assimilate within such a structure nor strictly opposes it. Rather, disidentification is a strategy that works on and against the dominant ideology."[46] As Verdi, Garcia, Rios, and Luis J. Rodriguez suggest, gangs may aid many working-class, gay Latino men in resisting the psychic and material conditions of their subaltern status in the United States, helping them to achieve a sense of belonging, power, and personal sovereignty. The gay men in *Homeboy* also understand many heterosexual, male-dominated gangs as homophobic subcultures that can endanger their lives—because of their own sexuality and the violent activities of gang members—but they refuse to set gang life against their sexuality because of the advantages these gangs offer them. The men of *Homeboy* identify with their gangs because doing so allows them to achieve the community-building and (de)colonial projects they desire.

Identifying with a gang intolerant toward their sexuality does not mean these men internalize self-hatred or homophobia either. Rather, disidentification as a survival strategy allows the men to identify selectively with a subculture that ameliorates their positions as second-class citizens in their barrios and the US nation-state while disidentifying with the ideologies of the gang that demand violent bigotry toward gay men. As many of the men of *Homeboy* suggest—particularly Larry Apodaca—this disidentification process, which to some may appear as contradictory confusion, remains a relatively satisfactory way of negotiating heterosexual gangs. Apodaca, for instance, whom the documentary codes as the "hardest" of the men in *Homeboy*, refuses to allow the homophobic ideologies of heterosexual gang life to impede his sexual and romantic pursuits. As he comfortably says, "[A]ll I do is date [male] gang members." For Apodaca, disidentification enables him to circumvent the coloniality of gender's capacity to regulate his sexuality while in a heterosexual gang. Instead, he develops an alternative epistemology and ontology that refuse to understand homosexuality and hypermasculine, heterosexual gang life as mutually exclusive.

Of course, disidentification is not an all-encompassing emancipatory survival strategy that can always or entirely negate the psychological trauma and physical danger gay men in heterosexual gangs can encounter. As Muñoz claims, "[D]isidentification is *not always* an adequate strategy of resistance or survival for all minority subjects.... [O]n other occasions, queers of color and other minority subjects need to follow a conformist path if they hope to survive a hostile public sphere."[47] Although, for Apodaca, disidentifying with gang life allows him to acquire its (de)colonial rewards while simultaneously positioning himself outside the gang sphere that criminalizes gay sexuality, the ability to disidentify with a gang may not always be a feasible or easily attainable option for every gay man. Many gay gang members might find—and understandably so—the homophobia within heterosexual gangs so psychologically traumatic that they may view disidentifying with these gangs a mentally and an emotionally unbearable option. Nonetheless, while disidentification might not prove viable for some gay gang members, the survival strategy does contain (de)colonial possibilities for others, and provides a hermeneutic for conceiving of the possibility of gay men who participate in homophobic heterosexual gangs.

To some, disidentification may resemble passing, and the gay gang members in *Homeboy* might not necessarily seem like gay men who disidentify with gangs, as much as they appear to be passing as "straight-acting" gang members. As Muñoz makes clear, however, passing and disidentification are not opposed to one another, but often transpire concurrently. According to Muñoz, passing "implicates elements of the disidentificatory process.... Like disidentification itself, passing can be a third modality where a dominant structure is co-opted, worked on and against. The subject who passes can be simultaneously identifying with and rejecting a dominant form."[48] As Muñoz insinuates, passing frequently includes disidentification, featuring a subject who both identifies with and rejects a dominant ideology. In many ways, then, acts of disidentification almost always feature some form of passing, though passing itself does not always constitute disidentification. To disidentify, subjects must consciously choose to identify with the majoritarian sphere and make use of its attributes while rejecting the notion that aspects of their identity compromise their ability to participate in that sphere. Because disidentification works as a *personal* survival strategy, disidentification is often private and includes passing. However, strictly passing for the sake of passing, while a personal survival strategy, does not require people to identify with the majoritarian sphere and reject its ideologies that preempt their participation in that space. Conversely, the gay gang members of *Homeboy* have all chosen to join gang life and identify as gang members because of the community, power, and resistance that gangs offer them. Many develop alternative ontologies and epistemologies that reject the presumption that their sexualities foreclose the possibility of claiming membership in heterosexual gangs.

The Rearticulation of *El Loco*

Homeboy features men who maintain the status quo aesthetics and norms that compose and regulate normative gender and sexuality in heterosexual, male-dominated gangs. But in publicly suturing gay sexuality to these aesthetics and norms, which in most gang cultures and in the dominant American imagination code as heterosexual, the documentary destabilizes bigoted ideologies that deem gay men incompatible with gang life and hypermasculinity. In *Gender Trouble*, Butler writes: "[T]he reconceptualization of identity as an *effect*, that is, as *produced* or *generated*, opens up possibilities of 'agency' that are insidiously foreclosed by positions that take identity categories as foundational and fixed."[49] For Butler, an identity (such as man or woman) reifies itself through the repetitive performance of that identity, meaning that an identity and the norms and aesthetics that compose that identity have the potential to shift and change continuously. As a result of these performative facets, Butler locates possibilities for reconfiguring identities, and their norms and aesthetics: "The critical task is, rather, to locate strategies of subversive repetition enabled by those constructions, to affirm the local possibilities of intervention through participating in precisely those practices of repetition that constitute identity, and, therefore, present the immanent possibility of contesting them."[50] By appropriating the normative performances that constitute an identity, and re-performing them in ways supposedly contradictory to that identity, the performer destabilizes the restrictive ideologies of the identity and reshapes its logics, norms, and aesthetics.

Homeboy displays men who conspicuously (via publicly declaring their statuses or histories as gay gang members in Dinco's film) disidentify with and perform—or have previously performed—a Latino gang member identity. In doing so, *Homeboy* operates as a (de)colonial cultural product that destabilizes and refashions the idea of a male gang member, enabling alternative conceptions where gay sexuality does not negate a man's ability to gangbang as a hypermasculine loco.[51] As Apodaca emphatically says, "The only thing I did was switch... from [pursuing] female to male. That's all. The *only* thing different from me. *That's it*" (Figure 4.2).[52] Apodaca, like many of the gay men of *Homeboy*, maintains a violent, hypermasculine gang life because of its (de)colonial rewards. In publicizing his alternative ontology and epistemology—evident at the coagulation of his sexuality, gang membership, and hypermasculine cholo aesthetic—Apodaca joins the other men of *Homeboy* in enabling the documentary to rearticulate gay sexuality away from stereotypical evocations of frailty and femininity and into a signifier for hypermasculinity.

The desire of Apodaca and many of the other men to date gang members also allows *Homeboy* to yoke with past cultural products that

Figure 4.2 *Larry Apodaca explains how gay sexuality does not compromise his hypermasculinity or capacity to live as a violent gang member. Video image supplied by the author.*

configure the cholo aesthetic into an image that signifies not just "admiration and fear," but sexual attraction as well.[53] While admiration and attraction resemble each other—and attraction often includes admiration—admiration denotes a sense of esteem, whereas attraction conveys an allure possibly arousing sexual or romantic interest. Before *Homeboy*, previous cultural products had partaken in this reshaping of cholo fashion aesthetics. One example is the film *Quinceañera*, which depicts two white men who sexually desire their Latino neighbor *because* of his cholo style. Similarly, the video-poem *El Abuelo* (2008) features Joe Jiménez reciting verse expressing his affinity for planchando so that he may "throw down a rowdy crease" (starch creases in Ben Davis pants and white t-shirts) and "captivate a Southside homeboy's wandering eye."

Homeboy participates in this same metamorphosing movement, as the men of the documentary relay that, for them, the cholo aesthetic does not invoke fear as much as romantic and sexual arousal. Garcia, for instance, says, "The one that turns my head in the beginning is . . . the bald guy or the shaved-head look with the tattoos. . . . That's the one that always catches my eye." Avila, to an even broader extent, distinguishes between men who dress like Latino gang members and actual gang members. Whereas Apodaca maintains that he only pursues men in gangs, Avila says,

> They really don't have to be gang members. They just have to have that look, bald head, straight-looking [read masculine], tattoos . . . just that machoism. . . . I don't care how good-looking the guy is. If he's got plucked eyebrows or he has any little femininity to him . . . it just totally turns me off.

Because of the frequency of comments such as these by Garcia, Apodaca, and Avila in the documentary, *Homeboy* contributes to the recent trend of representing cholo aesthetics as signifying romantic and sexual attraction, as much as intimidating hypermasculinity.

Although *Homeboy* is not alone in its many rearticulations of the Latino gang member, the documentary is distinct from *El Abuelo*, *Quinceañera*, and other gang and "homeboy" cultural products that reconceptualize normative aesthetics, ideology, and sexuality in gang and "street" life—such as the fictional films *On the Downlow*, *La Mission*, and *Moonlight*, and the artwork of Alex Donis and Hector Silva. In

Rethinking Chicana/o and Latina/o Popular Culture, Daniel Enrique Pérez writes that Donis and Silva use art to "assign effeminate roles to stereotypical macho men. In essence, they queer the macho," which "destabilizes the straight/gay and *macho/maricón* binary."[54] Likewise, Richard T. Rodríguez writes that Silva's art deconstructs "gender norms that commonly frame Chicano/Latino masculinity and crucially alters the ways in which the homeboy aesthetic has been made always already heterosexual or rendered antithetical to homosexuality."[55] Rodríguez later asserts that Silva's artwork facilitates fantasies where "a gay man may situate himself as the desiring subject in the symbolic mirror held up in Silva's work."[56] As he explains, "there are many ways to be caught up in the sequence of [Silva's] images.... The subject also has the ability to try out alternative identities and desires... imagining himself as part of a lustful brotherhood... that departs from the heteronormative premise of the homeboy aesthetic."[57] In this psychoanalytic hermeneutic, people viewing Donis's or Silva's artwork—or, as a corollary, any cultural product that queers the Latino cholo/"homeboy"—may create fantasies where they adopt various identities and enact multiple possibilities, attaining a jouissance that normative gang ideologies and cultures attempt to preempt.

While these fantasies, art pieces, and fictional films destabilize, and raise new lines of inquiry about, gender, masculinity, and sexuality in gang life, these representations are not without limitations. Admittedly, those threatened by the suggestion that gay men might gangbang— namely, heterosexual, homophobic, predominantly male gangs—may displace the possibility of hypermasculine gay men in gang life in that these cultural products *insinuate* gay locos—in contrast to *Homeboy*, which *affirms* them. Moreover, the adoption of a cholo or "homeboy" aesthetic, whether in cultural production or reality, does not automatically equate to gang membership. Avila makes this clear in explaining his willingness to pursue men who resemble gang members even if they are not in a gang. Any gay man can appropriate cholo aesthetics without participating in and having to navigate a homophobic, heterosexual gang. So, although Donis's and Silva's "homeboys," or characters like Jes and Che Rivera of *La Mission*, may resemble (but are not) gang members, this cultural production cannot approximate the severity of *Homeboy*'s intervention in gang culture, and its capacity to destabilize hegemonic ideologies of normative gender and sexuality in heterosexual gangs.

The Poetics of Documentary

Homeboy carries a certain veracity because of its documentary form and inclusion of actual current and former gang members. The film, however, does not entirely remove the veil between fiction and reality, and has its limits. In composing the mise-en-scène of a frame, directors manipulate objects and actors in a three-dimensional space. But, once the camera films this setup, the three-dimensional presentation transforms into a representation of reality. Despite *Homeboy*'s documentary form evoking a heightened realism, Dinco's film and the documentary form in general are still a calculated doctoring that produces representational images of the real. Documentaries do not provide an unadulterated window, and they still have elements of fiction. As Paula Rabinowitz says,

> [D]ocumentary rhetoric—despite being overlaid with a gloss of objectivity gleaned from its assignation as nonfiction... also derives from agitprop. Its function is to induce feeling, thought, and action. As such, it seems to me that documentary presents itself as much more performative than even fictional forms.[58]

Despite the perception that documentary is solely fact-based, neutral, non-fictional, and "non-performative," documentary usually harbors a political partisanship that erases any presumed objectivity.

In *Homeboy*, the viewer can identify several instances of propagandist construction that color assumptions of *Homeboy*'s impartiality. For example, in every shot of Rios, the frames always include background posters pinned to the wall that advocate gay pride or advertise gay homeboy websites or nightclubs (Figure 4.3). Additionally, Dinco divides *Homeboy* into three chapters: the first covering how and why the men joined their gangs, the second focusing on their identities as gay gang members, and the last detailing the reasons why some of them chose to leave gang life. But before each chapter commences, the film features long takes where the camera zooms in on various pieces of Silva's homoerotic homeboy artwork. In these shots that convey *Homeboy*'s political agenda, the viewer can identify its lack of objectivity and locate its ties to fictional representation.

Still, as Rabinowitz argues, since traditional fictional products "efface their constructions through naturalizing gestures, the response

Figure 4.3 *The filling of the frame with gay homeboy and cholo imagery emphasizes the documentary's partisanship in its queering of the homeboy/cholo aesthetic and figure. Video image supplied by the author.*

within the audience is contained; but in shifting the site of documentary from the object of vision to the subject of action by insisting on the dynamic relationship of viewer to view, documentary forms invoke performance within their audiences as much as within their objects."[59] Although documentary includes aspects of fiction, the form insists on the "dynamic relationship of viewer to view" and uses the same agitprop that negates its neutrality to stimulate action in ways that traditional fiction cannot. As such, despite *Homeboy*'s inability to detach itself completely from fictional film, its qualities as documentary produce a *sense* of immediacy and affect within the viewer to a degree that Donis's and Silva's artwork and that standard fiction do not.

Notwithstanding the documentary form's galvanizing qualities, documentary has a deplorable history rooted in colonialism. Chandan C. Reddy explains that documentary originates from colonial projects where the form was a tool for "'racializing' and exoticizing its objects, separating them from their historical context and the filmmaker and distancing the viewer from the locations depicted on screen, no matter how 'nearby' that ethnography might take place."[60] Because of documentary's "racializing" and "exoticizing" characteristics, the form helped justify "egregious acts of White violence by rendering people as exotic others that require 'western' cultural development."[61] Admittedly, *Homeboy* may inadvertently reproduce this effect of documentary, as its gang-exploitation conventions inhibit the film from socioeconomically contextualizing its subjects. Consequently, for nontargeted audiences, *Homeboy* may rationalize "White violence" against Latina/o/xs, and a colonial "development" of Latina/o/x cultures, because of how *Homeboy* features violent Latino gang members and uncovers homophobia in Latina/o/x spaces. *Homeboy* may also participate in fetishizing, exoticizing, and objectifying gay gang members for a non-gang or non-Latina/o/x audience, but these possibilities do not mean critics, scholars, and filmmakers should abandon *Homeboy* and the documentary form. Rather, documentary's flaws are precisely why critics and scholars remain key in cultural analysis. Not only do critics and scholars hinder those who would use a documentary such as *Homeboy* against gang members and Latina/o/x communities, but they also reveal the value in certain documentaries rife with exoticizing and objectifying characteristics. In spite of *Homeboy*'s limits, Dinco's documentary offers an avenue for theorizing: heterosexual hypermasculinity in gangs and its reliance on homophobia; how and why gay men persist in homophobic, heterosexual gangs; and how cultural products espousing violent hypermasculinities can themselves facilitate (de)colonial projects. As Rabinowitz implies, agency may reside in objectification as well: "[W]hat is so bad about objectification? Objects can speak also—listen to the commodities in *Capital*—and what they say perhaps undoes the subject itself."[62]

With Rabinowitz's suggestion in mind, I read the men in *Homeboy* as using its documentary form in a way similar to how Muñoz reads Pedro Zamora on MTV's *The Real World* (1994).[63] Noting the objectifying and mediated traits of reality television and *The Real World*'s application process, Muñoz argues that Zamora disidentified with both the show and its application protocols to enter a public stage where he could import a political intervention.[64] In disidentifying with *The Real World*, Zamora used the "televisual dissemination of such performances [to allow] for the *possibility of counterpublics*—communities and relational chains of resistance that contest the dominant public sphere."[65] Similarly, I submit that the men of *Homeboy* disidentify with the colonial history and traits of documentary to access a medium where their presence in *Homeboy* facilitates the film's status as a (de)colonial cultural product. By publicly avowing hypermasculine, violent gay gang members in heterosexual gangs, *Homeboy* not only challenges the logic of the coloniality of gender that organizes heterosexual gang life. As this chapter soon shows, the film also develops a gang counterpublic.

The Queer Macho Is Not yet Freed

Although the men of *Homeboy*'s disidentifications with heterosexual gang life showcase their capacity to reject and circumvent the homophobic components of the coloniality of gender and its power over their lives, they do not fully delink from this coloniality. These men's valorization of hypermasculinity and their insistence that their sexuality does not compromise this masculinity or their capability to participate in gang life means that they are not entirely revolutionary, but instead (de)colonial. In many ways, the men of *Homeboy*'s power to attain community in gang life, to resist homophobic bigotry outside their gangs, and to (de)colonize themselves from normative ideologies about sexuality in gang culture hinges on upholding several of the adverse qualities of a hypermasculinity that harms others and informs patriarchal hegemony. Daniel Enrique Pérez writes that, in Donis's and Sílva's artwork, "as the macho approximates a queer identity, he is freed from some of the negative traits associated with his image: misogyny, violence, stoicism."[66] These negative traits, however, are not limited only to sexuality, because they also implicate gender. Though the men of *Homeboy* are gay, they perform a hypermasculinity that does not shed these damaging qualities that Pérez mentions. The majority of the men of *Homeboy* maintain a stoic attitude and boast about their violent lives. For example, when underscoring his violent hypermasculinity, Apodaca brags about how, shortly before interviewing for *Homeboy*, a rival gang member pulled a gun on him. At the end of the day, these men either are or were violent gang members troubled by the same (and further) inequalities that plague straight, working-class Latino men and that help toxify subaltern masculinities. While many of the men reveal how they queer gang violence and crime to resist hate crimes and homophobia outside their gangs, gang citizenship regularly entails activity that may directly or indirectly harm other innocent, multiply marginalized persons in the barrio. None of the men ever deny partaking in this type of behavior.

Moreover, because the coloniality of gender not only entails "the subordination of females in every aspect of life," but also the devaluing of what Woman signifies, many of the men subscribe to the misogynous aspects of the coloniality of gender, even if not explicitly vocalizing a hatred of women.[67] The men's rearticulation of the Latino gang member implicitly comes at the expense of femininity—a performance that Woman signifies in the coloniality of gender—and feminine gay men. In the documentary, many of the men are incessant about their distance from femininity, and *Homeboy* never makes any redeeming statement about feminine men—only demonizing assertions, such as with Avila, who expresses distaste at any man who has "plucked eyebrows or . . . any little femininity to him." For this reason, the men and the documentary construct femininity as antithetical to gang life and as an unworthy gender performance. In spite of this disgust for femininity, none of the men provide any indication that they hate actual women. Yet this absence may partially stem from the fact that no meaningful discussion of women ever materializes in *Homeboy*. This is yet another of the film's troubling adherences to the gang-exploitation genre. As I have explained earlier in this book, in their representations and discussions of gangs, cultural producers and academics too often eclipse gang girls.

Ultimately, eliding Latina gang members furthers the homogenizing conception of gangs as exclusively male spaces. It also deprives women of benefitting from a subculture and counterpublic that they may crave in ways similar to, or even vastly different from, those of gay male gang members. For instance, upon witnessing the closing sequence of *American Me* where the viewer learns that Julie was once a gang girl, Fregoso writes,

> [T]he history of Chicana membership in gangs . . . unfolds not on the screen, but in my mind. The final weathered look in Julie's eyes sparks the painful silent memory of the female gang members I have known: Chicanas surviving and resisting *la vida dura* (the hard life). I often wonder why the story of Julie's oppression and resistance, why the pain of her rape, is not up there, on the Hollywood screen, looking at me.[68]

As Fregoso's comments imply, while recent films and artwork have begun to rearticulate the Latino gang member and/or homeboy, they have often subsumed gang girls. *Homeboy*'s representation of gay men differs from previous gang-exploitation films that elide sexual desire between men—or that displace this desire under a rape paradigm that indicates hypermasculine power and not sexuality. But the movie adheres to gang-exploitation conventions in overlooking an opportunity to provide a more nuanced intervention that attends to undertheorized issues of sexuality and non-male genders. Nevertheless, despite *Homeboy*'s limitations in its gang-exploitation film conventions and its use of the documentary form, the movie still invaluably provides a rare avenue through which to theorize masculinity and sexuality in gang life. It also helps construct a counterpublic for a population of multiply marginalized men who struggle to find a receptive space where they may understand and negotiate the multiplicity of their identities.

Gauging *Homeboy*'s Counterpublic

In disclosing their histories with heterosexual gangs in *Homeboy*, the men enable the documentary to create a counterpublic for gay men who cannot—or may not elect to—disidentify with gangs, and one aimed at dismantling homophobia in gang culture. Nancy Fraser argues that, in forming counterpublics, subaltern people "invent and circulate counter discourse, so as to formulate oppositional interpretations of their identities, interests, and needs."[69] In the circulation of this counter discourse, subaltern persons oppose and potentially reconfigure the "exclusionary norms of the 'official public sphere,' elaborating alternative styles of political behaviors and alternative norms of public speech."[70] In its formation of a counterpublic, *Homeboy* facilitates a counter discourse that contests the "exclusionary norms" of heterosexual gangs to envision "alterative styles" of involvement in gang life.

In its creation of this gang counterpublic, *Homeboy* has not matched the exhibition or viewership of previous Hollywood gang-exploitation films that homogenize gangs as heterosexual spaces incompatible with gay sexuality. When *American Me* premiered in 1992, for example, the film opened with a wide release (playing in 830 theaters across the United States), received praise from famed movie critic Roger Ebert—who compared the film to the American classic *The Godfather* (1972)—and benefitted from the emerging star power of Olmos, who had previously co-starred in *Blade Runner* (1982).[71] On the other hand, *Homeboy*, as well as other recent Latina/o/x films about gay homeboys/gang members— like *On the Downlow*, *Quinceañera*, and *La Mission*—premiered with limited releases at independent film festivals, and remains generally acknowledged only inside Latina/o/x circles. But these limited releases do not discount *Homeboy*'s destabilization of normative gender, sexuality, and ideology in gang culture, nor its counterpublic potentiality. The documentary has a propensity for generating meaningful discussions in Latina/o/x barrios, among gay and white populations, and within gangs.

Homeboy premiered in 2012 at Outfest in Los Angeles, an LGBTQ film festival that began in 1982.[72] Since screening at Outfest, *Homeboy* has played at several Latina/o/x and LGBTQ film festivals—primarily in California, the state with the largest Latina/o/x population. These screenings include Cine+Mas, a San Francisco-based Latina/o/x film festival; the Latin Quaker Queer Film Festival in Whittier; the Long Beach Q Films Festival; The Q-Sides (a San Francisco Bay Area lowrider and Latina/o/x art exhibition); the Santa Clara Annual Queer Film Festival; Out Like That! in New York City; and foreign festivals, such as the Belgian film festival Cine Zuid and EuroPride in Oslo, Norway. In addition to independent LGBTQ and Latina/o/x film festivals, *Homeboy* also often screens at colleges, universities, and cultural centers across the United States, such as San Diego State University, the University of Southern California, and the Cathedral Center of St. Paul in Echo Park.[73] During these screenings, Dinco usually holds question and answer sessions and organizes panels featuring former gang members or poets that write on gay Latino gang members or homeboys. These screenings and panels construct an environment designed to invite critical discussion on, and a reimagining of, gay sexuality in gangs, and to dismantle homophobia in other heterosexual societies.[74]

In its national exhibition, *Homeboy* has garnered a respectable amount of coverage in the United States, producing a discourse on the intersectional identities of the men of *Homeboy*, and the importance of fighting racism and homophobia so that these men and others like them can find belonging and love. *Homeboy* attained coverage, reviews, and recommendations in many local and national news outlets, such as *Silver Lake Star*, *Huffington Post*, *Queerty*, and *Big Gay Picture Show*.[75] Additionally, *Univision*, the New York-based, Spanish-language broadcast television and news network, interviewed Dinco, Rios, and Romero for an article recognizing the obstacles gay men in gangs face, and promoting *Homeboy* for heterosexual and Spanish-speaking audiences. As Dinco says in this interview, the documentary can help not only "gay men, but also heterosexuals, so that they can understand them."[76]

Along with attempting to further *Homeboy*'s heterosexual viewership, many of these articles discuss how *Homeboy* contests stereotypes about gay men and gang life, and enables multiple audiences to identify with the men of *Homeboy*, even when some audiences are not gay, Latina/o/x, or gang members. For instance, a white writer for the *Long Beach Post* claims that *Homeboy* "sho[o]ts down ... images that have proliferated since the 90s in showcasing gay men—loud, bitchy, and exclusively white" and also demonstrates that "[t]hese men, much like the feeling I held when being taunted as a kid growing up in the mountains, just want someone to care about them."[77] Not only does the film succeed in diversifying images of gay men across masculinity and race, but as this reviewer's comments suggest, *Homeboy* also excels in sentimentalizing gang membership to humanize people who gangbang—potentially impelling viewers to help enact meaningful, systemic change.

Homeboy's warm reception has resulted in other gay men joining the men of Dinco's film in publicizing their presences and experiences as gang members. For example, the *Press Telegram* featured an article promoting the documentary that incorporated an interview from a gay man named Manuel, who, after viewing the film, decided to share his past difficulties with accepting his sexuality, which he believed incompatible with his gang member identity: "I kept saying to myself that I wasn't gay because I had a girlfriend and was only doing it because I was in prison."[78] According to Manuel, restrictive prison conditions explained away his sexual encounters with other men, and assisted him in denying what he has now accepted: his gay sexual orientation. Ultimately, Manuel's story and the aforementioned commentary on *Homeboy* testify to the consequence of, and *Homeboy*'s success in, creating a counterpublic for gay gang members to participate in as a strategy for surviving the homophobia and whiteness pervading Latina/o/x and gay spaces. As in Manuel's case, such pressures may result in the denial or suppression of sexual identity.

While this review of *Homeboy*'s exhibition and reception establishes the documentary's resonance with Latina/o/x, gay, and—specifically—gay gang member audiences, one of *Homeboy*'s most noteworthy interventions lies in its capability to precipitate critical discussion at the site that necessitates disidentification for the men of *Homeboy*: the heterosexual, homophobic, male-dominated gang. Although Dinco exhibits the film across the United States and in other countries, screening *Homeboy* alongside discussion panels with former gang members, and primarily in Southern California areas like Los Angeles, Long Beach, and Echo Park, indicates an attempt to target, and combat homophobia in, heterosexual gangs. Despite its growing gentrification, Echo Park, for example, still houses the long-standing Chicana/o/x gangs the Diamond Street Locos, Head Hunters, Big Top Locos, Echo Park Locos, and Frogtown Rifa. Measuring *Homeboy*'s viewership among active gang members and the documentary's effects on gangs remains an exceedingly difficult venture, because doing so requires persons to out themselves as participants in highly criminalized activity in a nation with a surplus of gang injunction laws.[79] Nevertheless, evidence of *Homeboy*'s capacity to intervene in and influence heterosexual gangs does exist, primarily online, where the internet affords at least some anonymity.

One of the most notable locales where gang members' discussions of *Homeboy* materialize is *Streetgangs.com*, a popular website among gang members that not only houses news and information on current policing, racial, political, and legal matters pertaining to gangs, but also provides a forum for gang members of many races and ethnicities across the United States to engage in dialogue. Often, these conversations range from topics such as tagging, nascent gangs, and recent robberies to gang politics, deceased gang members, and emerging policing hotspots. After learning of *Homeboy* and watching its trailer, one user created a thread discussing gay sexuality in gangs and gay gang members' abilities to gangbang as hypermasculine, violent locos. Although some persons in this discussion avowed homophobic ideologies that stigmatize gay men as fragile, feminine, and weak, *Homeboy* sparked a conversation that led many not only to affirm gay gang members, but also to rethink any rationale that considers gay sexuality as compromising a gang member's violent hypermasculinity and reputation. For instance, one person writing under the handle "TomTom" says, "[W]ell-known riders [pull] gay shit like that and still being well respected."[80] Another user writing as "Cliffard" corroborates opinions like "TomTom"'s by citing Kody Scott, who refers to a Hoover Crip Gangster named "Fat Rat" as "a hood star, a hood legend," despite Fat Rat's same-sex history.[81] Although *Homeboy* has not duplicated the scale of exhibition of traditional gang-exploitation films, the documentary has created a counterpublic where persons in and out of gangs rethink homophobic ideologies that read gang identity as almost always heterosexual and antithetical to gay sexuality; recognize the importance of creating a receptive space for multiply marginalized men like those of

Dinco's film; and further encourage gay gang members to extend this counterpublic's potentiality through sharing their own histories in gangs.

When viewing Pedro Zamora's presence on *The Real World*, Muñoz says,

> I imagined countless other living rooms within the range of this broadcast and I thought about the queer children who might be watching this program at home with their parents. This is the point where I locate something other than the concrete interventions in the public sphere. Here is where I see the televisual spectacle leading to the possibility of new counterpublics, new spheres of possibility, and the potential for the reinvention of the world from A to Z.[82]

Like Muñoz's hope for Zamora's counterpublic, I also imagine a vision for *Homeboy*, one where Dinco screens his documentary at numerous sites across the United States, with many gay and straight Latino men as audience members, some having gangbanged and some not, but, perhaps, having friends or family members participating in la vida loca. In this vision, audience members witness and relate to others the stories of these men in *Homeboy*. In doing so, they increase *Homeboy*'s extensions, enabling gay gang members across the United States to identify with and participate in this counterpublic, discerning in this space not only a community to call their own, but also strategies for transforming bigoted ideologies that would dare to brand a loco a maricón.

5 | THE QUEER UTOPIAN FUTURITY OF FAILED GANG MEMBERS

IN THE FINAL SCENE OF TADEO GARCÍA'S 2004 FILM *ON THE Downlow*, a Two Six clica of Little Village, Chicago captures a former Latin King, Angel, and holds him hostage in a basement. Moments later, a Two Six named Isaac steadies a pistol before Angel's face, preparing to murder this rival gang member. Fearing his death, Angel, on his knees, cries out,

> Isaac, man. Isaac, you can't do this, man. We're supposed to be together, man, please! You and me, man, forever, man. Isaac, me and you man! You can't do this, man, please! Isaac, I love y—.

Unbeknownst to the rest of the Two Six, Isaac and Angel love each other and are in a romantic relationship, compromising Isaac's ability to murder this ex-Latin King. When begging for his life, Angel nearly openly proclaims his relationship with Isaac, supplicating his partner not to shoot him, with homoerotic appeals in front of Isaac's gang leader, Reaper, and other members of the Two Six. The film suggests, however, that the Two Six leader deduces the implications of Angel's entreaties, for before Angel can finish the word "you" and publicize his love for Isaac, Reaper kills him. Reaper's choice to shoot Angel at this precise moment implies that the gang leader pulls the trigger not only because of Angel's prior affiliation with the Latin Kings, but also (and implicitly primarily) because his relationship with Isaac demolishes Isaac's capacity to succeed at the Two Six's expectations of violent, heterosexual masculinity. In response to the murder of his partner, Isaac kills Reaper, and later puts a gun to his own head to commit suicide, to die alongside Angel.

In this film, the statements made by the men of *Homeboy* ring true: gay men in heterosexual, male-dominated gangs face deathly punishment. There is no disidentifying in this movie. Angel and Isaac fail in their gangs and barrio, in part because of the rivalry between the Two Six and the Latin Kings, but also—and perhaps more so—because of their inability to rearticulate gay sexuality into a signifier for violent hypermasculinity in a manner and to a degree that the Two Six leader finds sufficient.

As documented throughout this book, violent hypermasculinities play a crucial role in gang members enacting (de)colonial projects, in and through gang life, and in achieving subcultural citizenship in their clicas. Although many male-dominated, heterosexual gangs deem violent hypermasculinity inaccessible to women and gay men, the book has revealed how these "non-normative" gang members appropriate, refashion, queer, and gender gang violence, crime, and hypermasculinity. In doing so, they claim citizenship in these gangs and initiate (de)colonial projects—even if it means reproducing a toxicity that harms other multiply marginalized persons. But of course, not every non-normative gang member succeeds in male-dominated, heterosexual gangs that espouse violent hypermasculinity and misogynist and homophobic ideologies. Nevertheless, this book does not presume that failing in such gangs forecloses the possibility of these subcultures offering generative rewards for non-normative gang members.

Consequently, this chapter re-envisions how male-dominated, heterosexual, and homophobic gangs that idealize violent hypermasculinity might facilitate (de)colonial projects. I thus now shift toward gay gang members in *On the Downlow* who, unlike la Heredera, Lucía, and the men of *Homeboy*, do not co-opt and/or succeed in gangs and their barrios, but instead fail in them. In theorizing their failure, I distinguish between failure and refusal. Failure bespeaks an attempt that ultimately does not succeed or does not satisfactorily meet expectations. As readers will see throughout this chapter, the gay gang members of *On the Downlow* attempt to fulfill the expectations of what it means to be a successful gang member in their barrio through maintaining cholo aesthetics, participating in and bragging about violence, performing masculine stoicism, and closeting their sexuality. Although their efforts are futile, I read an antinomy in these men's failures in their gangs and barrio. I contend that queer failure generates alternative types of (de)colonial projects—different from the normative models available in gangs, but perhaps just as rewarding. In particular,

On the Downlow imagines how failing in male-dominated, heterosexual gangs and the homophobic barrio may facilitate the construction of a utopian futurity.[1] In their utopian futurity, the gay gang members of *On the Downlow* achieve a temporary (de)colonial freedom through fantasizing about a life outside of the racial and sexual constrictions of the coloniality of gender that organizes their gangs and barrio. In this way, Chapter 5 illuminates how (de)colonial projects need not always entail conventional notions of success, and shows how male-dominated, heterosexual gangs that glamorize hypermasculinity, violence, and crime might precipitate (de)colonial projects through failure.

Forging Utopian Futurity Through Queer Present Failure

In analyzing the connections gang and barrio failure have with utopian futurity, this chapter draws from Jack Halberstam's, José Muñoz's, and Lee Edelman's conceptions of queerness, failure, success, utopian futurity, and (no) future. Muñoz claims that, for queer persons, the "present is not enough. It is impoverished and toxic for queers and other people who do not feel the privilege of majoritarian belonging, normative tastes, and 'rational' expectations."[2] Part of the reason the present remains "impoverished and toxic for queers" centers on their failure in heteronormative society. As Muñoz says, "Queer failure is often deemed or understood as failure because it rejects normative ideas of value."[3] Adhering to the normative values referenced by Muñoz establishes success in a heteronormative present. For Halberstam, these "normative ideas of value" in heteronormative societies lead "to the equation of success with advancement, capital accumulation, family, ethical conduct, and hope."[4] Although barrios may have standards of success distinct from and similar to the model Halberstam proposes, participating in the present as a docile subject entails abiding by a pertinent society's definition of success, which may require not only ethical behavior and the acquisition of capital, but also the creation of family. This familial prerequisite, however, mandates a heterosexual, reproductive, and nuclear family, which, for many queer studies theorists, epitomizes the fulcrum of queer failure.

In his foundational polemic *No Future: Queer Theory and the Death Drive*, Edelman proclaims that queers have no future because of their inability to partake in traditional forms of reproductive futurism—a term that describes heterosexual reproduction that "preserves the absolute privilege of heteronormativity," and conserves the child as "the perpetual horizon of every acknowledged politics."[5] For Edelman, the child represents the future, and success in heteronormative societies demands the advancement of the cult of the child. For this reason, Edelman defines queerness by its rejection of reproductive futurism, and he regards the child as the future, rendering people (regardless of their sexuality) who choose not to or cannot participate in conventional modes of heteronormative reproductive futurism queer.[6] Because queerness does not "figh[t] for the children"—and, by extent, the future—Edelman links queerness to the death drive: "a place, to be sure, of abjection expressed in the stigma, sometimes fatal, that follows from reading that figure literally."[7] As the realm of habitually lethal persecution, the death drive structures the road toward the queer's "no future."

Edelman's statements on queerness, reproductive futurism, and the child as the future have substantially shaped how academics conduct queer studies scholarship, but many have also critiqued Edelman for subsuming the intersection between race and the future. For instance, Muñoz takes issue with Edelman's diatribe against an op-ed that Sylvia Ann Hewlett and Cornel West published in the *Boston Globe* in 1998, which argues for "creating the conditions that allow parents to cherish their children" to "ensure our collective future."[8] Edelman lambastes Hewlett and West for a "self-serving" and "redundant" politics that will mortgage the present "to a *fantasmatic* future in the name of the political 'capital' that those children will thus have become."[9] Despite West's extensive scholarship on race, racism, and white supremacy and, as Muñoz says, "the topic of race that is central to the actual editorial" that West and Hewlett write, Edelman neglects how Hewlett and West's propositions reply to the US coloniality that curtails children of color's futures.[10] As Muñoz points out, Edelman's critique "is flawed insofar as it decontextualizes West's work from the topic that has been so central to his critical intervention: blackness."[11]

Edelman's oversight accents Muñoz's larger concerns with *No Future*: its theories "of queer temporality that fail to factor in the relational relevance of race and class" and "merely reproduce a crypto-universal white gay subject that is weirdly atemporal."[12] In other words, though Edelman posits that the future belongs to the child, his argument disregards how the "future is only the stuff of some kids. Racialized kids, queer kids, are not the sovereign princes of futurity."[13] Joining with Muñoz in bristling at the lack of intersectionality in Edelman's polemic,

Halberstam contends that *No Future* reads as misogynist in its ramifications for women. As Halberstam asserts,

> Edelman always runs the risk of linking heteronormativity in some essential way to women, and perhaps, unwittingly, woman becomes the site of the unqueer: she offers life, while queerness links up with the death drive; she is aligned sentimentally with the child and with "goodness," while the gay man in particular leads the way to "something better" while "promising absolutely nothing."[14]

For Halberstam, *No Future* positions women as protectorates of the hegemony of the child and the future, through the capacity to bear children.

These critiques of Edelman are worth mentioning because of their relevance to my book's argument about *On the Downlow* and on the connection between utopian futurity and (de)colonial failure in gangs. *On the Downlow* does not just envision the possibility of *a* future for gay men that Edelman views as non-existent. This movie also imagines a utopian futurity for gay *Latino* men—one that responds to a death drive that operates along racial and classed, as much as sexual, lines.[15] In this way, this chapter's interpretation of *On the Downlow* troubles Edelman's postulations on the antagonism between the future and queerness, and expands on Muñoz's theorization of how queers of color construct utopian futurities out of present failure.

Muñoz repudiates viewing queer failure pessimistically, or foreclosing the future for queers. Differing from Edelman, Muñoz sees the future not as the realm of the child, but as "queerness's domain," because queerness "is a structuring and educated mode of desiring that allows us to see and feel beyond the quagmire of the present."[16] Because queerness hinges on the desire for futurity (possibilities beyond those in the present), queerness "is a longing that propels us onward" as an "ideality that can be distilled from the past and used to imagine a future."[17] Thus, since queerness "is primarily about futurity and hope" and "essentially about the rejection of a here and now and an insistence on potentiality or concrete possibility for another world," queerness appropriates failure to erect utopian futurities—the Edenic, affective moments in the present that envision an array of idyllic, future possibilities.[18] In this way, according to Muñoz, the "politics of failure are about doing something else," and accord "escape and a certain kind of virtuosity."[19] For Muñoz, the redeployment of failure in pursuit of "escape" and "virtuosity" forms utopian futurities unencumbered by the disciplinary regulations of heteronormativity. These utopian futurities permit queers to "conceptualize new worlds and realities that are not irrevocably constrained by the HIV/AIDS pandemic and institutionalized state homophobia."[20] Likewise, Halberstam deems queer failure subversive to hegemonic ideologies and ontologies, even if recognizing that failure may also entail a "host of negative affects, such as disappointment, disillusionment, and despair."[21] As Halberstam says, failure "allows us to escape the punishing norms that discipline behavior and manage human development," and "can be used to recategorize what looks like inaction, passivity, and lack of resistance in terms of the practice of stalling the business of the dominant."[22] Oppositional and emancipating in the construction of a utopian futurity—even if this futurity eventually dissipates—queer failure "recognizes that alternatives are embedded already in the dominant and that power is never total or consistent."[23]

Applying Muñoz's and Halberstam's theories about failure as subversive and liberating as much as it is overbearing to *On the Downlow* discloses how gay gang members are not "irrevocably constrained" by the heteronormative and heterosexual precepts, or by the definitions of success, of certain barrios and gangs. In the context of this film, success in the barrio and in gangs for men predominantly centers on violent, heterosexual hypermasculinity. But differing from the other texts this book has so far examined, in this movie, the gang and barrio that idealize violent, heterosexual masculinity facilitate (de)colonial projects for gay men not through success but, paradoxically, through failure. Failing in the heterosexual, hypermasculine, and violent gang and barrio initiates the construction of a utopian futurity where gay men may, if sometimes only temporarily, escape psychologically and physically abusive homophobia, excessive poverty, and the pressure to perform violent hypermasculinity.

The Latin Kings and Two Six of Little Village

Set in the predominantly Latina/o/x neighborhood of Little Village, *On the Downlow* focuses on a pair of gay men from two of the most prominent contemporary Latina/o/x gangs in Chicago: the Latin Kings and Two Six. Founded by Ramon "King Papo" Santos, the Latin Kings first emerged as a Puerto Rican gang in the Humboldt Park area of the West

Side of Chicago in the 1950s but has since branched out into other cities (primarily New York) to become one of the largest Latina/o/x gangs in the United States.[24] As of now, the US Department of Justice estimates the Latin Kings' membership at 20,000 to 35,000.[25] The gang commonly wears black- and gold-colored clothing and has adopted a five point crown as its primary symbol. According to the gang, the crown "symbolizes our royalty among men; our sovereignty and our Kingdom among Nations.... Each of the Coronet's five points has a special meaning. They represent Love, Honor, Obedience, Sacrifice, and Righteousness."[26] As a Puerto Rican Chicago gang, the Latin Kings often embrace the culture of the Taíno civilization—an indigenous nation native to Puerto Rico—such as in the gang's ranking system. Certain members carry the title of Sun King, Corona, Inca, and Cacique, the last of which is a Spanish transliteration that derives from the Taíno word kasike, a term that referred to the chief of the Taíno.[27]

In their initial formation, the Latin Kings understood themselves as a revolutionary group espousing what I would label a (de)colonial ideology, and remnants of this mindset persist in contemporary Latin Kings clicas. New members must demonstrate their willingness to adhere to the gang's rules and creed by signing a contract. This document stipulates that the Latin Kings' "purpose was and is for the progress, upliftment, and freedom of our people—the Third World people. Our duty is to learn so that we may teach, to seek liberation of our oppressed brothers and sisters, to unite and stand up against those who seek to deny our rightful existence, not only in the level of economic progress, but also cultural acceptance."[28] The Latin Kings see themselves as challenging and circumventing the power of those who "seek to deny our rightful existence" through drawing upon the power of what they call "Brown Force": the legacies and souls of "millions of Brown Men and Women" who "have given their life in the fight for liberation" and "against colonialism, hunger, ignorance, and for the human dignity of our People."[29] Antonio "King Tone" Fernandez, a former Supreme Inca who headed the New York faction of the Latin Kings in the 1990s, perhaps best vocalized how these revolutionary ideologies of the 1950s Chicago Latin Kings still permeated the gang several decades later in an interview with *Workers World*:

> We call ourselves kings and queens to promote a sense of worth and self-respect. Latinos are always made to feel that we are worthless. What we are saying is that Latinos are kings and queens of

their own lives. Just like Puerto Ricans are the true kings and queens of Puerto Rico—not the United States who invaded our land.[30]

For Fernandez, the Latin Kings provided an avenue through which Puerto Ricans could challenge the sub-ontological existence that US coloniality imposes on many Latina/o/xs.

Though the Latin Kings originated as a Puerto Rican gang, the gang's quest to unite their "oppressed brothers and sisters" and "establish progress, upliftment, and freedom" for "Third World People" resulted in the gang migrating out of Humboldt Park to engage other Latina/o/x ethnic groups. In March 1964, the Bohemian real estate agent Richard A. Dolejs began a rebranding campaign of South Lawndale, Chicago, a village sharing its eastern border with the emerging Mexican American enclave of Pilsen. Dolejs's aim was to distance perception of the town from any association with the black population of North Lawndale. Amezcua writes that the real estate agent proposed renaming the town "Little Village" to "evoke the small Czech and Slavic villages 'from which his forebears came.'"[31] For Dolejs, embracing the "white, even if immigrant" cultures of South Lawndale "could sever any association with Black [North] Lawndale."[32] Though South Lawndale did rename itself Little Village, the town did not anticipate the westward Mexican American migrations from Pilsen, ultimately leading to Little Village becoming a primarily Mexican American area by the 1980s. After forming the Latin Kings in the 1950s, Santos and other founding members of the gang journeyed south in the 1960s to recruit this emerging Mexican American population in Little Village. The result was Santos establishing Little Village's first Latin Kings chapter, and transforming the Latin Kings from a Puerto Rican to Latina/o/x gang.[33]

Despite the Latin Kings purporting to advocate for the "liberation" of their "oppressed brothers and sisters" and to unite Latina/o/xs in the fight against coloniality, the gang epitomized the (de)colonial paradox in their contradictory attacks against Latina/o/xs who refused to join them or were members of other gangs. Today, Little Village houses only three main gangs: the Latin Kings, the Two Six, and the Cullerton Deuces—a smaller Mexican American gang inhabiting the Marshall Square section of the east side of the town. The Two Six transformed into a gang as means of defending themselves against the Latin Kings, as the latter preyed upon Latina/o/xs who rejected the invitation into the gang. Founded by David, Tyrone, and Alfonso Ayala in the early 1970s, the Two Six were initially a softball club that called themselves the Two-Six Boys. But after the Latin Kings began victimizing the boys in the west end of Little Village, the Ayala brothers re-organized the softball team into a gang and began recruiting.[34] Under the leadership of Alfonso, the Two Six sported black and beige colors and adopted the two and six dice; the spade, clover, and diamond; the cross guard sword; and the Playboy and Nesquik bunnies, as well as Bugs Bunny, as their symbols.[35] After Alfonso was shot and killed in 1981, David led the gang for a short time. He was arrested, however, and sentenced to life in prison without the possibility of parole, for overseeing a hit on a Latin King that resulted in the deaths of two civilians uninvolved in gangs.[36] This Latin King/Two Six rivalry that began in the 1970s continues today, and is a conflict on which *On the Downlow* offers a queer take in its portrayal of Isaac (a Two Six) and Angel (a Latin King).

Love in the Barrio

To mitigate the risks of dating each other, Angel drops out of the Latin Kings and joins the Two Six, though this new membership does not nullify the dangerous homophobia the pair must navigate in Little Village and in the Two Six. Ultimately, as mentioned earlier, the Two Six leader, Reaper, discovers Angel's history in the Latin Kings and charges Isaac to murder him. Reaper, however, resorts to killing Angel himself. Isaac cannot carry out the order, because he loves Angel. Isaac subsequently commits murder-suicide, shooting Reaper in revenge, before putting the pistol to his own head.

At the onset of this narrative, *On the Downlow* opens with a montage of Little Village, to establish the film's main setting. Over the first few minutes, the movie displays a range of closeups and long shots of streets and walkways filled with car and pedestrian traffic; littered garbage and industrial smog; Spanish signage; a taquería, and paleteros and fruit-and-vegetable street vendors; multiple high-arching churches and a mural of the Virgin Mary; Chicago police cars and officers; run-down apartment buildings; and several gang members, some of them throwing gang signs or cruising in lowriders. These images help portray Little Village as a space where gangs, Catholicism, and the police have prominent presences. As Bill Johnson González says, this montage "suggests that the neighborhoods are also zones of bleak life possibilities, restricted mobility, dead ends, and police surveillance and punishment."[37] Through these images, *On the Downlow* conveys that this barrio offers little possibility of upward mobility, and only minimal life chances that the United States constricts through repressive state apparatuses and white capitalism.

These images contrast with the shots that *On the Downlow* cuts to at the end of this first montage. In the next montage, the film displays shots of open, unpolluted skies and luscious greenery; analogous middle-class homes with crisply-cut lawns and American flags decorating their doors (suggesting the American Dream, suburban uniformity, and equality); SUVs that imply family, an insinuation that later materializes with images of a white (presumably) brother and sister playing basketball; only white people; uncongested, clean sidewalks; and a dog (also white) frolicking in a front yard off-leash. Whereas the previous montage emphasized a low-income/working-class status by featuring many shots of businesses and working people, in this montage several images characterize the space as recreational. Although the basketball-playing brother and sister are minors, and the dog (a toy breed, not a working breed) likely cannot contribute to labor for human income, their play renders the neighborhood free from the burden of work—a place of pleasures, unhampered by the police. The montage contains only one man working (cutting his lawn)—though, for many homeowners, this action may evoke leisure, rather than labor. Regardless, the lawn that he cuts connotes financial wealth and privilege—as do the suburban homes—in a way that the shots of Little Village do not. González observes that these suburban images are "visual metaphors" for an "ideology of a democratic standard of living, a package of material goods, civil rights, and social equality that America ideally was to deliver to *every* citizen."[38] But the absence of people of color in this second montage conveys the opposite of this ideology: only white people can obtain this "democratic standard of living." Thus, the juxtaposition of these two montages imparts a critique of the coloniality the United States imposes onto persons of color inhabiting neighborhoods like Little Village, purporting that distribution of wealth and upward mobility operate racially to enable the prosperous life chances of some, while diminishing those of others.

Though critiques of economic inequality permeate the film's entire diegesis, *On the Downlow* does not just represent these two neighborhoods as financially disparate. Rather, the film further distinguishes these neighborhoods in suturing violent hypermasculinity and homophobia, which do not appear in the white district, to the barrio. *On the Downlow*'s opening references to Catholicism's influence in Little Village appear apt, once the film intimates how the religion engages gay sexuality in a confrontation between Isaac and his mother. Isaac's mother, whom Isaac complains to Angel about for repeatedly "telling me about all the God-almighty sins of the world," argues with her son before he leaves the house to attend a gang party. This argument occurs against a religious backdrop, with an oversized crucifix, an altar, and votive candles filling the right third of the frame. Isaac's mother yells at him for gangbanging and hanging out with "pandilleros... especialmente ese tal Angel" (gang members... especially that Angel). Before the mother invokes Angel's name, she pauses for several seconds at "tal," hinting at her awareness of his relationship with Isaac, and insinuating that she does not know what to call Angel—a boyfriend, special friend, lover, maybe even a derogatory epithet for gay men. In either case, afterward, the mother condemns her son's behavior, yelling, "¡Qué es un mal muy grande!" ("That is a great evil!"), and claiming that Isaac "tir[a] [su] vida a la basura" (throws his life in the trash). But Isaac's mother's speechlessness at Angel renders her words a double entendre, implying that gay sexuality "es un mal muy grande" as much as gangbanging is, and that Isaac "tir[a] [su] vida a la basura" for sexually criminal reasons, as well. As a result, this religious mother and the Catholic props in the scene reinforce the Church's presence in the barrio—an element the film never portrays in the white middle-class neighborhood—and indicate that Catholicism's stances on gay sexuality contribute to and support homophobia in Little Village and in the Two Six.

In *On the Downlow*, this homophobia materializes in the public sphere as well as in the private. When representing sexual intolerance in the public sphere of the barrio, the film—in part because of the racial, class, and sexual spatial dichotomies it constructs—implies that white persons who enter this predominantly Latina/o/x vicinity are also susceptible to its ideologies about sexuality and violent hypermasculinity. In one scene, Angel and Isaac visit a grocery store, where they happen upon a Latino clerk and white patron discussing gay sexuality. The clerk tells the customer that he and his wife attended a movie theater, but that they could not watch the film because "two faggots were sitting right there" and "swapping spit." The Latino man exclaims that he wanted to assault them, and the white man concurs, saying that "they ought to make that shit illegal." While the two men speak with each other, the camera repeatedly cuts to Angel and Isaac, who feel disgruntled and decide to leave. Outside, Angel wants to return "to beat his ass," but Isaac replies that "it ain't worth it" because "it's just words." According to Isaac, Angel needs to "just forget it" and "deal with it," because Isaac can ignore the bigotry.

In this exchange between Isaac and Angel, the movie expresses that, in the barrio, gay men—even those who gangbang—have limited means for resisting homophobia. Isaac's ambiguous words "it ain't worth it" are not just the pacification adage frequently preceding impending fistfights. Instead, the phrase leaves the viewer wondering why, unlike with the men of *Homeboy*, Isaac believes gay men cannot successfully perform violent hypermasculinity in a way that combats homophobia outside their gangs. What does the second "it" in Isaac's statement refer to? If they defend gay men, would violent retribution against bigots not raise concerns within Angel and Isaac's gang, and the barrio, about their hypermasculinity (and, thus, sexuality)? Might the Latino clerk pay renta to the Two Six and thus find himself in a position to disclose Angel and Isaac's relationship? Will the possible outing of their sexuality in Angel's resistance to homophobia invite lethal consequences from their fellow gang members and other violent, heterosexual men? In the end, Angel and Isaac's only option is to accept this intolerance as an ordinary part of their lives, if they are to live in this neighborhood.

This scene also possibly blurs the film's dichotomies between white and Latina/o/x spaces and cultures. Although the white suburban area does not feature a single instance of homophobic discourse or, initially, violent hypermasculinity, white characters in this barrio still espouse hatred for gay men—such as the patron who bemoans watching gay men kiss in public. In this same vein, Angel encounters a similar event with his white male co-workers at a motorcycle repair shop. Needing to finish fixing a motorbike before joining Isaac at a gang party, Angel beseeches the two men for aid. When one of the men helps Isaac, however, he begins grumbling about a "fag" customer who "is always looking at me funny." The man continues, "I hate fags. They're the ones spreading all that AIDS shit. You know, it's getting so that you can't have sex naturally with a girl unless you're wearing a fucking rubber." After an awkward silence, Angel feels compelled to jibe, "Fuck yeah! . . . How do these assholes think that ass-fucking each other is better than fucking a nice hot babe?" For the white man, gay men contaminate heterosexual intercourse through sexually transmitted diseases and, in doing so, hinder heterosexual men from performing their masculinity through having unprotected sex with women. On the one hand, this scene coincides with the grocery store conversation in painting gay men as powerless to resist homophobia in Little Village. Not only does Angel decide he must accept this language, as Isaac recommends to him, but to preempt others from questioning his presumed heterosexuality and hypermasculinity, he needs to publicly spread homophobia as well.

This motorcycle shop discourse also dovetails with the white patron's bigotry in the grocery store in problematizing the routine assumption that whites and white culture are devoid of homophobia or are more sexually inclusive than communities of color. In these two scenes, the white characters are as homophobic as the Latino clerk. On the other hand, the white characters code as working-class/low-income, and reside in the barrio—the only place in the film where this type of language manifests. As such, the film also suggests that only working-class/low-income whites or whites in locations of color are homophobic, and middle- and upper-class whites and areas are free from this attitude. In doing so, *On the Downlow* re-inscribes the logic of the racial contract—the narrative that criminalizes many people of color and their cultures to excuse and rationalize colonialism/coloniality.

In *The Racial Contract*, Charles Mills argues, "The norming of space is partially done in terms of the *racing* of space, the depiction of space as dominated by individuals (whether persons or subpersons) of a certain race. At the same time, the norming of the individual is partially achieved by *spacing* it [the individual], that is, representing it as imprinting with the characteristics of a certain kind of space."[39] According to Mills, the racial contract sutures culture and behavior to spaces and to people. Persons who arrive from a certain region carry with them the culture of their previous location, potentially "racing" other areas they travel to for the "better" (if white settlers) or the "worse" (if people of color). At the same time, locales "space" the human, meaning that a person who journeys to another locality will adopt the cultural characteristics of that place that others have "raced." Although this logic theoretically applies to both whites and people of color, and their corresponding spaces, in European colonial projects, the theory of "spacing" the human disproportionally pertained to lands populated by people of color. This disparity stemmed from a racist fear that the "savage" culture of people of color would infect the culture, ethics, and standards of living of whites in proximity to people of color or whites who occupy their lands. This same logic continues when racial contracts appear in coloniality, as well. As a result, the philosophy of spacing and racing exonerates the white colonizer for mobilizing physical and cultural genocide, and for instilling inequitable distributions of power, given the supposed need not only to "advance" subaltern persons but also to protect whites.[40] Because *On the Downlow* limits homophobia to working-class/low-income whites living in the barrio—or those whom the barrio has "spaced"—the film potentially corroborates and aligns with the racist, colonial ideology of the racial contract.[41]

The Gang and Barrio as Panopticon

Despite *On the Downlow* relegating homophobia and violent hypermasculinity to Little Village, and sexual inclusivity to white suburbia, the barrio does not foreclose gay sexuality. As Richard T. Rodríguez argues, *On the Downlow* "negate[s] a common tendency to conclusively render subjectivity as topographically determined."[42] Angel and Isaac's gay sexuality in Little Village reveals how the barrio does not determine sexual desire, though this inability to shape sexual orientation does not equate to freedom from the psychological, emotional, and physical oppressions that certain topographies cultivate. Rodríguez acknowledges as much when he argues that gay persons may inhabit "[m]inor architectures," which he defines as "peripheral locations in which nonnormative sexual practices unfold."[43]

In *On the Downlow*, gay sexuality often manifests in "minor architectures" because of Little Village's and the Two Six's homophobia, such as in an onscreen kiss between Angel and Isaac. In an early scene where Isaac returns a cellphone to Angel, the two gang members kiss outside of Angel's apartment (Figure 5.1). This kiss transpires in public but at night, in front of several dumpsters, which a rotting, wooden fence partially encloses—forming a minor architecture in the barrio. The low-key lighting and mise-en-scène of this scene accentuate gay men's position in the neighborhood. This kiss must occur under the protective covering of darkness, in secret, and out of the purview of surveillance, because the barrio and Two Six regard gay men as unacceptable and shameful. Situating the men's kiss against garbage and a decaying fence also connotes that these two men are where Little Village and the Two Six believe gay men belong (in the trash heap),

Figure 5.1 *Isaac and Angel embrace within the safety of Little Village's minor architecture. Video image supplied by the author.*

indicating their expulsion of "waste," and portending Angel and Isaac's future embrace of their failure in the gang and the barrio. Similarly, the debilitated wooden fence foreshadows Angel and Isaac's march toward the racial, classed, and sexual death drive that they will succumb to.

Of course, Angel and Isaac do not limit their time together in Little Village to its minor architecture, but their appearances in "major architecture" (non-peripheral locations) underscore how Little Village and the Two Six's panopticism disciplines and regulates sexuality and violent masculinity to promote barrio and gang member success. Theorizing the operational power of Jeremy Bentham's panopticon prison, Foucault writes that the panopticon induces "a state of consciousness and permanent visibility that assures the automatic functioning of power."[44] Once subject to this visibility, a person imprisoned in the panopticon "assumes responsibility for the constraints of power" and, thus, "becomes the principle of his own subjection."[45] Although Angel and Isaac eventually escape—if temporarily—the panopticism of the homophobic barrio, when inhabiting the spaces of major architecture in Little Village, Angel and Isaac's visibility coerces them into altering their behavior to feign violent, heterosexual masculinity—such as when the two visit major architecture in the barrio for a lunch date.

Contrasting with the mise-en-scène and cinematography of the garbage kiss scene, this meal between the two transpires in an open, outdoor eating area alongside many businesses and a highway full of traffic (Figure 5.2)—the opposite of peripheral, less-populated minor architectures that accord escape from surveillance. The scene also features warm, natural daylight and brighter color, joining with the rest of

174 | Clicas

Figure 5.2 *The restaurant or "major architecture" where Angel and Isaac share their lunch in full view of the barrio. Video image supplied by the author.*

the setting to accent Angel and Isaac's presence in major architecture. Although Angel and Isaac do not kiss or show physical affection in this scene, intimate acts are not necessary for gay sexuality to materialize onscreen, just as heterosexual characters in literature and film need not exhibit sexual or romantic intimacy for audiences to interpret them as heterosexual. The congestion of the streets and the diner parking lot in this scene, however, insinuate that Angel and Isaac must abide by the barrio and Two Six's stipulations for sexuality and hypermasculinity, for the gazes of multiple subjects in the vicinity police them.

The film emphasizes this panoptic regulation when Reaper drives by and catches Isaac eating with Angel. Reaper demands to know if Angel was ever a member of the Southside Latin Kings, and inquires about Angel's potential "badass" hypermasculinity, because Reaper cannot "be rolling with no pussies" in the Two Six. After Angel assuages his concerns about his past gang history and his violent hypermasculinity by informing Reaper of the type of gun he carries, Reaper feels confident about Angel's ability to achieve gang member success. In this film, "success" entails a heterosexual orientation, performing violent hypermasculinity, and maintaining a cholo visage and stoic demeanor. Consequently, Reaper grants permission for the Two Six to later jump Angel into the gang. Reaper's gaze and subsequent words mark how—when inhabiting major architecture in the barrio and in sight of the barrio's and the Two Six's potential gaze—Angel and Isaac must always abide by the coloniality of gender's normative codes of gender and sexuality. Otherwise, they could succumb to a death drive that operates across racial, classed, and sexual lines, and that may manifest in Reaper murdering Angel and Isaac as a consequence of their romantic relationship.

Failure Is Your Domain

Despite Angel and Isaac's attempts to perform violent hypermasculinity and closet themselves, they ultimately fail in the barrio and as gang members. While the two maintain a cholo aesthetic, carry guns, participate in gang fights, and boast about their toughness, they also violate the barrio's and gang's ideas of normative sexuality, nullifying whatever slight measure of success they achieve. This failure precipitates a perennial paranoia that affects Angel and Isaac's behavior in major architecture, causes them psychological and emotional trauma, and steers them to minor architecture for safety. Ironically, however, failing in the Two Six and the barrio also facilitates the construction of utopian futurities for the two men. Paradoxically, failure, rather than success, enables Two Six gang life to initiate non-conventional (de)colonial projects. In their utopian futurities, Angel and Isaac circumvent much of the Two Six's demands to perform violent hypermasculinity and maintain masculine stoicism, as well as the gang's and Little Village's intolerance for gay men. Failing at the harsh expectations of violent hypermasculinity and heterosexuality frequently impels the two men to leave the barrio and visit the white middle-class neighborhood from the second montage. When in this area, they repose in their car, drinking sodas, and discussing their gang failure and desire for a world beyond the one they inhabit in Little Village. Once more, Muñoz understands queerness as "primarily about futurity and hope," which, in this hope for a future beyond the disheartening present, generates a utopian futurity that "lets us imagine a space outside of heteronormativity" and other perils, such as those emerging from "institutionalized state homophobia."[46] In the time they share with each other in Angel's car in this white middle-class neighborhood, Angel and Isaac satisfy Muñoz's requirements for the construction of queer utopian futurities.

When commenting about his desire for a life and future in a neighborhood like the white suburban one he and Angel frequently visit, Isaac claims that "out here, I can relax," nodding to how a future in this environment would not feature the constant pressure to abide by the Two Six and Little Village's expectations of violent hypermasculinity and heterosexuality. In white suburbia, the two men spend time together in broad daylight and open spaces, and do not fear disciplinary subjects like Reaper, Angel's co-workers, or the grocery clerk and patron who may fatally penalize gay sexuality. In fact, no person in the white neighborhood ever exhibits homophobia or mentions expectations for sexuality. Removed from the Two Six and barrio, the two gang members hope for and visualize a future that abandons their gang's constrictions on their sexual desire and its demand to perform violent hypermasculinity.

This environment, where the two envision Edenic fantasies, operates as a site where Angel and Isaac reveal what Nicole M. Guidotti-Hernández calls "flexible ideas of Mexican masculinities."[47] Unraveling normative hypermasculine affect, Angel and Isaac remove the veil of masculine stoicism by confessing their false bravado and failure as gang members. For example, in one scene in the white locale, Angel, who initially brags about his violent hypermasculinity and ability to kill people, admits his doubts about whether he could murder someone unless in self-defense, changing his original assurance to "maybe" and later to "I don't know." Eventually, he even concedes that his hypermasculine performance is bogus, and confesses the fright he felt during a past gun fight. In relaying this confrontation to Isaac, Angel mocks himself for pulling his "gun out" and "talking shit" when he was not intending to shoot anyone but "was just trying to get away." Likewise, Isaac discloses that—despite his tough demeanor—he, too, has never killed anyone and that, when he saw Reaper murder a person, he "just stood there, frozen." Isaac also goes so far as to declare his desire to leave the Two Six, saying "it just doesn't feel right."

In dreaming of an idyllic future and revealing their fear of violence, their reservations about killing people, and their struggle to perform the hypermasculinity of Two Six gang life, the two men create a utopian futurity where expectations of gang member success or fear of failure do not encumber them. Instead, they jettison their gang member facades and laugh off their failures. Should gang members in the barrio hear their words, these confessions would likely warrant violent penalties. In the men's utopian futurity, however, these revelations only elicit liberatory giggles because, at this moment in the diegesis, they exist outside the Two Six's control. Failing in gangs and in the barrio has ironically precipitated a utopian futurity that, at least temporarily, frees Angel and Isaac from the Two Six and Little Village's regulation of their lives.

Angel and Isaac do not just hope for a future free from a restrictive gang life that mandates violent hypermasculinity and heterosexuality. Their utopian futurity also allows them, especially Isaac, to fantasize about and long for life chances that circumvent the racial and classed components of the death drive that coloniality imposes on them. As Isaac says to Angel's question about why Isaac always wants him to park in front of the same middle-class home,

> 'Cause we live in a fucking sewer, man, that's why. That neighborhood we live in? It's dirty, bro! . . . Fuck, man. This? This is a fucking neighborhood, bro. I mean, this is nice. I dream of owning a house like that, man, in a neighborhood like this. . . . It's quiet. I can hear fucking birds chirping. There are no birds in our neighborhood, just fucking pigeons, feeding off of everything else.

For Isaac, parking the car in front of this house enables him to obtain a utopian futurity where he can psychologically migrate away from the impoverished, unhygienic, rowdy living conditions of Little Village. In this utopian futurity, he can dream of middle-class property ownership, a white-picket fence, and a freshly trimmed lawn, and enjoy a tranquility not available to him in the barrio, which does not contain chirping birds but pigeons that he deems parasitical, "feathered rats." This utopian futurity that assists Angel and Isaac in temporarily escaping the economic inequality of coloniality occurs because their failure to succeed in the Two Six and in Little Village drives them, as Muñoz might say, to do "something else": seek out refuge in white suburbia.[48] By finding a safe haven through failure, the two men temporarily negate much of the classed, racial, and sexual hardship they face in the Two Six and barrio. In this way, gang membership, violence, crime, and hypermasculinity facilitate (de)colonial projects not through success, but through failure.

This utopian futurity does not restrict their sexuality and psychologically alleviates, if ephemerally, much of the systemic racism and penury they encounter in the barrio. Nevertheless, Angel and Isaac's utopian futurity cannot *entirely* escape the subaltern racial/ethnic status and gangs that haunt them. On one occasion, when Angel and Isaac loaf in front of the middle-class house, a policeman who knows Angel from Little Village accosts the two men, despite them not engaging in any criminal activity. The officer asks Angel, "You're not going to roll this house?" Once Angel denies that they intend to commit burglary and a call comes through the cop's radio, the officer drives off but not before uttering to Angel in mockery of a Caló accent, "I'll catch you later, esé." Angel and Isaac's signifiers of criminality and low-income status (their beatdown car, race/ethnicity, and cholo fashion style) cast them as infiltrators in this white middle-class community where they create utopian futurity, attracting disciplinary action from this white location's repressive state apparatuses that enforce its own panopticon. The policeman's harassment of Angel also spotlights the race/space ideology that Mills explains. Because Angel and Isaac are gangbanging trespassers, the cop's behavior may strive to impede them from "racing" the neighborhood, which the film's opening implies that Angel and Isaac have temporarily done previously.

In their first sequence together, Angel and Isaac burst into this white space fleeing Latin Kings, not wanting to reveal that Angel conspires with a Two Six or disclose their romantic relationship. The Latin Kings invade the middle-class location, where they shoot at Angel and Isaac and engage them in a fistfight. The altercation creates the only instance of violent hypermasculinity seen in this neighborhood and disrupts its serenity, as homeowners in their front yards observe in shock. In representing Angel and Isaac as importing crime and violence into this peaceful abode, *On the Downlow* re-inscribes both facets of the race/space portion of the racial contract. In this film, not only might Latina/o/x barrios "space" white persons detrimentally, but Latinos also "race" white space in a harmful manner.

Regardless of the potential for reading a racial contract in the film, the reaches of neither the State nor the gang nullify Angel and Isaac's utopian futurity. Rather, much as this utopia enables them to reject and disregard the barrio's and gang's expectations of violent hypermasculinity and heterosexuality, their utopian futurity also allows Angel and Isaac to evade gang and State extensions into their sanctuary. In their utopian futurity, the two men laugh about and ridicule the police officer's attempt to regulate them in the same way that they mock their own hypermasculine facades. In doing so, they transform police harassment into a joke that generates jovial affects that contribute to the comforting atmosphere of their utopian futurity. Relatedly, because they retreat to a location that the Latin Kings are unfamiliar with, Angel and Isaac eventually lose the gang in the winding roads of suburbia, the two men's utopian futurity literally providing them with the avenues to escape gangs' clutches, as they never encounter gangs again in the middle-class neighborhood.

Queer Contradictions

Notwithstanding the film's exploration of a liberating (de)colonial failure, *On the Downlow* invokes a narrative of ethnic and cultural betrayal when depicting Angel and Isaac's utopian futurity. And, despite its queering of the gang member figure, it potentially trades in alternative forms of homophobia. Although the film critiques how wealth accumulation operates racially in the United States, *On the Downlow* represents its gay Latinos as indifferent to or unaware of how the white middle-class neighborhoods that they desire partially secure their financial and social privileges through benefitting from the white capitalism and systemic racism that suppress many Latina/o/xs in the United States. Although the United States' capitalist colonial structure constrains its own people, Angel and Isaac are seemingly willing to buy into this inequitable system and renounce Latina/o/xs and Latina/o/x spaces for the manifold advantages of white society.

Indeed, when discussing his hope for a future beyond the barrio, Isaac admits that his disaffection stems not just from his economic status, but from his proximity to "all these fucking 4 × 4 Mexicans, crowding up the place, blaring their music and shit." Poverty, homophobia, and expectations of violent hypermasculinity are not the only culprits that cause Isaac to establish utopian futurity in a white space. In this white neighborhood, he can dream of a future where he may escape not only working-class/low-income Mexican people, but their aesthetics and culture as well. His revulsion at them "blaring their music" lies not with volume, as he attends parties with Chicana/o/x hip-hop blasting, but with the style, implying that he finds the music more common south of the US-Mexico border, such as norteño or corridos, disgusting—especially, since he invokes nationality in using the term Mexican, as opposed to Chicana/o/x, Mexican American, or Latina/o/x. Qualifying "Mexicans" with "4 × 4" also signals a demonization of a working-class/low-income aesthetic, possibly entailing the attire of manual labor or a rundown work truck. As such, his words signify that he desires a future where he can not only reap white society's financial and sexually inclusive rewards, but also enjoy its lack of working-class/low-income Mexican culture and people. For these reasons, neither Isaac nor Angel fully delinks from the ideologies of coloniality—even if rejecting its sexual components. Their circumvention of its power is born out of frustration from the material and psychological effects this system imposes on them. Their ideological subscriptions and/or indifferences to certain components of coloniality do not suggest a total rejection of its continued presence, only a desire to escape the subaltern status it imposes on them. In this way, their utopian futurity in whiteness epitomizes the contradictory elements of the (de)colonial.

Isaac, in particular, lusts for this white world so fervidly that he suggests he prefers a white future over Angel, hinting that he might forsake him, if necessary, to attain one. When Angel (who lives alone) offers Isaac the chance to escape from his Catholic mother by inviting Isaac to move into his apartment, Angel stands before his balcony, opens his arms, and says to Isaac, "What do you think? . . . All this could be yours. . . . Ain't no use in staying in hell when you know where the door to heaven is." Despite having the opportunity to leave his likely homophobic mother and attenuate the bigotry he faces in the private sphere, Isaac turns in aversion. He does not think much of the "this" that he could have because, as Isaac says, he would only have "a beautiful porch" that, at the end of the day, still overlooks "the hood." Angel's offer does not contain the white world that Isaac yearns for. Isaac therefore rebuffs the invitation, implying that living with his partner does not entice him, unless he can accomplish this goal in a white space. Isaac even indicates that he would abandon Angel, if he must, to acquire the white future he romanticizes. After hearing how passionately Isaac discusses his aspirations for living in a white residential neighborhood like the one they visit together, Angel—concerned Isaac may leave him—asks, "[W]hat happens to me?" In response, Isaac says, "I don't know. What happens to you?" Although Isaac immediately pacifies Angel by telling him, "You know you're my boy," Isaac's refusal to live with Angel in the barrio renders his reassurances dubious. Furthermore, his distaste for "4 × 4 Mexicans" and his romanticization of whiteness leave the viewer pondering if Angel's race and ethnicity factor into Isaac's threat to forsake him.

Although Isaac's troublesome conversations with Angel corroborate an affinity for white society—perhaps even over a Latino who does not display bigotry or violence toward him and, instead, loves him—Isaac and Angel's desire for a future removed from Little Village and the Two Six is not without reason. As Anzaldúa famously says in her disavowal of "vendida" accusations, "Not me sold out my people but they me."[49] In a barrio and gang so antagonistic to gay men that Angel and Isaac fear for their safety and feel compelled to disseminate homophobia to protect themselves, the two gang members, in many ways, have no choice but to cultivate a relationship with, and inhabit the spaces of, whiteness, for these are the only places where the movie conveys they may physically and psychologically survive.

In spite of this association of gay Latino men with whiteness, which some might read as an alternative form of homophobia, *On the Downlow* seemingly attempts to beseech Latina/o/xs to confront homophobia in the barrio and in gangs to promote sexual inclusivity. The film most powerfully conveys this apparent agenda in the evanescence of Angel and Isaac's utopian futurity and their fall to the death drive. As Muñoz says, utopian futurity "has been prone to disappointment" and "is always destined to fail."[50] The potential for the continuation of Angel and Isaac's utopian futurity disintegrates in the film's climax, when Reaper murders Angel. Again, because Reaper kills Angel immediately before Angel can finish openly proclaiming his love for Isaac ("You can't do this, man, please! Isaac, I love y—"), the film intimates that Reaper pulls the trigger not only because of Angel's history with the Latin Kings, but also, and likely more so, because Angel will declare his and Isaac's romantic relationship. Making their love public would violate the Two Six's adherences to the laws of the coloniality of gender that govern sexuality and masculinity. This is an infraction that the gang cannot openly tolerate, and that warrants death if discovered because—as the previous chapter explains—gay sexuality often panics the masculinities, sexuality, and, thus, gender identities of heterosexual male gang members. Thus, Angel and Isaac—after Isaac commits suicide since he cannot live without his partner—succumb to a death drive that claims their lives at the intersection of race, class, gender, and sexuality. In this way, the film visualizes Lugones's contentions about the violence of heterosexuality in coloniality. In *On the Downlow*, heterosexuality and fragile masculinity's insecurity have "perverse, violent, demeaning" effects that result in "a turning of people into animals," ultimately transforming Reaper into a heterosexual monster who contributes to the deaths of multiple people in the Two Six.[51]

In depicting these characters' deaths in this manner, *On the Downlow* accentuates the lethal power and effects of the coloniality of gender, and urges viewers to challenge this type of bigotry and hate crime. Although this exhortation requires the destruction of utopian futurity, this breakdown does not render utopian futurity worthless for Angel and Isaac. Muñoz argues that, despite eventual dissipation, utopian futurity still provides "a certain mode of virtuosity that helps the spectator exit from the stale and static lifeworld" and its "alienation, exploitation, and drudgery."[52] Even if only temporarily curative, failing in the Two Six and Little Village precipitates Angel and Isaac's "exit" from certain components of the coloniality constricting their lives. The film, thus, imagines the potential methods gay men may rely on to escape psychologically from oppressive barrios and gangs, and how (de)colonial projects need not always entail conventional notions of success.

Moreover, the remainder of *On the Downlow*'s final scene suggests—despite Angel's and Isaac's deaths, and Edelman's insistence on no queer future—*the* and *a* future for gay men in male-dominated, heterosexual gangs. After Isaac commits suicide, the two remaining Two Six in the basement look over Isaac's, Angel's, and Reaper's dead bodies before locking eyes and holding each other's hands, insinuating another romantic relationship between men in gangs. The film immediately ends on this shot, intimating not only *the* future where gay men preside in the Two Six but also their futurity—a realm of unknown possibilities that may hold *a* future where Angel's and Isaac's martyred bodies have reshaped for the better how heterosexual male gang members conceive not only of their own sexualities and gender identities, but of those of gay men, as well.

Ultimately, *On the Downlow* discloses the manifold ways that gang life may precipitate a sense of (if partial and temporary) freedom from the coloniality that structures the lives of multiply marginalized persons. In its representations of gay gang members, the film features an antinomy, suggesting that heterosexual, homophobic, male-dominated gangs might ironically facilitate (de)colonial projects for gay men not through succeeding, but through failing in gang life. Failing at the Two Six's and Little Village's expectations of gender and sexuality leads Angel and Isaac to construct utopian futurities that provide a range of—even if temporary—liberations. Although *On the Downlow* focuses on gay men, the revelation that gangs may precipitate (de)colonial projects through failure as much as success applies to women as well. While la Heredera and Lucía may succeed in gang life, women might also mobilize (de)colonial projects through failure in gangs. *On the Downlow* thus demands that critical gang studies re-envision its conventional conceptions of resistance in gang life, and refrain from dismissing "non-normative" gang members as abject outsiders, imploring scholars to consider instead how these gang members might navigate—and what they may gain from—abjection.

AFTERWORD

The Immigrant/Gang Member Binary in Latina/o/x Literature and Film

CARY JOJI FUKUNAGA'S *SIN NOMBRE* VISUALIZES AMERICAN FRIGHT, the specter that haunts this entire book: extraordinarily violent and sexually predatorial Mara Salvatrucha gang members from Mexico. Midway through the film, the head of the local MS clica, Lil Mago, leads an assault against unsuspecting Central American migrants riding the rooftops of "la Bestia," a freight train that travels across northern and southern Mexico and often claims the limbs and lives of riders who fall from it.[1] After robbing several migrants on la Bestia, Mago singles out a young Honduran woman named Sayra, whom he pistol whips, mounts, and attempts to rape at gun point. Mago's vicious sexual attack on Sayra is only one of the many monstrous actions he performs throughout the film—including the attempted rape and successful killing of a young Mexican woman, and the ordering of his clica to dismember a rival gang member and to feed his body parts to dogs.

These representations of Mara Salvatrucha gang members as terrifying monsters who reap sadistic pleasure in violence permeate much of contemporary political discourse, such as in former president Donald Trump's 2018 interview with National Public Radio, in which he says of the gang:

> They kidnap. They extort. They rape and they rob. They prey on children. They shouldn't be here. They stomp on their victims. They beat them with clubs. They slash them with machetes, and they stab them with knives. They have transformed peaceful parks and beautiful, quiet neighborhoods into blood-stained killing fields. They're animals.[2]

US political discourse and cultural production that portray gang members—and specifically Mara Salvatrucha gang members from south of the US-Mexico border—as undocumented, violent animals help create narratives and sentiments that inform and support anti-immigration legislation and nativist hegemony, which ultimately help render undocumented immigrants what Martha D. Escobar calls a "flexible, and thus exploitable, labor force."[3] In other words, the presumption that Latin American immigrants are violent gang members, and that a porous US-Mexico border enables Mara Salvatrucha's clandestine entrance into the nation, buttresses the argument for criminalizing undocumented immigration—thus helping to impose a status of illegality onto the undocumented that ultimately transforms them into cheap, exploitable, and disposable labor.

For this reason, the gang member remains a figure of liminality in United States. As much as the State demonizes and appears to wish to destroy gangs, the State maintains an investment in preserving gang members as "controlling images": "repetitive stereotypes that also possess the power to influence action and policies against people of color."[4] Recuperating the image of the Latina/o/x and Latin American gang member enables the State to further what Leo Chavez terms the "Latino Threat Narrative"—a nativist view that equates the Latinization of the United States with "the devolution of society," and helps legitimate "action and policies against people of color," oftentimes against Latin American immigrants.[5] In this way, the gang member approximates the role of the "marginal person" in Orlando Patterson's theorization of hegemonic society. As Patterson explains, the "marginal person, while a threat to the moral and social order, was also essential for its survival."[6] While the Latina/o/x gang member might undermine State power, the gang member's mere existence functions as a recuperative tool for the State's many systems of disempowerment over others, such as in the criminalization of Latin American immigration to maintain the Anglicization of the US nation-state, and undocumented immigrants' statuses as exploitable, flexible, and deportable labor. This capacity to recuperate gangs illuminates how just the existence of the Latina/o/x gang member encapsulates the core contradictions of what I am labeling the (de)colonial. While much of the literature and film by and/or about gang members that this book studies showcase how gang life and culture might enable gang members to circumvent the extent to which coloniality regulates their lives, this circumvention hinges on their creation of a subculture whose existence reinforces how other systems of disempowerment affect other subaltern persons.

Contemporary Latina/o/x literature and film seem well-attuned to this detrimental role that Latin American and Latina/o/x gangs have in the dominant American imagination and the State's criminalization of Latin American immigrants, and consequently often disassociate immigrants from gang members. Movies and books such as *Sin Nombre*, *A Better Life* (2011), *Greencard Warriors* (2013), *The Tattooed Solider*, and *When I Walk through That Door, I Am* demonstrate the habitual gang member/immigrant dichotomy that often pervades Latina/o/x literature and film. Within this genre, the gang member/immigrant dichotomy appears as a frequent trope that serves to challenge the Latino Threat Narrative and anti-Latin American immigrant sentiment through inviting sympathy for immigrants, whom these texts portray as honest, hard workers deserving of citizenship. These positive depictions of Latin American immigrants, however, typically engage in what Lisa Marie Cacho calls "valuing." According to Cacho, "[R]ecuperating social value *requires* rejecting the other Other. Ascribing readily recognizable social value always requires the devaluation of an/other, and that other is almost always poor, racialized, criminalized, segregated, legally vulnerable, and unprotected."[7] Although Latina/o/x literature and film featuring the immigrant/gang member dichotomy might strive to contest the belief that Latin American immigrants are violent criminals who will harm American citizens, these texts cast immigrants as virtuous, familial, and socially productive persons *against* the Latina/o/x and Latin American gang member. The immigrant/gang member trope regurgitates many of the routine representations of gang members as extraordinarily violent and sexually perverse, to suggest that Latin American immigrants are not *that* type of Latin American or Latina/o/x. Unlike many of the gang narratives this book covers, these texts rarely gesture toward the material and abstract effects of coloniality that cultivate gang membership or suggest what gang members might attain from gang life that warrants their violent and criminal lifestyles. In effect, the immigrant/gang member trope in Latina/o/x literature and film seems to argue that Latin Americans are good people who can beneficially contribute to the United States and are, instead, themselves victims of barbaric gang members—just like American citizens are—and, thus, require and deserve US asylum. Indeed, Jimmy Santiago Baca's epic poem *When I Walk through That Door, I Am*, for instance, rests on the premise that its speaker and her four-year-old son flee San Salvador "to escape the wrath of the gangs"—which the poem implies as Mara Salvatrucha—that murder her husband.[8] Admittedly, representations such as Baca's are not necessarily without reason. Several scholars have shown how Latin American gang members target immigrants and "chúntaros," a term that references anyone "who stands for the rural backwardness that Mexico was trying to shed in the 1990s."[9]

But though these texts might have grounds for representing Latin American and Latina/o/x gang members as antagonistic toward immigrants, Latina/o/x literature and film that engage the immigrant rights struggle through valuing are, as Escobar says, "fundamentally relational and violent" because, "regardless of how well intentioned and/or expanded the category of 'good' (im)migrant becomes," binaries between "good" and "bad" Latina/o/xs and Latin American immigrants "participat[e] in passing judgment over persons' deservingness."[10] For Escobar, these binaries that appear in immigrant rights discourse and in cultural products, such as "felons/families, criminals/children, gang member/hard-working mothers," "assume that these categories are mutually exclusive; that 'felons' are not part of families, that 'criminals' are not children, that 'gang members' are not hard-working parents."[11] For this reason, the immigrant/gang member dichotomy and others akin to it partake in "constructing (im)migrants as innocent" while "normalizing the violence that occurs to those" on the negative end of the binary.[12]

To avoid reifying relational valuing, Escobar suggests that immigrant rights discourse should embrace a "structural analysis of power relations" that "directs our attention from individual acts of 'crime' towards the ways that the creation of 'crime' serves social and political purposes."[13] The Latina/o/x gang narratives this book has explored adopt a similar critical framework. Though *My Father Was a Toltec*, *Locas*, *Homeboy*, and *On the Downlow* feature Latina/o/x gang members who victimize other multiply marginalized persons, these texts begin to unravel how the material and abstract effects of the coloniality of gender cultivate gang membership, and the accompanying violence and harm toward other disempowered groups. These narratives, together with this book's analyses of the texts, do not aim to excuse this maltreatment of other multiply marginalized people. Instead, they endeavor to spotlight the intersectional systemic impetuses that must disintegrate in order to eradicate gang violence, toxified masculinities, and racialized, classed, gendered, and sexual inequalities. But these texts are about gang membership, not Latin American immigration and, accordingly, do not feature the typical gang member/immigrant trope in the way traditional immigration narratives do. In contrast, Javier Zamora's poetry collection *Unaccompanied*, which tells the story of his migration from El Salvador to the United States, merges the gang member and immigrant, collapsing the traditional valuing binary to approximate the "structural analysis" Escobar calls for, and rearticulating the masculinity of America's vaunted boogeyman lying south of the US-Mexico border: Mara Salvatrucha.

Birthing and Deporting the US Gang Problem

The story of Mara Salvatrucha begins on October 15, 1979, when the Revolutionary Government Junta (RGJ) of El Salvador overthrew the tyrannical military regime of Carlos Humberto Romero. Once in power, the RGJ began replicating the despotism of the Romero administration. It employed militias and death squads to spy on, kidnap, torture, and murder government protestors and citizens whom the RGJ believed were communist sympathizers, as well as to suppress the leftist group the Farabundo Martí National Liberation Front (FMLN). On March 24, 1980, after months of civil unrest, the RGJ assassinated Óscar Romero, archbishop of San Salvador, during mass, because of his demands that the military and death squads refuse orders to murder civilians. The fury following his death precipitated the FMLN's increased insurrection against the RGJ, sparking the Salvadoran Civil War. With the war underway, the RGJ forced many Salvadorans into the military, while others tried to escape guerrilla warfare tactics that included counterinsurgency bombings and mortar attacks against innocent people.[14]

The United States exacerbated the death and terror Salvadorans faced during the civil war by supporting the right-wing military dictatorships of the RGJ. As William Wheeler explains, for the United States, the Salvadoran Civil War presented "the threat of another communist victory in its backyard."[15] After its failure in the Vietnam War, the United States could not allow the FMLN to secure victory. The Salvadoran government, "by whatever means, *had* to win the war, or the country's [United States'] security would be unacceptably threatened."[16] For this reason, the Carter, Reagan, and Bush administrations provided over 4.5 billion dollars in military aid to the Salvadoran government during the civil war, often training the country's military and placing US officers in leadership roles in the Salvadoran military.[17] The United States' intervention in the war would become a global controversy after El Mozote Massacre, an atrocity where the Salvadoran Atlacatl Battalion—an army unit that US military advisers created, supplied, funded, and directed—murdered over eight hundred civilians in El Mozote on December 11, 1981.[18] The Reagan administration later denied the Massacre, displacing the event as FMLN propaganda. Despite dismissing its culpability, the United States' participation in the Salvadoran Civil War helped create the deadly environment that would drive Salvadorans to flee to the US—the country where these refugees would form Mara Salvatrucha.

The majority of Salvadoran refugees immigrated to Los Angeles, many of them suffering from mental illness after becoming accustomed to seeing dismembered and decapitated bodies on the roads of El Salvador during the civil war. The immigrants often arrived isolated, with little to no family left, as many of their kin had "disappeared" or died in the civil war. If children or teenagers arrived with their parents, the parents rarely had time to see them and find comfort. To support themselves and their children, parents worked long hours, often for wages well under the federal minimum, since the United States refused to recognize Salvadoran immigrants as refugees and imposed an undocumented status upon them. Without family in their lives, Salvadoran youth were often left alone to experience culture shock, undocumented life, and coloniality in the United States. Because they were Salvadoran in a city whose Latina/o/x population was primarily Mexican American, these youth also struggled to identify with other Latina/o/xs in Los Angeles. Many Mexican Americans alienated them, ridiculing their Spanish (for using "vos" instead of "tú") and the Salvadoran boys' masculinity. In El Salvador, the popular fashion aesthetic among boys and young men favored close-fitting pants and shirts. Many were also accustomed to wearing uniforms to school—a sartorial practice not prevalent in the Los Angeles public school system. One Salvadoran young man, for example, says that at school classmates teased him with questions like, "How can you wear those tight-ass pants?" and "Are you a mama's boy?"[19] The Salvadoran immigrant youths also found themselves victim to the many Mexican American gangs of Los Angeles.

Responding to this isolation and discrimination, the Salvadoran youths grouped together to form a gang of their own to provide themselves community, belonging, and protection in a way that affirmed their masculinity. They called themselves the Mara Salvatrucha Stoners (MSS). This gang was not yet the typical cholo gang, or even a gang, as contemporarily understood. MSS did not vie for territory or engage in violent crime, though they did fight to defend themselves from other Los Angeles cholo gangs. MSS was a stoner/party crew—a type of gang whose purpose hinges on having fun, getting high and drunk, throwing parties, and making friends. But while MSS was a stoner/party crew, they adopted a darker ideology and aesthetic than was typical of stoner/party crews of the era, perhaps as a result of the psychological trauma from the Salvadoran Civil War. MSS dabbled in satanism, dressed extensively in black, grew their hair long, and preferred listening to heavy metal. A palimpsest of this history manifests when contemporary Mara Salvatrucha clicas flash devil horns—extending the index and pinky fingers while folding the middle two—to signify the gang. MSS's drug use and frequent and escalating fights with Los Angeles cholo gangs, however, resulted in many MSS gang members spending time in jail or prison, where they had to shave their heads and wear prison uniforms. Once inside, their proximity to Mexican American cholos led to many MSS members adopting the cholo aesthetic, and mirroring the identities and ideologies of a traditional street gang member. Upon their release, these Salvadorans helped spread the cholo gang culture into MSS to the point where the former stoner/party gang would begin to evolve into Mara Salvatrucha during the mid-to-late 1980s. By the mid-1990s, Mara Salvatrucha had fully become another conventional cholo gang of Los Angeles.[20]

Mara Salvatrucha began to spread to El Salvador once Bill Clinton signed the Illegal Immigration Reform and Immigrant Responsibility Act of 1996 (IIRIRA). The act increased the number of persons in the United States who were eligible for deportation, by expanding the category of "aggravated felonies" to include crimes that carried a one-year sentence, such as shoplifting. Non-citizens who committed aggravated felonies—both prior to and after the passage of the IIRIRA—were now deportable. The IIRIRA also denied noncitizens who overstayed their visas the capacity to extend their time in the United States, whereas, before the IIRIRA, overstayed noncitizens could simply pay a fine to adjust their residence status. Under these new laws, the undocumented population grew from five to twelve million in the next ten years—five million of whom would have qualified for "legal status" had Clinton not signed the bill.[21] With these new immigration laws in place, the United States deported thousands of Salvadorans, many of whom were Mara

Salvatrucha gang members, back to a war-torn El Salvador still toiling in the aftereffects of the civil war that ended in 1992.

This post-war El Salvador acted as a petri dish for gang membership. As Juan José Martínez D'Aubuisson explains,

> The country was in ruins, its infrastructure reduced to rubble, its social fabric irremediably torn. El Salvador was a country of orphans, of the unemployed, the crippled and the maimed. And while the state tried to pick up the pieces, army combatants and guerillas alike found themselves out of work.[22]

After the war, El Salvador—its economy hamstrung—struggled to absorb its former militants and its maimed citizens, and failed to destroy the weaponry of the war. This left former fighters who were inured to, yet traumatized by, violence with minuscule options for reentry into society and with an array of arms available for use. The deported members of Mara Salvatrucha descended on this environment, providing these persons a medium through which to release their frustration and trauma, and a violent means of securing money and food in an impoverished nation. Mara Salvatrucha spread uncontrollably. The United States, despite having partly fomented this upheaval in El Salvador and having birthed Mara Salvatrucha, had, in effect, deported its "gang problem" to this postwar nation.

Although Mara Salvatrucha now operates primarily in the Northern Triangle of Central America (Guatemala, Honduras, and El Salvador), US cultural production, media, and politicians regularly recuperate and sensationalize the gang in order to create support for anti-immigration and anti-Latin American/Latina/o/x legislation. After MS gang members murdered seventeen-year-old Brenda Paz—a former member turned FBI informant—media outlets like *National Geographic* and *Newsweek* began referring to MS as "the most dangerous gang in America."[23] Far-fetched rumors about the gang quickly followed this appellation, such as the myth that Mara Salvatrucha gangs castrate male enemies or play soccer with the heads of victims they kill—though scholars of MS like Sonja Wolf and T. W. Ward find no merit in these claims, and contend that most Mara Salvatrucha gang members do not murder people.[24] The gang also developed a reputation for misogyny and for violence against women—which in part arose from male members commonly tattooing "Trust No Bitch" onto themselves—relegating women members to domesticity, and beating gang girls for cooking terribly, not properly washing clothes, and neglecting children.[25] While several MS clicas deserve their reputation for violent misogyny, many researchers and scholars agree that depictions of the gang that homogenize MS members as predatorial rapists, such as those made in *Sin Nombre* and by Trump, are unfounded, because the gang rarely engages in sexual violence. Steven Dudley, for example, notes that Mara Salvatrucha widely "prohibits rape of female companions or relatives of gang members," owing this stance to "experiences in jails where it [MS] and its family members were raped on a regular basis."[26] Likewise, Ward finds that some MS clicas lethally punish members who rape women, often stabbing them for their behavior.[27]

Regardless of how factual or sensationalized these beliefs about Mara Salvatrucha are, these narratives about MS—as well as similar tales about other Latin American and Latina/o/x gangs—have migrated into Latina/o/x literature and film as a way of cultivating sympathy for immigrants and disassociating them from gang members. And though these texts might have grounds for castigating members of MS and other Latin American/Latina/o/x gangs, the immigrant/gang member dichotomy often disregards the structural analysis of power relations that Escobar advocates for, in favor of engaging the immigrant rights struggle through a method that ultimately hinges on valuing. Zamora's *Unaccompanied*, however, discloses how Latina/o/x immigration literature and film might partake in the immigrant rights struggle while neither relying on this binary nor reproducing hyperbolic accounts about gang membership and gang masculinities. Zamora not only rearticulates the MS masculinities that are often sensationalized as always violent and sexually perverse, but also shows how to critique the violence MS gang life enacts on Salvadorans in a way that emphasizes the State's accountability in fomenting the environment for this violence to prosper.

Approximating Decoloniality

Early in his poetry collection, Zamora reconceptualizes the normative way Latina/o/x literature incorporates the figures of the immigrant and gang member with the poem "Second Attempt Crossing." Rather than representing MS gang members as always harmful toward immigrants, this poem that details Zamora's migration to the United States lovingly memorializes a Mara Salvatrucha gang member named

"Chino" as selfless, protective, and caring toward the young Zamora. The poem tells of a night when Chino, who sleeps aside Zamora, abruptly flees after another migrant shouts "¡La Migra!"[28] Zamora writes that after Chino realizes he remains behind, Chino, unlike the other immigrants, "sprinted back toward me," carrying him on his shoulders to escape "the white trucks, then their guns."[29] Eventually, however, immigration enforcement runs Chino and Zamora down. Reflecting on this moment of capture, Zamora writes,

> So I wouldn't touch their legs that kicked you,
> you pushed me under your chest,
> and I've never thanked you.
>
> Beautiful *Chino*—
>
> the only name I know to call you by—
> farewell your tattooed chest: the M,
> the S, the 13.[30]

In these stanzas, Zamora rejects the frequent antagonism between immigrants and gang members, and instead introduces what Guidotti-Hernández calls "transnational masculinity" into the immigrant/gang member relationship in Latina/o/x literature. For Guidotti-Hernández, transnational masculinity refers to "the emotional bonds and relationships that Mexican men built with other men and their extended networks during their migrations to the United States."[31] In "Second Attempt Crossing," Zamora visualizes a Salvadoran version of this transnational masculinity that rearticulates the MS gang member. Rather than approximating the violent, sexually perverse masculinity normally seen in other representations of Mara Salvatrucha gang members, Chino displays a masculinity that distinguishes him from the other migrants in Zamora's group—one that casts him as self-sacrificing, tender, and devoted to the young Zamora. For this reason, Zamora sees Chino's MS tattoos not as symbols of tyrannical violence and terror. Rather, for Zamora, they are markers that connote protection, safekeeping, warmth, and the facilitation—not the hindering—of Zamora's migration to the United States. In this way, the poem's depiction of MS gang aesthetics resembles, if for different reasons, the men's rearticulation of cholo aesthetics in *Homeboy*. Zamora may not read gang aesthetics as sexually titillating like the men of *Homeboy* do. Like them, however, he rearticulates gang aesthetics away from intimidation and toward some type of attractiveness. Zamora's attraction to, and affectionate relationship with, "Beautiful *Chino*" does not end in the moment of flight delineated in "Second Attempt Crossing" but continues during Zamora's successful migration to the United States—the poem explaining that Chino and Zamora speak twice monthly on the phone, until gang violence one day claims Chino's life.

In portraying his warmhearted relationship with a Mara Salvatrucha gang member, Zamora engages the immigrant rights struggle—visualizing and critiquing the illicit violence migrants encounter from State apparatuses—without relying on a valuing binary that necessitates Chino's devaluation. While Chino ultimately succumbs to gang violence, which admittedly, for some, might still suggest an investment in some form of valuing (the reformed/conflicted gang member versus the perverse ones), cultural production that aims to challenge sensationalist portrayals of gang members, and yet entirely refrains from the violence of gang life, only reads as disingenuous. Still, even in its inclusion of Chino's death from gang violence, Zamora's poetry collection nevertheless ventures away from the valuing intrinsic to the traditional gang member/immigrant binary insofar as it gestures toward a "structural analysis of power relations" that cultivate gang membership and violence.

In "El Salvador"—the poem succeeding "Second Attempt Crossing"—Zamora juxtaposes Chino's narrative with a critique of repressive state apparatuses and Mano Dura (Iron Fist) policies that help foment gang membership and a violent, dangerous environment for Salvadorans. Contemplating a return to El Salvador, the speaker reflects on the country's conditions and politics:

> please don't let cops say: *he's gangster,*
> Don't let gangsters say: *he's wrong barrio.* Your barrios
>
> stain you with pollen. Every day cops and gangsters pick at you
> with their metallic beaks, and presidents, guilty.
>
> Dad swears he'll never return, Mom wants to see her mom,
> and in the news: black bags, more and more of us leave.
>
> Parents say: *don't go; you have tattoos. It's the law; you don't know what law means there.*[32]

In juxtaposing gang members and police in the first two stanzas, the poem suggests that the State is just as responsible for the black body bags and violence afflicting El Salvador as are the gangs that cultural production often scapegoats for the nation's hazardous conditions. Indeed, the poem's invocation of both gangs' and the police's use of "metallic beaks" (suggesting firearms) that place the lives of Salvadoran residents in "black [body] bags," and cause "more and more of us" to flee the country, seems to gesture toward the Salvadoran police's practice of confiscating guns from gangs and selling them to rival gangs, as well as toward the police/gang war that has resulted in the deaths of fifty-three "suspected gang members" for every one cop murdered in shoot-outs with gangs.[33] While the poem understands gangs as a problem that harms innocent Salvadorans, it also nods toward a structural analysis of the power relations that breed this gang violence in references to the corrupt policing and Mano Dura policies that the speaker finds "presidents, guilty" of initiating.

El Salvador combats gangs through a Mano Dura approach that has only worsened gang violence and crime and proliferated gang membership—in part because of the notoriously inhumane prison conditions in the nation, and Mano Dura's inability to address the systemic impetus for gang membership. Mano Dura began in 2003 with one of the "presidents, guilty" that Zamora's poem alludes to: Francisco Flores, who initiated the mass incarceration of gang members. Under Flores, Mano Dura's measures enabled police to arrest and charge suspected gang members for minor infractions, and the supporting laws lengthened prison sentences for minors associated with gangs. This new legislation also allowed courts to try gang-affiliated minors as young as twelve as adults. This legislation also outlawed gang tattoos, which the speaker of "El Salvador" references with the lines, "*don't go; you have tattoos. It's the law; you don't know / what law means there.*" In these lines, the speaker insinuates that, though he is not a gang member, the State may interpret his tattoos as gang-related, leading to his arrest and possible imprisonment or even death in the police/gang war. As Carlos Martinez says, Mano Dura had three goals: "To ban gangs. To ban being a gang member. And it also allowed police to arrest people for their appearance."[34] Once Flores left office, his successor Antonio Saca—another of the "presidents, guilty"—amplified this criminalization and punishment legislation, creating "Súper Mano Dura," a mindset that later president Salvador Sánchez Cerén, after briefly breaking from Mano Dura, would continue.[35]

But rather than ban "being a gang member," Mano Dura proliferated gang membership and exacerbated El Salvador's trouble in combatting gangs. Prisons in El Salvador are infamously overcrowded, often have debilitating infrastructure, underpay guards (thus incentivizing the acceptance of bribes), have few or no rehabilitation programs, and struggle to regulate and police incarcerated persons. Imprisoning gangs in these highly congested spaces with meager supervision enabled them to strengthen their bonds, develop greater group cohesion, and spread gang membership to others previously uninvolved in gang life. Additionally, as Wolf argues, "The large-scale incarceration of gang members put street-based gang youth under greater pressure to provide for their imprisoned peers and families, but the growing social intolerance towards these groups further shrank their opportunities for legitimate work. Gang members therefore stepped up their illicit income-generation activities."[36] Gang members on the outside attempted to alleviate their peers' deplorable living conditions in prison and also assisted their families by providing money and goods. But because legitimate employment opportunities that provide sufficient financial security are not widely available in El Salvador, gangs attained these resources through criminal means. Because Mano Dura ignored the systemic impetus for gang membership, its initiatives spiked gang violence, crime, and membership, rather than reducing them. Zamora's poetic critiques of gang violence—and simultaneous allusions (as well as greater attention) to Mano Dura and the presidents behind its policies—suggest that his poem finds the State's reaction to gangs the primary reason for Salvadorans filling "black bags" or emigrating.

By gesturing toward these systemic impetuses that multiply and worsen gang violence in El Salvador, as well as rearticulating the figure and masculinity of the Mara Salvatrucha gang member, Zamora's poetry reveals how the gang member and the immigrant need not always have an antagonistic relationship in texts that engage the immigrant rights struggle. I am not suggesting that Latina/o/x literature and film should never portray gang members as harmful toward immigrants. Indeed, doing so is duplicitous and unrealistic. I am, however, arguing that Zamora's work shows how productive representations of immigrants need not rely on an immigrant/gang member valuing dichotomy. His poetry collection discloses how Latina/o/x immigration literature might critique how gang membership afflicts innocent persons in a way that refrains from pathologizing people in gangs and, instead, spotlights the systemic impetuses cultivating and propagating gang violence and crime.

With his critique, Zamora's poetry perhaps comes the closest to approximating Quijano's, Walsh's, and Mignolo's conceptions of decoloniality out of all the texts *Clicas* studies. The gang members of *My Father Was a Toltec*, *Locas*, *Homeboy*, and *On the Downlow* might use gang life in some way to circumvent the extent to which coloniality materially, ontologically, emotionally, and psychologically afflicts their lives. But none of these works—if to a different degree and in different forms—is able to delink entirely from coloniality. Many of the gang members of these texts still adhere to various aspects of the epistemologies of coloniality—even if rejecting others—and harm multiply marginalized persons in their circumvention of the material and abstract effects of coloniality. For these reasons, these gang members epitomize the (de)colonial. Gang life might facilitate certain forms of escape and resistance, but the power this subculture provides ultimately relies on ideological contradictions. In contrast, Zamora's "Second Attempt Crossing" and "El Salvador" more closely approach the idea of decoloniality: "epistemic disobedience" that demonstrates "power within the colonial matrix to undermine the mechanism that keeps it in place requiring obeisance."[37] Zamora's poems reject the normative gang member/immigrant valuing dichotomy that conceals and upholds the mechanisms of power keeping racialized systems of oppression like coloniality in place. But as Maria Lugones explains, coloniality is never *just* racial but is mutually constitutive—and operates at the intersection—of race, class, gender, and sexuality, a phenomenon that the term "the coloniality of gender" highlights. As Lugones says, the coloniality of gender "was as constitutive of the coloniality of power as the coloniality of power was constitutive of it."[38]

Zamora's poems do an excellent job of delinking from the racially troubling aspects of the immigrant/gang member dichotomy, as well as of envisioning alternative gang masculinities. But, whether through the (de)colonial or decoloniality, gang texts that feature as much of a critical investment in gender and sexuality as they do in race and class would wondrously expand our capacity to understand how coloniality influences and cultivates gang life in material and abstract ways. In this way, the literary and filmic gang narratives this book extrapolates help show how cultural production and humanist methodologies might contribute to and advance the academic study of gang membership, violence, and crime. Too often has critical gang studies elided questions of gender and sexuality when focusing upon gang subcultures—presuming these spaces uninhabitable sites for anyone not subscribing to a normative, heterosexual, male ideal. The literature and film by and/or about Latina/o/x gang members that *Clicas* studies, however, suggest otherwise.

SELECTED FILMOGRAPHY

American Me. Directed by Edward James Olmos. Universal Pictures, 1992.

The Ballad of Gregorio Cortez. Directed by Robert M. Young. Embassy Pictures, 1982.

A Better Life. Directed by Chris Weitz. Summit Entertainment, 2011.

Boulevard Nights. Directed by Michael Pressman. Warner Bros., 1979.

Bound by Honor. Directed by Taylor Hackford. Buena Vista Pictures, 1993.

Boyz n the Hood. Directed by John Singleton. Columbia Pictures, 1991.

Bruising for Besos. Directed by Adelina Anthony. AdeRisa Productions, 2016.

Colors. Directed by Dennis Hopper. Orion Pictures, 1988.

El Abuelo. Directed by Dino Dinco. Frameline, 2008.

End of Watch. Directed by David Ayer. Open Road Films, 2012.

Foxy Brown. Directed by Jack Hill. American International Pictures, 1974.

Gang Related. Directed by Jim Kouf. Orion Pictures, 1997.

Greencard Warriors. Directed by Miriam Kruishoop. Screen Media, 2013.

Havoc. Directed by Barbara Kopple. New Line Cinema, 2005.

Homeboy. Directed by Dino Dinco. Alphadogs, 2012.

La Mission. Directed by Peter Bratt. Global Cinema Distribution, 2009.

La Vida Loca. Directed by Christian Poveda. Ad Vitam Distribution, 2008.

LA 92. Directed by Daniel Lindsay and T. J. Martin. National Geographic Channel, 2017.

Menace II Society. Directed by the Hughes Brothers. New Line Cinema, 1993.

Mi Vida Loca. Directed by Allison Anders. Sony Pictures, 1993.

Moonlight. Directed by Barry Jenkins. A24, 2016.

On the Downlow. Directed by Tadeo García. Iconoclast Films, 2004.

Quinceañera. Directed by Richard Glatzer and Wash Westmoreland. Sony Pictures Classics, 2006.

Real Women Have Curves. Directed by Patricia Cardoso. HBO Films, 2002.

Set It Off. Directed by F. Gary Gray. New Line Cinema, 1996.

Sin Nombre. Directed by Cary Joji Fukunaga. Focus Features, 2009.

Sweet Sweetback's Baadasssss Song. Directed by Melvin Van Peebles. Cinemation Industries, 1971.

Training Day. Directed by Antoine Fuqua. Warner Bros., 2001.

Zoot Suit. Directed by Luis Valdez. Universal Pictures, 1981.

NOTES

Chapter 1: Gang Subcultures as (De)colonial Praxis

1. I use the term "coloniality" in the theoretical tradition that Latin American and Latina/o/x scholars developed for assessing the persistence of colonial relations after the "end" of formal colonialism. I elaborate on the concept later in this chapter.
2. Coined by James Diego Vigil in 1983, multiple marginality "analyzes oppression along various axes" and suggests that a person's multiple identities (race, gender, sexuality, etc.) intersect to determine the degree of marginalization one experiences in society (Vigil, *Multiple Marginality and Gangs*, 2). A Latina may face multiple marginalization in that she may experience discrimination as racialized sexism and gendered racism. The framework is akin to Kimberlé Crenshaw's theory of intersectionality, an idea that, as Vivian M. May says, arises from the "insights and practices of Black Feminist and women of color theoretical and political traditions," such as the thinking put forth in the 1977 Combahee River Collective Statement (3). For May, intersectionality "approaches lived identities as interlaced and systems of oppression as enmeshed and mutually reinforcing" (3). Though intersectionality has become a central tenet of humanist feminist studies, the social sciences tend to favor the concept of multiple marginality. Because this book operates at the interstices of the humanities and social sciences, I use both terms.
3. See, for instance, Sharron Angle's "The Wave," a campaign advertisement circulated during her 2010 run for the US Senate that depicts Latino gang members as harming white American women and children. Years later, Donald Trump would disseminate similar rhetoric in his campaign speeches decrying Mara Salvatrucha and advertisements featuring Luis Bracamontes.

4. This book uses the terms (de)colonial, decolonial, decoloniality, decolonize, and decolonization. When I use (de)colonial, I am specifically referring to the paradoxical resistance in the gang narratives the book analyzes. I absent the parentheses when referring to the field's traditional understanding of decolonial, decoloniality, and decolonization.
5. Ortega, "Decolonial Woes and Practices of Un-Knowing," 511.
6. Ortega, "Decolonial Woes and Practices of Un-Knowing," 505.
7. Ortega, "Decolonial Woes and Practices of Un-Knowing," 512. Other examples of these contradictions include antiracist/decolonial academics participating in US universities that benefit from the prison industrial complex or the maquiladora industry in Mexico. Angela Davis, for instance, has documented how public California universities often use furniture that prisoners build for low wages in exploitative and unsafe working conditions (36). Many US universities also use teaching and/or sporting equipment manufactured by Nike, RCA, Acer, and Sony, all of which, as Alica Gaspar de Alba shows, have ties to maquiladoras, factories that help enable the femicide against young Mexican women (64).
8. Ortega, "Decolonial Woes and Practices of Un-Knowing," 505.
9. Pérez, *The Decolonial Imaginary*, 7.
10. Stuart Hall has documented the scholarly dismissal of criminality and deviancy, and explained the importance of considering crime as subaltern agency in studies of Marxist resistance. See Hall's "Black Crime, Black Proletariat."
11. I define toxic/toxified masculinity as psychologically, emotionally, and physically violent masculinities that dominate or exhibit hostility toward women, gay persons, femininity, and others of disempowered statuses and identities. In most cases, I favor the word "toxified" when theorizing this type of masculinity amongst Latina/o/x persons, to foreground the systemic violences and inequalities that cultivate toxic masculinities amongst Latina/o/xs and other marginalized groups. For more on the origins and debates on the use of the term toxic masculinity, see Harrington.
12. See Mirandé's *Hombres y Machos*, and Luibhéid and Cantu Jr.'s *Queer Migrations*.
13. Aldama and Aldama, "Decolonizing Latinx Masculinities," 5.
14. Lugones, "The Coloniality of Gender," 1.
15. Throughout this project, I invoke the terms "citizenship" and "citizen-subject" when referring to gang members' participation in their gangs. When using these terms in this way, I refer to the critical race theory concept of "equal citizenship"—the principle that "every individual is presumptively entitled to be treated by the organized society as a respected, responsible, and participating member" (Lawrence III, 59).
16. Cuevas, *Post-Borderlandia*, 19.
17. Dean and Lane, "Homosexuality and Psychoanalysis," 7.

18. Cohen, "Punks, Bulldaggers, and Welfare Queens," 438; Dean and Lane, "Homosexuality and Psychoanalysis," 21.
19. Cuevas, *Post-Borderlandia*, 20.
20. Rodríguez, "X Marks the Spot," 210.
21. Rodríguez, "X Marks the Spot," 210.
22. Wolf, "Mara Salvatrucha," 68.
23. Wolf, "Mara Salvatrucha," 68.
24. Bruneau, Introduction to *Maras*, 5.
25. Bruneau, Introduction to *Maras*, 5.
26. Many current and former gang members use pen names to author autobiographies or memoirs about their previous gang life, such as an ex-Latin King who writes under the name Reymundo Sanchez and has published *My Bloody Life: The Making of a Latin King*; *Once a King, Always a King*; and coauthored with Sonia Rodriguez *Lady Q: The Rise and Fall of a Latin Queen*.
27. Pérez, *The Decolonial Imaginary*, 20.
28. Addison, "QFilms Review," https://lbpost.com/news/lgbtq/qfilms-review-homeboy-unabashedly-explores-gay-latino-gang-members/.
29. Hall, "Black Men, White Media," 54, emphasis in original.
30. Delgado, "Legal Storytelling," 2413.
31. Orlando Patterson, *Slavery and Social Death*, viii.
32. Bruneau, Introduction to *Maras*, 18–19.
33. Clarke et al., "Subcultures, Cultures, and Class," 44.
34. Clarke et al., "Subcultures, Cultures, and Class," 45, emphasis in original.
35. Weber, *Basic Concepts in Sociology*, 117.
36. Fanon, *The Wretched of the Earth*, 38–39.
37. Mills, *The Racial Contract*, 11.
38. Mills, *The Racial Contract*, 11.
39. Mills, *The Racial Contract*, 56.
40. Thiong'o, *Decolonising the Mind*, 3.
41. Fanon, *Black Skin, White Masks*, 89.
42. Fanon, *Black Skin, White Masks*, 89.
43. Fanon, *Black Skin, White Masks*, 93.
44. Maldonado-Torres, "On the Coloniality of Being," 254.
45. Kelley, Introduction to *Discourse on Colonialism*, 27.
46. For more on the initial theorization of coloniality, see Quijano; Mignolo; and Mignolo and Walsh.
47. Maldonado-Torres, "On the Coloniality of Being," 243.
48. Maldonado-Torres, "On the Coloniality of Being," 243; Méndez, "Decolonial Feminist *Movidas*," 76.
49. Tuck and Yang, "Decolonization Is Not a Metaphor," 4.
50. Tuck and Yang, "Decolonization Is Not a Metaphor," 4–5.
51. While the concept of coloniality remains, for the most part, unchallenged in the academy, the idea of internal colonialism has precipitated much

debate. For more on the conversations about internal colonialism, see Barrera, Barrera et al., Acuña (1972), Acuña (1981), Gilbert G. González, Almaguer (1971), Alamguer (1989), and Pinderhughes.
52. Wacquant, *Urban Outcasts*, 3.
53. Oyěwùmí, *The Invention of Women*, 121.
54. Ortega, "Decolonial Woes and Practices of Un-Knowing," 507.
55. Lugones, "The Coloniality of Gender," 7.
56. Lugones, "Towards a Decolonial Feminism," 743.
57. Lugones, "The Coloniality of Gender," 13.
58. Lugones, "The Coloniality of Gender," 13.
59. Lugones, "The Coloniality of Gender," 11.
60. Lugones, "The Coloniality of Gender," 7.
61. Lugones, "The Coloniality of Gender," 9, 8.
62. Lugones, "The Coloniality of Gender," 12; Lugones, "Toward a Decolonial Feminism," 743.
63. Lugones, "Toward a Decolonial Feminism," 745.
64. Lugones, "The Coloniality of Gender," 11.
65. Lugones, "The Coloniality of Gender, 10.
66. Lugones, "The Coloniality of Gender," 12.
67. Lugones, "The Coloniality of Gender," 12.
68. Lugones, "Towards a Decolonial Feminism," 746.
69. Mignolo and Walsh, *On Decoloniality*, 121.
70. Tuck and Yang, "Decolonization Is Not a Metaphor," 19, emphasis in original.
71. Tuck and Yang, "Decolonization Is Not a Metaphor," 7.
72. Tuck and Yang use the phrase "repatriation of land" to define how scholars should use the term decolonization (7). Some might challenge Tuck and Yang's definition of decolonization in its reliance on the word "repatriation." In its traditional sense, decolonization signals the colonized *seizing* their stolen land from the colonizer, not the colonizer returning stolen land. In this conception, decolonization is not something granted by the colonizer, but *rather won by the colonized* through the use of violence. For more on this understanding of decolonization, see Fanon's *The Wretched of the Earth*.
73. Mignolo, *The Darker Side of Western Modernity*, xxvii.
74. Mignolo and Walsh, *On Decoloniality*, 222.
75. Mignolo and Walsh, *On Decoloniality*, 106.
76. Maldonado-Torres, "On the Coloniality of Being," 261.
77. Mignolo and Walsh, *On Decoloniality*, 114.
78. Mignolo and Walsh, *On Decoloniality*, 17.
79. Fanon, *The Wretched of the Earth*, 36.
80. Mignolo and Walsh, *On Decoloniality*, 17, 115.
81. Cuevas, "Fighting the Good Fight," 131, 132.

82. Cuevas, "Fighting the Good Fight," 147.
83. Cuevas, "Fighting the Good Fight," 147, 131.
84. Cuevas, "Fighting the Good Fight," 147.
85. Mignolo and Walsh, *On Decoloniality*, 108.
86. Clarke et al., "Subcultures, Cultures, and Class," 45, emphasis in original.
87. Wolf, "Mara Salvatrucha," 79.
88. Wolf, "Mara Salvatrucha," 79–80.
89. Wolf, "Mara Salvatrucha," 80.
90. The Lynwood Vikings was a notorious police gang in the 1970s, featuring many members who would later hold high-ranking, prestigious political and law enforcement positions—such as Paul K. Tanaka, who became mayor of Gardena and undersheriff in the Los Angeles County Sheriff's Department. For more on the Vikings, see O'Conner and Daunt, as well as Sullivan.
91. For more on the Executioners, see Silva.
92. Vigil, *Barrio Gangs*, 7.
93. Rodríguez, "Queering the Homeboy Aesthetic," 130.
94. Rodríguez, "Queering the Homeboy Aesthetic," 127–128.
95. Ramírez, *The Woman in the Zoot Suit*, 56.
96. Mendoza-Denton, *Homegirls*, 154.
97. Rivera Fellah, "Graciela Iturbide's Cholos/as Series," 321.
98. Hebdige, *Subculture*, 17.
99. Hebdige, *Subculture*, 17.
100. Hebdige, *Subculture*, 2, 90.
101. Mendoza-Denton, *Homegirls*, 157.
102. Mendoza-Denton, *Homegirls*, 157.
103. Hernández, *Aesthetics of Excess*, 17.
104. For more on how mental, emotional, and sexual trauma in gang members' families drives them to join gangs, see Vigil's *Barrio Gangs*; Moore's *Going Down to the Barrio*; and Sánchez-Jankowski.
105. Wacquant, *Urban Outcasts*, 211.
106. Wolf, "Mara Salvatrucha," 70. For more on how violence in gangs strengthens kinship bonds and cohesion between members, see Brown; Dudley; Savenije; and Wacquant.
107. Ward, *Gangsters without Borders*, 145.
108. Many readers will wonder about the connections between fatal gang violence and the (de)colonial consequences I am outlining. On the one hand, as many scholars in critical gang studies (such as Ward and Klein) note, gang members rarely kill each other. On the other hand, when gang members die from fratricidal violence or live their lives in ways that put them at greater risk of lethal police violence, these deaths also possibly have liberating consequences. The United States exercises biopolitical control over the racial Other, a power that Michel Foucault defines as "the right to make live and

to let die" (*Society Must Be Defended*, 241). The State letting people of color die often materializes through the fatal violence of repressive state apparatuses and/or through what Rob Nixon calls "slow violence"—described as a "violence that occurs gradually and out of sight, a violence of delayed destruction that is typically not viewed as violence at all," such as the long-term effects of toxic waste and mass poverty in barrios (2). Gang members who conduct their lives in manners that accelerate this slow violence by engaging in fatal wars with rivals or by amplifying their chances of repressive state apparatuses murdering them are thus, potentially, seizing the biopolitical power of the State over their lives—electing to "let die" on their own terms. For more on how gang members might "defy sovereign powers and material forms of subjugation" through a "pathological embrace of death," see Gilberto Rosas's *Barrio Libre* (119, 127).

109. Wacquant, *Urban Outcasts*, 68.
110. Gregorio Cortez was a Mexican American maize farmer in Texas during the late-nineteenth and early-twentieth centuries. On June 12, 1901, Sheriff W. T. "Brack" Morris visited Gregorio and his brother Ronaldo's farm, accusing them of stealing a caballo (stallion). Gregorio responded that he recently acquired a yegua (mare), which Morris did not comprehend and ultimately led to a heated argument that culminated with Morris shooting Ronaldo. Gregorio shot and killed Morris in retribution and later fled the pursuit of the Texas Rangers on foot and on horseback, travelling over 400 miles in ten days in one of the longest manhunts in US history. The Texas Rangers eventually captured Gregorio, whom a jury convicted of second-degree murder, the judge sentencing him to life in prison. In 1913, Governor Oscar Colquitt pardoned him, although, shortly after his release, Gregorio was poisoned to death at dinner. Throughout the Southwest, many Mexican Americans and Chicana/o/xs consider Cortez a folk hero, as his legacy lives on through a great variety of cultural forms, most famously in the song "El Corrido de Gregorio Cortez," Americo Parédes's novel *With His Pistol in His Hand*, and Robert Young's film *The Ballad of Gregorio Cortez*.
111. Navarro, *Machos y Malinchistas*, 20, viii.
112. Brown, *Gang Nation*, xxiii.
113. For studies of gangs that ignore women or gay persons, view gang girls only as sex objects who are subordinate to male gang members, or reduce women in gangs to social maladjustment, see Thrasher; Campbell; Cohen; Short and Strodtbeck; and Swart.
114. For an extensive history of the zoot suit counterculture and the Zoot Suit Riots, see Shane White and Graham White; Alvarez; Ramírez; and Acuña.
115. Fregoso, "Re-Imagining Chicana Urban Identities," 72.
116. Fregoso, "Re-Imagining Chicana Urban Identities," 72.
117. Ramírez, *The Woman in the Zoot Suit*, 19.
118. Ramírez, *The Woman in the Zoot Suit*, 19.

Notes to Pages 35–42 | 207

119. Fregoso, "Re-Imagining Chicana Identities," 89.
120. Brown, *Gang Nation*, xxxiii.
121. Brown, *Gang Nation*, xxxiv, emphasis in original.
122. Vigil, "Urban Violence," 227.
123. Miranda, *Homegirls in the Public Sphere*, 3, 4.
124. Miranda, *Homegirls in the Public Sphere*, 79.
125. Miranda, *Homegirls in the Public Sphere*, 81.
126. Valdez, "Southern California Latino Gangs," 32.
127. Peterson, "Girlfriends, Gun-Holders, and Ghetto-Rats," 78.
128. Moore, *Going Down to the Barrio*, 53.
129. Galván, *The Chola Loca*, 16.
130. Galván, *The Chola Loca*, 163.
131. Rivera Fellah, "Graciela Iturbide's Cholos/as Series," 322.
132. Johnson, "Taking Over the School," 88.
133. Johnson, "Taking Over the School," 88–89.
134. Johnson, "Taking Over the School," 89.
135. Johnson, "Taking Over the School," 89.
136. Pérez, *Rethinking Chicana/o and Latina/o Popular Culture*, 163.
137. For more on the activo/pasivo ideology and its role in Mexican and Chicana/o/x cultural systems, see Almaguer's "Chicano Men."
138. Pérez, *Rethinking Chicana/o and Latina/o Popular Culture*, 163.
139. Aldama, "Penalizing Chicano/a Bodies," 83.
140. For a further analysis of homosocialism/eroticism between Santana and J. D., see Newman.
141. Thomas, *Down These Mean Streets*, 55, emphasis in original.
142. Thomas, *Down These Mean Streets*, 56.
143. Brown, *Gang Nation*, 16.
144. Brown, *Gang Nation*, 18.
145. Francisco J. Galarte's analysis of the 2008 murder of Angie Zapata—a transwoman whom Latino gang member Allen Andrade killed after believing Zapata deceived him into sexual activity with her—showcases how the State has used the popular assumption that homophobia and transphobia are "compulsory parts of Mexican American culture and gang culture" to enact anti-Latina/o/x and anti-immigration legislation, ostensibly to protect trans and gay folks (61). This book's unveiling of gay gang members/narratives hopes to rearticulate that common presumption, showing that gay sexuality is not always incompatible with gang membership.
146. Panfil, *The Gang's All Queer*, 3.
147. Panfil, *The Gang's All Queer*, 3.
148. Panfil, *The Gang's All Queer*, 7.
149. Panfil, *The Gang's All Queer*, 8, 9.
150. Panfil, *The Gang's All Queer*, 109.

151. Panfil, *The Gang's All Queer*, 15.
152. Rosario, "When Is a Gang Not a 'Gang,'" 34.
153. Given the plentitude of 1960s and 1970s prison literature, many will wonder why prison writers or prison gangs do not receive attention in this project. Although social revolutionaries like George Jackson, Angela Davis, Eldridge Cleaver, and Jack Henry Abbott are eminent for their revolutionary thought, none of them was a gang member when theorizing prison radicalization. Prison gangs, coloniality in prison, and the gender/sexual cultural codes of prison substantially differ from gangs and gang violence in the barrio and, thus, warrant a separate book project. Though not always (if at all) focusing on prison gangs, for scholarship on prison literature and resistance, see Franklin; Olguín; Hames-García; and Dylan Rodríguez.
154. Cacho, *Social Death*, 17.

Chapter 2: The Shared Experience of (De)colonial Gang Life

1. Martínez D'Aubuisson, "Asi viven y mueren," https://www.revistafactum.com/asi-viven-y-mueren-las-mujeres-pandilleras-en-el-salvador.
2. Martínez D'Aubuisson, "Asi viven y mueren," https://www.revistafactum.com/asi-viven-y-mueren-las-mujeres-pandilleras-en-el-salvador.
3. The limited number of textual representations of gay men in gangs and their socialities in currently available cultural production leads this chapter to focus on women and heterosexual men in gangs. Nonetheless, the chapter's analyses are applicable to and have consequences for the study of gay men in gangs.
4. Martínez, "Shifting the Site," 229, 241, emphasis in original.
5. Martínez, "Shifting the Site," 227.
6. For more on the whitewashed or "race traitor" condemnations Chicanas/Latinas face when critiquing heteropatriarchy in their ethnic communities, see Blackwell's *¡Chicana Power!* and Richard T. Rodríguez's *Next of Kin*.
7. O'Connor and Corrado, *Compliments of Chicagohoodz*, 87.
8. "Greaser Gangs: The Start of Old School White Gangs," https://www.kulturevulturez.com/old-school-white-greaser-gangs.
9. The Latina/o/x Two Six gang, which presently still exists, also uses the Playboy bunny. For more on the Two Six, see Chapter 5. Also, see O'Connor and Corrado for further information on the use of the Klansman symbol in white Chicago gangs of the twentieth century.
10. Gunderson, "Sweaters and Other Strange Ephemera," https://news.wttw.com/2017/05/18/sweaters-and-other-strange-ephemera-chicago-s-1970s-street-gangs.

11. Gunderson, "Sweaters and Other Strange Ephemera," https://news.wttw.com/2017/05/18/sweaters-and-other-strange-ephemera-chicago-s-1970s-street-gangs.
12. Quoted in Breen, "Chicago Gangs," https://www.dnainfo.com/chicago/20170329/englewood/chicago-gangs-knitted-sweaters-varsity-patches.
13. Gunderson, "Sweaters and Other Strange Ephemera," https://news.wttw.com/2017/05/18/sweaters-and-other-strange-ephemera-chicago-s-1970s-street-gangs.
14. Mid-twentieth century Chicago gangs also used "compliment cards" to promote their gang. They would often host parties and advertise them through passing out cards displaying the gang's name, symbols, and members' nicknames. Typically, gangs would also dump bundles of these cards in rivals' territories, or after committing crimes against other gangs to disrespect them. For more on compliment cards, see Gunderson and O'Connor and Corrado.
15. Black gangs in Chicago also emerged in response to racial hostility from the Irish and Italians. The fashion aesthetics of black gangs, however, did not usually resemble Latina/o/x, Irish, and Italian styles. Rather than wear varsity sweaters, black gangs of this era adopted the beret as their standard fashion. The color of the beret signaled membership in a particular gang. The Gangster Disciples, for instance, wore a blue beret, whereas the Blackstone Rangers wore a red one.
16. Italian immigrants viewed Chicago's urban renewal initiatives as an opportunity to banish the growing Mexican and black American population from the Near West Side, to reclaim the area as Italian space. Mike Amezcua explains that Italian immigrants successfully lobbied for urban renewal demolition to occur in the eastern portions of the Near West Side—sections where Mexican Americans and blacks lived—rather than in the Little Italy areas in the west (47–48). For more on the racialization of this urban renewal, and how Mexican Americans resisted and made sense of their displacement, see Amezcua.
17. Watson, *Romantic Violence in R-World*, 7.
18. Watson, *Romantic Violence in R-World*, 7.
19. Watson, *Romantic Violence in R-World*, 7.
20. O'Connor and Corrado, *Compliments of Chicagohoodz*, 18.
21. O'Connor and Corrado, *Compliments of Chicagohoodz*, 18.
22. Cartwright, "Toltec Civilization," *Ancient History Encyclopedia*, https://www.worldhistory.org/Toltec_Civilization.
23. Castillo, *My Father Was a Toltec*, xviii.
24. Salas, *Soldaderas in the Mexican Military*, 3.
25. Castillo, *My Father Was a Toltec*, xviii.
26. Castillo, *My Father Was a Toltec*, 3, emphasis in original.
27. Castillo, *My Father Was a Toltec*, 6.

28. For more on the support of the Confederacy in Bridgeport, see Pacyga.
29. Amezcua, *Making Mexican Chicago*, 4.
30. O'Connor and Corrado, *Compliments of Chicagohoodz*, 16; Kass, "Gangs that Came to Rule," *Chicago Tribune*, https://www.chicagotribune.com/news/ct-xpm-2012-06-22-ct-met-kass-0622-20120622-story.html.
31. For more on how Atlantic immigrants espoused racism against blacks and Latina/o/xs as a strategy for attaining upward mobility and assimilating into whiteness, see Amezcua and Omi and Winant.
32. Castillo, *My Father Was a Toltec*, 3, emphasis in original.
33. Fanon, *The Wretched of the Earth*, 94.
34. Casas, "An Account, Much Abbreviated," 68.
35. Maldonado-Torres, "On the Coloniality of Being," 247–248.
36. Pérez, "Sexuality and Discourse," 168.
37. Pérez, "Sexuality and Discourse," 168.
38. Pérez, "Sexuality and Discourse," 164.
39. The possibility of subaltern women performing and queering subaltern masculinities applies to this argument. This book adheres to Jack Halberstam's conception of masculinity as not beholden to a single gender but as an independent cultural phenomenon that any gender may perform. For this reason, the subaltern masculinities this book discusses that potentially entail the "possession" of women as a method for aggrandizing masculinity apply to multiple genders. *Clicas* further explores this topic of subaltern female masculinity later in this chapter in analyzing the daughter-speaker's entrance into gang life, as well as in much more detail in Chapter 3.
40. Pérez, "Sexuality and Discourse," 169.
41. As much as sexual relations with white women may function as an ironic (de)colonial response, these activities may also suggest internalized racism and reinforce psychological colonization. I do not, however, interpret the daughter-speaker's father's philandering with white women as internalized racism—especially because of his membership in a gang named after an indigenous nation, and his history of warring with whites. For some people, this theorization of the connections between women and subaltern masculinities may read as "sympathizing" with, "defending," or "excusing" subaltern men who understand rape against both white women and women of color as acts of racial resistance, as Eldridge Cleaver argues in *Soul on Ice*. While this chapter does not share Cleaver's argument, it tackles this subject to consider the possible role of the coloniality of gender in some subaltern men's violent assaults against women.
42. Castillo, *My Father Was a Toltec*, 6.
43. Castillo, *My Father Was a Toltec*, 6.
44. An alternative reading of "The Toltec" might interpret the character "mami" not as the father's wife but his own mother. Reading "The Toltec" as a standalone poem invites this interpretation, but because I am reading "The

Toltec" as part of a collective ensemble of poems that form an overarching narrative, I interpret the "mami" character as a reference to the daughter-speaker's mother—especially since the "Toltec chapter" centers on three main characters (the father, his wife, and their daughter) and maintains the daughter as the speaker for every poem in that chapter.
45. Pérez-Torres, *Movements in Chicano Poetry*, 124.
46. Estill, "In Father's Footsteps," 54.
47. Castillo, *My Father Was a Toltec*, 4.
48. The poem's title also invokes the Greek mythological figure Electra (King Agamemnon and Queen Clytemnestra's daughter and princess of Argos) and the Electra complex. Psychoanalyst Carl Jung theorized the Electra complex as the opposite of the Oedipus complex, suggesting that a girl psycho-sexually competes with her mother for her father.
49. Fregoso, "Re-imagining Chicana Identities," 76.
50. Castillo, *My Father Was a Toltec*, 5.
51. Castillo, *My Father Was a Toltec*, 6.
52. Fraser, "Rethinking the Public Sphere," 57.
53. Fraser, "Rethinking the Public Sphere," 57.
54. Fraser, "Rethinking the Public Sphere," 57.
55. Fregoso, "Re-imagining Chicana Identities," 76.
56. Fregoso, "Re-imagining Chicana Identities," 77.
57. Castillo, *My Father Was a Toltec*, 6.
58. Castillo, *My Father Was a Toltec*, 6.
59. Castillo, *My Father Was a Toltec*, 6.
60. Navarro, "Revisiting the Boulevard."
61. Castillo, *My Father Was a Toltec*, 6.
62. Anzaldúa, *Borderlands/La Frontera*, 39.
63. Much of Latina/o/x literature and film features the trope of a mother (or sometimes a grandmother) internalizing or adhering to heteropatriarchy and functioning as a patriarchal agent who regulates the lives of young Latina daughters, such as in Junot Díaz's *The Brief Wondrous Life of Oscar Wao*, Adelina Anthony's *Bruising for Besos*, and *Real Women Have Curves* (2002). This literary and filmic trope reflects the gendered, differential treatment that many Latina daughters encounter from mothers in traditional, heteropatriarchal Latina/o/x families, whereas young boys often receive less supervision and discipline, and incur greater praise.
64. Méndez, "Decolonial Feminist *Movidas*," 76.
65. For some readers, *My Father Was a Toltec*'s representation of absent fatherism might invite comparisons to Daniel Patrick Moynihan's infamous *The Negro Family: The Case for National Action*, which identified and attempted to theorize absent fatherism in working-class black families. Representing and examining absent fatherism in a racially minoritarian family is not in and of itself problematic, especially in autobiographical poems that portray

the author's actual childhood history. Indeed, the gang narrative tradition often highlights broken homes and absent parents as common factors that cultivate gang membership. What distinguishes these gang texts from the racially troubling "Moynihan Report," however, is that it is typical for gang narratives to recognize and theorize how systemic racism, white capitalism, and other aspects of coloniality encourage absent fatherism in working-class families of color. Examples that do so include Luis J. Rodriguez's and Jesmyn Ward's memoirs *Always Running* and *Men We Reaped* (both of which this book later discusses). Moynihan, on the other hand, argued that absent fatherism materialized in black urban communities because black women are too masculine and aggressive, therefore driving black men away from the home. For more on the racial politics of Moynihan's thesis, see Collins.

66. Paredes, "The Evolution of Daughter-Father Relationships," 136.
67. For elaboration on the variance and detailed meanings of machismo, see Chapter 3.
68. García, "Studying Chicanas," 192.
69. Cantú, "Entre Hombres/Between Men," 166.
70. Fregoso, "Re-imagining Chicana Identities," 76.
71. Fregoso, "Re-imagining Chicana Identities," 77.
72. Ward, *Men We Reaped*, 131.
73. Paz, *The Labyrinth of Solitude*, 36.
74. Paredes, "The Evolution of Daughter-Father Relationships," 138.
75. Franco, "Beyond Ethnocentrism," 507.
76. Castillo, *My Father Was a Toltec*, 7.
77. Castillo, *My Father Was a Toltec*, 8, emphasis in original.
78. Ana Castillo, email message to author, May 11, 2022; Amezcua, *Making Mexican Chicago*, 48.
79. O'Connor and Corrado, *Compliments of Chicagohoodz*, 64.
80. O'Connor and Corrado, *Compliments of Chicagohoodz*, 65.
81. Fanon, *Black Skin, White Masks*, 89.
82. Fanon, *Black Skin, White Masks*, 94.
83. Castillo, *My Father Was a Toltec*, 8, emphasis in original.
84. George Lipsitz, "Con Safos," 47.
85. Castillo, *My Father Was a Toltec*, 8.
86. Castillo, *My Father Was a Toltec*, 12.
87. Castillo, *My Father Was a Toltec*, 12.
88. Pérez, "Sexuality and Discourse," 171.
89. Chapter 3 provides a more nuanced analysis of the history of domestic violence against Latinas, and the ways that the US nation-state perceives their bodies as violable. In doing so, the chapter also analyzes in further detail how gangs might provide Latinas an avenue for combatting domestic violence.

90. Castillo, *My Father Was a Toltec*, 13.
91. Castillo, *My Father Was a Toltec*, 15.
92. Castillo, *My Father Was a Toltec*, 15.
93. Castillo, *My Father Was a Toltec*, 15–16, emphasis in original.
94. Stallings, *Funk the Erotic*, 63, 5.
95. Miranda, *Homegirls in the Public Sphere*, 79–80.
96. Pérez, *The Decolonial Imaginary*, 118.
97. Castillo, *My Father Was a Toltec*, 8, emphasis in original.
98. Castillo, *My Father Was a Toltec*, 11.
99. Estill, "In Father's Footsteps," 55, my emphasis.
100. Castillo, *My Father Was a Toltec*, 15.
101. Estill, "In Father's Footsteps," 55.
102. Anzaldúa, *Borderlands/La Frontera*, 80–81.
103. Anzaldúa, *Borderlands/La Frontera*, 80.
104. Castillo, *My Father Was a Toltec*, 6.

Chapter 3: The Toxified Female Masculinities of (De)colonial Gang Girls

1. See Rubio and Campbell for more on the scholarly obsession over, and exaggeration of, women's sexual statuses in male-dominated gangs.
2. Ward, *Gangsters without Borders*, 123.
3. Pérez, *Rethinking Chicana/o and Latina/o Popular Culture*, 152.
4. Moore, *Going Down to the Barrio*, 53.
5. For more on the Latin Kings, see Chapter 5.
6. Galván, *The Chola Loca*, 22.
7. The Echo Park Lobos are likely a literary allusion to the actual Latina/o/x gang the Echo Park Locos (ExP). ExP formed in Echo Park in the 1960s and was one of the main Latina/o/x gangs of this area during the 1980s and 90s. Gentrification and a 2013 gang injunction significantly reduced the gang's membership. Latina members of ExP starred in Allison Anders's 1993 girl gang flick *Mi Vida Loca*.
8. Halberstam, *Female Masculinity*, 13.
9. Halberstam, *Female Masculinity*, 13.
10. Halberstam, *Female Masculinity*, 9.
11. Halberstam, *Female Masculinity*, 2.
12. Halberstam, *Female Masculinity*, 2.
13. Halberstam, *Female Masculinity*, 114.
14. Halberstam, *Female Masculinity*, 117, 115. For a discussion of how television shows like *Lockup*, *Cops*, and *60 Days In* constitute pornography for white viewers, see Riofrio. Additionally, see Cruz for a striking analysis of how race play in BDSM culture and pornography fetishes black sexuality and implicates colonial and slave trade histories.

15. Halberstam, *Female Masculinity*, 229.
16. Hernández, "Fea, Firme y Formal," 168.
17. Cuevas, "Fighting the Good Fight," 147.
18. Cuevas, *Post-Borderlandia*, 55.
19. Rincón, "La Chicana," 17–18. For further accounts that elaborate on how machismo exhibits both positive and negative qualities, see Alcalde; Arciniega; and Mirandé's *Hombres y Machos*.
20. Tapia, "Machismo, Class, and National Oppression," 20.
21. Tapia, "Machismo, Class, and National Oppression," 20.
22. Totten, *Guys, Gangs, and Girlfriend Abuse*, 31.
23. Ward, *Gangsters without Borders*, 133.
24. Notable woman-authored African American contemporary street novels include Teri Woods's *True to the Game*, Sister Souljah's *The Coldest Winter Ever*, Wahida Clark's *Thugs and the Women Who Love Them*, Nikki Turner's *A Hustler's Wife*, and Vickie Stringer's *Dirty Red*.
25. Gifford, *Pimping Fictions*, 158.
26. Gifford, *Pimping Fictions*, 153.
27. Ramírez, *The Woman in the Zoot Suit*, 56, 20.
28. Ramírez, *The Woman in the Zoot Suit*, 68–69.
29. Rivera Fellah, "Graciela Iturbide's Cholos/as Series," 317.
30. Murray, *Locas*, 7.
31. Murray, *Locas*, 7, emphasis in original.
32. Murray, *Locas*, 7.
33. Murray, *Locas*, 9.
34. Murray, *Locas*, 9.
35. Murray, *Locas*, 19.
36. Murray, *Locas*, 31.
37. Murray, *Locas*, 20.
38. Murray, *Locas*, 40.
39. Ward, *Gangsters without Borders*, 135.
40. Murray, *Locas*, 32.
41. Murray, *Locas*, 29.
42. Murray, *Locas*, 7.
43. Murray, *Locas*, 94. In California Latina/o/x gang culture, Northern California Latina/o/x gangs wear red and Southern California gangs wear blue. Cholas often reflect these allegiances in their makeup and hair coloring, though as Mendoza-Denton explains, "Sureñas sometimes also dye their hair black" because blue hair codes as "punk" or "(mostly) white" (157). While Mendoza-Denton is correct in identifying that Southern California cholas shy away from wearing blue hair out of fear of suggesting they desire whiteness, it is important to note that many persons not from California or unfamiliar with these gang subcultures use Sureño and Norteño interchangeably with Southsider and Northsider. The words convey different meanings. Sureño

and Norteño are statuses that only incredibly violent and loyal gang members can earn while in prison, and that signify a specific relationship with the all-male prison gangs the Mexican Mafia and Nuestra Familia. To my knowledge, these prison gangs award these titles only to men.
44. Murray, *Locas*, 95.
45. Murray, *Locas*, 94.
46. Murray, *Locas*, 94.
47. Contemporary understandings of, and language for, gender have evolved beyond the biological determinism represented in *Locas*. Published in 1997, the book's deliberations on gender politics engage gender solely through cisgendered logics. For this reason, my extrapolation of this novel's representation of gender operates from the language of a cisgender hermeneutic.
48. Ramírez, *The Woman in the Zoot Suit*, 124.
49. Murray, *Locas*, 41.
50. Rodríguez, "Queering the Homeboy Aesthetic," 128.
51. Ramírez, *The Woman in the Zoot Suit*, 90–91.
52. Mendoza-Denton, *Homegirls*, 155.
53. Murray, *Locas*, 39.
54. Mendoza-Denton, *Homegirls*, 49.
55. Murray, *Locas*, 32.
56. Murray, *Locas*, 32, 33.
57. Murray, *Locas*, 95.
58. Murray, *Locas*, 95.
59. Miranda, *Homegirls in the Public Sphere*, 80.
60. Connell, *Gender and Power*, 133.
61. Murray, *Locas*, 52.
62. Murray, *Locas*, 150.
63. Murray, *Locas*, 151.
64. Murray, *Locas*, 107.
65. Murray, *Locas*, 161, emphasis in original.
66. Murray, *Locas*, 239.
67. The final section of *Locas* takes place in 1997, a year marking the onset of the gentrification of Echo Park. While the town still maintains a working-class Latina/o/x presence, today much of Echo Park is populated by hipsters and middle- and upper-class whites. Rising rent costs have resulted in many Echo Park gangs transforming into "weekend" gangs—a phenomenon where Echo Park (and other Los Angeles) gang members have moved east to San Bernardino, Riverside, and other areas of the Inland Empire and now "commute" into Echo Park and LA on weekends to gangbang. Murray published *Locas* before the development of weekend gangs, so this type of gang does not exist in her book. For more on the weekend gangs and gentrification of Echo Park, see Gerber.

216 | *Notes to Pages 108–116*

68. Brown, *Gang Nation*, 106.
69. Pérez, *Rethinking Chicana/o and Latina/o Popular Culture*, 152.
70. For other analyses that trace female masculinity in *Locas* and how Lobos women use the performance to claim citizenship, see Ibarraran-Bigalondo's "Chicano Gangs/Chicana Girls" and "Wolves, Sheep, and *Vatos Locos*."
71. The lack of cultural texts depicting male femininity in hypermasculine, male-dominated gangs makes analyzing the agential potential of male femininity in these contexts exceedingly difficult. The absence of cultural products representing male femininity in gangs, in part, arises from the distinct significations that femininity connotes when men, rather than women, perform femininity in many heterosexual, male-dominated gangs. In these gangs, male femininity threatens men's heterosexuality and gender identity in a way that female femininity does not—a dynamic I tease out in Chapter 4.
72. See Totten, Brown, and Daniel Enrique Pérez for more on femininity and women gang members.
73. Murray, *Locas*, 22.
74. Murray, *Locas*, 23.
75. Murray, *Locas*, 23–24.
76. Murray, *Locas*, 23.
77. Murray, *Locas*, 23.
78. Murray, *Locas*, 23.
79. Murray, *Locas*, 15.
80. Murray, *Locas*, 16, 17.
81. Murray, *Locas*, 27.
82. Murray, *Locas*, 28, emphasis in original.
83. Murray, *Locas*, 214.
84. Ellison, *Invisible Man*, 3.
85. Murray, *Locas*, 214.
86. Murray, *Locas*, 29.
87. Murray, *Locas*, 38.
88. Murray, *Locas*, 38.
89. Murray, *Locas*, 38.
90. Murray, *Locas*, 39.
91. Murray, *Locas*, 107.
92. Murray, *Locas*, 148.
93. Murray, *Locas*, 148.
94. Murray, *Locas*, 148.
95. Edelman, *No Future*, 3, emphasis in original.
96. Murray, *Locas*, 41.
97. Murray, *Locas*, 113.
98. Murray, *Locas*, 113.
99. Murray, *Locas*, 51.

100. Murray, *Locas*, 51–52.
101. Ibarraran-Bigalondo, "Chicano Gangs/Chicana Girls," 50, 52.
102. Brown, *Gang Nation*, 90.
103. Pérez, "Sexuality and Discourse," 169.
104. Rodríguez, *Next of Kin*, 52.
105. Murray, *Locas*, 4.
106. For further information about how the State systemically excludes undocumented women and their children from access to healthcare, as well as how undocumented persons internalize that they are unworthy of medical care, see Farfán-Santos.
107. In 1994, California voted to pass Proposition 187, which attempted to revoke health care and education services to undocumented persons. Thus, not only does the threat of deportation deter undocumented immigrants from obtaining adequate health care, but many states have also installed laws to deny undocumented persons medical care, with Proposition 187 as one of the most famous examples.
108. For more on the lack of/under prosecution of vigilantes committing violent crimes against undocumented persons, see Chávez, Cacho, and Larson.
109. Murray, *Locas*, 145.
110. Murray, *Locas*, 11.
111. Murray, *Locas*, 64.
112. Murray, *Locas*, 79.
113. Murray, *Locas*, 145, 81.
114. Ruiz, *Two Badges*, 164.
115. Venkatesh, *Gang Leader for a Day*, 173–174.
116. Cacho, *Social Death*, 40. In cases where the police do arrest and charge men who commit domestic violence against black and Latina women (especially in low-income, racialized spaces), the US court system often symbolically excuses and/or justifies this violence through the low/under prosecution rates of their abuses, thus maintaining the violability and vulnerability of these women. For more on this matter, see Escobar, Ferber, Crenshaw (1991), and Baca (2002).
117. Miranda, *Homegirls in the Public Sphere*, 83.
118. Murray, *Locas*, 144.
119. Méndez, "Decolonial Feminist *Movidas*," 76.
120. Murray, *Locas*, 19.
121. Murray, *Locas*, 35.
122. Freud, "Repression," 97, emphasis in original.
123. Freud, "Repression," 96.
124. Freud, "Repression," 96, emphasis in original.
125. Murray, *Locas*, 51.
126. Murray, *Locas*, 145.
127. Pérez, "Sexuality and Discourse," 161.

128. Murray, *Locas*, 86.
129. Murray, *Locas*, 86.

Chapter 4: (De)colonial Gay Locos, Disidentifications, and Counterpublics

1. Panfil, *The Gang's All Queer*, 2.
2. Although *Clicas* studies the cultural representations of gay men in heterosexual gangs, the lack of filmic or literary texts portraying gay gangs preempts this book from attending to gay men in gay gangs. For more on this subject, readers should see Panfil.
3. Muñoz, *Disidentifications*, 4.
4. Muñoz, *Disidentifications*, 11.
5. Olguín, *La Pinta*, 154.
6. Guerrero, *Framing Blackness*, 69–70.
7. Bogle, *Toms, Coons, Mammies, Mulattoes, and Bucks*, 175–176.
8. Lawrence, *Blaxploitation Films of the 1970s*, 19.
9. Lawrence, *Blaxploitation Films of the 1970s*, 19.
10. Olguín, *La Pinta*, 155.
11. Gunckel, "Gangs, Gone, Wild," 38.
12. Fregoso, *The Bronze Screen*, 133.
13. Fregoso, *The Bronze Screen*, 126.
14. Olguín, *La Pinta*, 161.
15. Olguín, *La Pinta*, 158.
16. Olguín, *La Pinta*, 170.
17. Fregoso, *The Bronze Screen*, 126.
18. Olguín, *La Pinta*, 170.
19. Córdova, "The Neoliberal Policy Regime," 56.
20. Ocampo, "Making Masculinity," 451.
21. McFarland, "Urban AlterNative Masculinity," 81.
22. Maldonado-Torres, "On the Coloniality of Being," 247–248; Pérez, "Sexuality and Discourse," 168.
23. Mirandé, *Hombres y Machos*, 77.
24. Mora, "Abjection and the Cinematic Cholo," 126.
25. Gardiner, "Masculinity, the Teasing of America," 1259.
26. Quoted in Butler, "Melancholy Gender," 166.
27. Butler, "Melancholy Gender," 168.
28. Butler, "Melancholy Gender," 169.
29. Butler, "Melancholy Gender," 168.
30. Lugones, "The Coloniality of Gender," 12.
31. Duggan, *The Twilight of Equality*, 50.
32. Butler, "Melancholy Gender," 168.
33. Cantú, "Entre Hombres/Between Men," 150.

34. Cantú, "Entre Hombres/Between Men," 150.
35. Cantú, "Entre Hombres/Between Men," 150.
36. Rodriguez, *Always Running*, 250.
37. Moore, *Going Down to the Barrio*, 90.
38. Moore, *Going Down to the Barrio*, 90.
39. Panfil, *The Gang's All Queer*, 87.
40. Panfil, *The Gang's All Queer*, 87.
41. Dudley, "MS13 in the Americas," 47.
42. Murray, *Locas*, 51.
43. Durán, "The Core Ideals," 110.
44. Durán, "The Core Ideals," 114.
45. Emphasis in original.
46. Muñoz, *Disidentifications*, 11.
47. Muñoz, *Disidentifications*, 5, emphasis in original.
48. Muñoz, *Disidentifications*, 108.
49. Butler, *Gender Trouble*, 201, emphasis in original.
50. Butler, *Gender Trouble*, 201.
51. In California Latina/o/x gang culture, the term "loco" references a person who epitomizes the idealized image of an incredibly hypermasculine and violent gang member.
52. Emphasis in original.
53. Rodríguez, "Queering the Homeboy Aesthetic," 128.
54. Pérez, *Rethinking Chicana/o and Latina/o Popular Culture*, 29, 12.
55. Rodríguez, "Queering the Homeboy Aesthetic," 131.
56. Rodríguez, "Queering the Homeboy Aesthetic," 133.
57. Rodríguez, "Queering the Homeboy Aesthetic," 133.
58. Rabinowitz, *They Must Be Represented*, 8–9.
59. Rabinowitz, *They Must Be Represented*, 9.
60. Reddy, "Home, Houses, Nonidentity," 368.
61. Reddy, "Home, Houses, Nonidentity," 368.
62. Rabinowitz, *They Must Be Represented*, 6.
63. Pedro Zamora was an openly gay Cuban American with AIDS who appeared on MTV's reality television show *The Real World* in 1994. During his time on this show, Zamora used the televisual platform to bring attention to HIV/AIDS and LGBTQ discrimination (Muñoz, *Disidentifications*, 152).
64. Muñoz, *Disidentifications*, 150.
65. Muñoz, *Disidentifications*, 146, emphasis in original.
66. Pérez, *Rethinking Chicana/o and Latina/o Popular Culture*, 29.
67. Lugones, "The Coloniality of Gender," 7.
68. Fregoso, *The Bronze Screen*, 134–135.
69. Fraser, "Rethinking the Public Sphere," 123.
70. Fraser, "Rethinking the Public Sphere," 116.

71. "American Me," https://www.boxofficemojo.com/release/rl2806220289/weekend.
72. Martinez, "Homeboy," http://www.homeboyfilms.com.
73. For a record of these screenings, see "Q-Sides"; Flynn; Danny Martinez; and "Screening of *Homeboy*."
74. Dinco, email message to author, February 13, 2016.
75. See Isaac; Mournian; Raymundo; and Sitz.
76. In the original: "hombres gay, sino también a los heterosexuales, para que los puedan entender"; Acevedo, "Pandilleros gay," https://www.univision.com/noticias/noticias-de-eeuu/pandilleros-gay-un-grupo-poco-conocido.
77. Addison, "QFilms Review," https://lbpost.com/news/lgbtq/qfilms-review-homeboy-unabashedly-explores-gay-latino-gang-members.
78. Valenzuela, "'Homeboy' Explores Gay Gang Members," https://www.presstelegram.com/2013/09/04/documentary-homeboy-explores-gay-gang-members-film-to-show-sunday-at-2013-qfilm-festival-in-long-beach.
79. As Ana Muñiz explains, "a gang injunction is a restraining order, not against an individual, but rather against an entire neighborhood. If subject to an injunction, alleged gang members are not allowed to engage in behavior that is otherwise legal, including congregating in groups of two or more and standing in public for more than five minutes" (5). Persons who disclose themselves as gang members in areas with gang injunctions risk the State legally curtailing their freedom, penalizing them, and incarcerating them for actions that a non-gang member can legally carry out.
80. "TomTom," comment on "New Documentary 'Homeboy' Explores Gay Gang Members," https://www.streetgangs.com/billboard/viewtopic.php?t=55386.
81. "Cliffard," comment on "New Documentary 'Homeboy' Explores Gay Gang Members," https://www.streetgangs.com/billboard/viewtopic.php?t=55386. Kody Scott, also known as Sanyika Shakur and "Monster," is a former member of a Los Angeles Crip gang who was incarcerated at San Quentin State Prison, Pelican Bay State Prison, and the California Institution for Men in Chino, California. After his release from prison, Scott was discovered dead at 57 in 2021 in Oceanside, CA, though no evidence of foul play was present (Brown, "'Monster' Kody Scott"). In 1993, he published an autobiography detailing his experiences as a gang member, *Monster: The Autobiography of an LA Gang Member*.
82. Muñoz, *Disidentifications*, 160.

Chapter 5: The Queer Utopian Futurity of Failed Gang Members

1. Readers may ponder how other post-2000 films, such as *Quinceañera*, *La Mission*, and *Moonlight*, that queer the homeboy or gang member, figure in

this chapter and relate to its exegesis of *On the Downlow*. All these films queer the homeboy/cholo aesthetic. They feature protagonists who, at least at one point, fail in the barrio or heteropatriarchal family—though, out of all the gay men in these films, Chiron of *Moonlight* perhaps approximates success the best. Still, only *Quinceañera* incorporates a gay protagonist who gangbangs: Carlos, a member of one of the local Echo Park gangs of Los Angeles. But because *Quinceañera* never explores Carlos's history, his presence, or his success or failure in his gang (or ever shows him with other gang members or participating in gang activity), that film does not factor into this book. For more on the queer politics of *Quinceañera* and films of the "queer homeboy" genre, see my article, "Queer Whiteness, the Chicana/o/x Family, and *El* Malinche in *Quinceañera*."
2. Muñoz, *Cruising Utopia*, 27.
3. Muñoz, *Cruising Utopia*, 173.
4. Halberstam, *Queer Art*, 89.
5. Edelman, *No Future*, 2, 3.
6. Edelman, *No Future*, 3.
7. Edelman, *No Future*, 3.
8. Quoted in Edelman, *No Future*, 112.
9. Edelman, *No Future*, 111, 112, emphasis in original.
10. Muñoz, *Cruising Utopia*, 94.
11. Muñoz, *Cruising Utopia*, 94.
12. Muñoz, *Cruising Utopia*, 94.
13. Muñoz, *Cruising Utopia*, 95.
14. Halberstam, *Queer Art*, 118.
15. Although Muñoz at times uses the terms "future" and "futurity" interchangeably, readers should not mistake them as always synonymous. In this chapter's analysis of *On the Downlow*, future accentuates fixity, a time that is not yet present but sure to occur, and that may not meet romanticized expectations of life beyond the present. Futurity accents potentiality, the array of future possibilities that have yet to, and may not, arrive. Moreover, as this chapter later explains, utopian futurity refers to the present, *affective* moments of idealizations, dreams, and visions of an idyllic future that one hopes will transpire.
16. Muñoz, *Cruising Utopia*, 1.
17. Muñoz, *Cruising Utopia*, 1.
18. Muñoz, *Cruising Utopia*, 11, 1.
19. Muñoz, *Cruising Utopia*, 174, 173.
20. Muñoz, *Cruising Utopia*, 35.
21. Halberstam, *Queer Art*, 3.
22. Halberstam, *Queer Art*, 3, 88.
23. Halberstam, *Queer Art*, 88.
24. Jones, "1964," https://www.chicagoganghistory.com/history/1964.

25. "The Latin Kings," https://www.justice.gov/entity-popup/file/432481#:~:text=Latin%20Kings%20associating%20with%20the,to%20be%2020%2C000%20to%2035%2C000.
26. "Latin King Manifesto," 4, http://archive.org/details/LatinKingsManifesto/page/n5/mode/2up.
27. O'Connor and Corrado, *Compliments of Chicagohoodz*, 281.
28. "Latin King Manifesto," 2, http://archive.org/details/LatinKingsManifesto/page/n5/mode/2up.
29. "Latin Kings Manifesto," 5, http://archive.org/details/LatinKingsManifesto/page/n5/mode/2up.
30. Quoted in Brown, *Gang Nation*, 139.
31. Amezcua, *Making Mexican Chicago*, 127.
32. Amezcua, *Making Mexican Chicago*, 127.
33. Jones, "1964," https://www.chicagoganghistory.com/history/1964. Today, Little Village now contains twenty-four chapters of the Latin Kings. For more on these gangs, see O'Connor and Corrado.
34. O'Connor and Corrado, *Compliments of Chicagohoodz*, 178.
35. O'Connor and Corrado, *Compliments of Chicagohoodz*, 178.
36. For more on his version of this event, see Ayala. David has always maintained his innocence of this crime and claims wrongful imprisonment.
37. González, "The Limits of Desire," 20.
38. González, "The Limits of Desire," 21, emphasis in original.
39. Mills, *The Racial Contract*, 41–42, emphasis in original.
40. For many racists, the logic of racing/spacing often pervades prison gang films that feature rape or other types of delinquent behavior. For instance, proponents of the racial contract might understand whites who rape in prison to be a result of a primarily black and Latina/o/x prison "spacing" whites.
41. Many post-2004 films that queer the homeboy or gang member also geographically orient hetero/homosexuality in a way that reproduces the racing and spacing elements of the racial contract. For more on this cinematic trope, see my article "Queering the Racial Contract."
42. Rodríguez, "The Architectures of Latino Sexuality," 85.
43. Rodríguez, "The Architectures of Latino Sexuality," 83.
44. Foucault, *Discipline and Punish*, 201.
45. Foucault, *Discipline and Punish*, 203.
46. Muñoz, *Cruising Utopia*, 11, 35.
47. Guidotti-Hernández, *Archiving Mexican Masculinities*, 3.
48. Muñoz, *Cruising Utopia*, 174.
49. Anzaldúa, *Borderlands/La Frontera*, 44.
50. Muñoz, *Cruising Utopia*, 9, 173.
51. Lugones, "The Coloniality of Gender," 12.
52. Muñoz, *Cruising Utopia*, 173.

Afterword: The Immigrant/Gang Member Binary in Latina/o/x Literature and Film

1. For more on la Bestia, see Óscar Martínez.
2. Gross, "Trump Uses MS-13," https://www.npr.org/2018/02/15/585937834/trump-uses-ms-13-to-sell-draconian-overhauls-of-border-issues-journalist-says.
3. Escobar, *Captivity Beyond Prisons*, 44.
4. Deckard et al., "Controlling Images," 584.
5. Leo Chavez, *The Latino Threat*, 45.
6. Patterson, *Slavery and Social Death*, 46.
7. Cacho, *Social Death*, 17, emphasis in original.
8. Baca, *When I Walk through That Door, I Am*, 5.
9. Rosas, *Barrio Libre*, 83. See Rosas and Saldaña-Portillo for superb analyses of how Latin American gang members extort and harm immigrants and chúntaros in Mexico and Central America.
10. Escobar, *Captivity Beyond Prisons*, 14, 13.
11. Escobar, *Captivity Beyond Prisons*, 3.
12. Escobar, *Captivity Beyond Prisons*, 62, 70.
13. Escobar, *Captivity Beyond Prisons*, 15, 95.
14. Ward, *Gangsters without Borders*, 1.
15. Wheeler, *State of War*, 31.
16. Danner, *The Massacre at El Mozote*, 132, emphasis in original.
17. Wheeler, *State of War*, 31.
18. For more on El Mozote Massacre, see Danner.
19. Ward, *Gangsters without Borders*, 54.
20. For more on this history, see Al Valdez; Ward; Wheeler; and Martínez D'Aubuisson's *A Year Inside MS-13*.
21. Wheeler, *State of War*, 41.
22. Martínez D'Aubuisson, *A Year Inside*, 7.
23. Campo-Flores, "The Most Dangerous Gang in America," 22. Paz provided the FBI with intel about Mara Salvatrucha, famously teaching them the language for MS stacking in a recorded video now widely available online, in exchange for clemency and assistance in leaving the gang. Though the FBI helped Paz leave MS and placed her in witness protection, Paz could not resist the allure of gang life, electing to return to her old clica. Eventually, MS discovered her collaboration with the FBI and stabbed Brenda, pregnant at the time, to death at the Shenandoah River in Virginia. For more on Paz, see Logan.
24. Ward, *Gangsters without Borders*, 104–105; Wolf, "Mara Salvatrucha," 77.
25. Martínez D'Aubuisson, *A Year Inside*, 39–40; Ward, *Gangsters without Borders*, 100.
26. Dudley, "MS13 in the Americas," 26.

27. Ward, *Gangsters without Borders*, 97.
28. Zamora, *Unaccompanied*, 9.
29. Zamora, *Unaccompanied*, 9.
30. Zamora, *Unaccompanied*, 9, emphasis in original.
31. Guidotti-Hernández, *Archiving Mexican Masculinities*, 5.
32. Zamora, *Unaccompanied*, 11, emphasis in original.
33. Wheeler, *State of War*, 61, 76.
34. Quoted in Wheeler, *State of War*, 53.
35. For more detail on Mano Dura legislation, see Wolf's *Mano Dura*.
36. Wolf, "Mara Salvatrucha," 78.
37. Mignolo and Walsh, *On Decoloniality*, 114.
38. Lugones, "The Coloniality of Gender," 12.

REFERENCES

Acevedo, Enrique. "Pandilleros gay, un grupo poco conocido." *Univision*, October 3, 2013. https://www.univision.com/noticias/noticias-de-eeuu/pandilleros-gay-un-grupo-poco-conocido.

Acuña, Rodolfo F. *Occupied America: The Chicano's Struggle Toward Liberation*. San Francisco: Canfield Press, 1972.

Acuña, Rodolfo F. *Occupied America: A History of Chicanos*. 2nd ed. New York: Harper & Row Publishers, 1981.

Addison, Brian. "QFilms Review: 'Homeboy' Unabashedly Explores Gay Latino Gang Members." *Long Beach Post*, August 22, 2013. https://lbpost.com/news/lgbtq/qfilms-review-homeboy-unabashedly-explores-gay-latino-gang-members.

Alcalde, Cristina M. "What It Means to be a Man? Violence and Homophobia in Latino Masculinities On and Off Screen." *Journal of Popular Culture* 47, no. 3 (2014): 537–553.

Aldama, Arturo J. "Decolonizing Predatory Masculinities in *Breaking Bad* and *Mosquita y Mari*." In *Decolonizing Latinx Masculinities*, edited by Arturo J. Aldama and Frederick Luis Aldama, 117–130. Tucson: University of Arizona Press, 2020.

Aldama, Frederick Luis. "Penalizing Chicano/a Bodies in Edward J. Olmos's *American Me*." In *Decolonial Voices: Chicana and Chicano Cultural Studies in the 21st Century*, edited by Arturo J. Aldama and Naomi H. Quiñonez, 79–97. Bloomington: Indiana University Press, 2002.

Aldama, Frederick Luis, and Arturo J. Aldama. Introduction to *Decolonizing Latinx Masculinities*, edited by Arturo J. Aldama and Frederick Luis Aldama, 3–20. Tucson: University of Arizona Press, 2020.

Almaguer, Tomás. "Chicano Men: A Cartography of Homosexual Identity and Behavior." *Differences: A Journal of Feminist Cultural Studies* 3, no. 2 (1991): 75–100.

Almaguer, Tomás. "Ideological Distortions in Recent Chicano Historiography: The Internal Model and Chicano Historical Interpretation." *Aztlán: A Journal of Chicano Studies* 18, no. 1 (1989): 7–28.

Almaguer, Tomás. "Toward the Study of Chicano Colonialism." *Aztlán: A Journal of Chicano Studies* 2, no. 1 (1971): 7–21.

Alvarez, Luis. *The Power of the Zoot: Youth Culture and Resistance during World War II*. Berkeley: University of California Press, 2009.

"American Me." *Box Office Mojo*. https://www.boxofficemojo.com/release/rl2806220289/weekend.

Amezcua, Mike. *Making Mexican Chicago*. Chicago: University of Chicago Press, 2022.

Angle, Sharron. "The Wave." *YouTube*. October 25, 2010. Video, :30 https://www.youtube.com/watch?v=tIkNAA2y4I4.

Anzaldúa, Gloria. *Borderlands/La Frontera: The New Mestiza*. 25th Anniversary ed. San Francisco: Aunt Lute Books, 1987.

Anzaldúa, Gloria, and Cherríe Moraga. *This Bridge Called My Back: Writings by Radical Women of Color*. 4th ed. Albany: SUNY Press, 2015.

Arciniega, G. M., Thomas C. Anderson, Zoila G. Tovar-Blank, and Terence J. G. Tracey. "Towards a Fuller Conception of Machismo: Development of a Traditional Machismo and Caballerismo Scale." *Journal of Counseling Psychology* 55, no. 1 (2008): 19–33.

Ayala, David. "Help Us Put an End to David's Wrongful Conviction." *Legal Fund for David Ayala*. https://legalfundfordavidayala.com.

Baca, Jimmy Santiago. *A Place to Stand*. New York: Grove Press, 2002.

Baca, Jimmy Santiago. *When I Walk through That Door, I Am: An Immigrant Mother's Quest*. Boston: Beacon Press, 2019.

Barrera, Mario. *Race and Class in the Southwest: A Theory of Racial Inequality*. South Bend: University of Notre Dame Press, 1979.

Barrera, Mario, Carlos Muñoz, and Charles Ornelas. "The Barrio as Internal Colony." *People and Politics in Urban Society* 6 (1972): 465–498.

Bhabha, Homi K. *The Location of Culture*. New York: Routledge, 1994.

Blackwell, Maylei. *¡Chicana Power! Contested Histories of Feminism in the Chicano Movement*. Austin: University of Texas Press, 2011.

Bogle, Donald. *Toms, Coons, Mammies, Mulattoes, and Bucks: An Interpretive History of Blacks in American Films*. New York: Viking Press, 1973.

Breen, Justin. "Chicago Gangs Used to Wear Varsity-Style Sweaters with Patches." *The Block Club*, March 31, 2017. https://www.dnainfo.com/chicago/20170329/englewood/chicago-gangs-knitted-sweaters-varsity-patches.

Brown, Kailyn. "'Monster' Kody Scott, Former L.A. Gang Member who Became a Bestselling Author, Found Dead at 57." *Los Angeles Times*, June 15, 2021. https://www.latimes.com/california/story/2021-06-15/monster-kody-scott-former-gang-member-best-selling-author-found-dead.

Brown, Monica. *Gang Nation: Delinquent Citizens in Puerto Rican, Chicano, and Chicana Narratives*. Minneapolis: University of Minnesota Press, 2002.

Bruneau, Thomas C. Introduction to *Maras: Gang Violence and Security in Central America*, edited by Thomas C. Bruneau, Lucía Dammert, and Elizabeth Skinner, 1–19. Austin: University of Texas Press, 2011.

Butler, Judith. *Gender Trouble: Feminism and the Subversion of Identity*. New York: Routledge, 1990.

Butler, Judith. "Melancholy Gender—Refused Identification." *Psychoanalytic Dialogues* 5, no. 2 (1995): 165–180.

Cacho, Lisa Marie. *Social Death: Racialized Rightlessness and the Criminalization of the Unprotected*. New York: New York University Press, 2012.

Campbell, Anne. *The Girls in the Gang*. 2nd ed. Cambridge: Blackwell Publishers, 1992.

Campo-Flores, Arian. "The Most Dangerous Gang in America." *Newsweek*, March 2005, 22–25.

Cantú, Lionel. "Entre Hombres/Between Men: Latino Masculinities and Homosexualities." In *Gay Latino Studies: A Critical Reader*, edited by Michael Hames-García and Ernesto Javier Martínez, 147–167. Durham: Duke University Press, 2011.

Cartwright, Mark. "Toltec Civilization." In *Ancient History Encyclopedia*. 2018. https://www.ancient.eu/Toltec_Civilization.

Casas, Bartolomé de las. "An Account, Much Abbreviated, of the Destruction of the Indies." In *The Norton Anthology of American Literature: Beginnings to 1820*, edited by Robert S. Levine. 9th ed., 68–71. New York: W. W. Norton & Company, 2017.

Castillo, Ana. *My Father Was a Toltec*. Albany: Anchor Books, 1995.

Chavez, Leo R. *The Latino Threat: Constructing Immigrants, Citizens, and the Nation*. Stanford: Stanford University Press, 2008.

Clark, Wahida. *Thugs and the Women Who Love Them*. Wahida Clark Publishing, 2012.

Clarke, John, Stuart Hall, Tony Jefferson, and Brian Roberts. "Subcultures, Cultures, and Class." In *Resistance Through Rituals: Youth Subcultures in Post-War Britain*, edited by Stuart Hall and Tony Jefferson, 1–79. New York: Hutchinson & Co., 1976.

Cleaver, Eldridge. *Soul on Ice*. New York: Delta, 1968.

Cliffard. Comment on "New Documentary 'Homeboy' Explores Gay Gang Members." *Streetgangs.com*, September 14, 2013. https://www.streetgangs.com/billboard/viewtopic.php?t=55386.

Cohen, Albert K. *Delinquent Boys: The Culture of the Gang*. New York: Routledge & Kegan Paul, 1956.

Cohen, Cathy J. "Punks, Bulldaggers, and Welfare Queens: The Radical Potential of Queer Politics?" *GLQ: A Journal of Lesbian and Gay Studies* 3, no. 4 (1997): 437–465.

Collins, Patricia Hill. *Black Feminist Thought: Knowledge, Consciousness, and the Politics of Empowerment*. 1st ed. New York: Routledge, 2009.
Combahee River Collective. "The Combahee River Collective Statement." In *How We Get Free: Black Feminism and the Combahee River Collective*, edited by Keeanga-Yamahtta Taylor, 15–27. Chicago: Haymarket Books, 2017.
Connell, Raewyn. *Gender and Power: Society, the Person, and Sexual Politics*. Stanford: Stanford University Press, 1987.
Córdova, Teresa. "The Neoliberal Policy Regime and Implications of Latino Studies Scholarship." *Aztlán: A Journal of Chicano Studies* 41, no. 1 (2016): 55–83.
Crenshaw, Kimberlé. "Demarginalizing the Intersection of Race and Sex: A Black Feminist Critique of Antidiscrimination Doctrine, Feminist Theory and Antiracist Politics." *University of Chicago Legal Forum*, no. 1 (1989): 139–167.
Crenshaw, Kimberlé. "Mapping the Margins: Intersectionality, Identity Politics, and Violence against Women of Color." *Stanford Law Review* 43, no. 6 (1991): 1241–1299.
Cruz, Ariane. *The Color of Kink: Black Women, BDSM, and Pornography*. New York: New York University Press, 2016.
Cuevas, T. Jackie. "Fighting the Good Fight: Grappling with Queerness, Masculinities, and Violence in Contemporary Latinx Literature and Film." In *Decolonizing Latinx Masculinities*, edited by Arturo J. Aldama and Frederick Luis Aldama, 131–150. Tucson: University of Arizona Press, 2020.
Cuevas, T. Jackie. *Post-Borderlandia: Chicana Literature and Gender Variant Critique*. New Brunswick: Rutgers University Press, 2018.
Danner, Mark. *The Massacre at El Mozote*. New York: Vintage Books, 1994.
Davis, Angela Y. *Are Prisons Obsolete?* New York: Seven Stories Press, 2003.
Dean, Tim, and Christopher Lane. "Homosexuality and Psychoanalysis: An Introduction." In *Homosexuality and Psychoanalysis*, edited by Tim Dean and Christopher Lane, 3–42. Chicago: University of Chicago Press, 2001.
Deckard, Natalie Delia, Irene Browne, Cassaundra Rodriguez, Marisela Martinez-Cola, and Sofia Gonzalez Leal. "Controlling Images of Immigration in the Mainstream Black Press: The Discursive Power of the 'Illegal Latino.'" *Latino Studies* 18, no. 4 (2020): 581–602.
Delgado, Richard. "Legal Storytelling: Storytelling for Oppositionists and Others: A Plea for Narrative." *Michigan Law Review* 87 (1989): 2411–2441.
Dudley, Steven. "MS13 in the Americas: How the World's Most Notorious Gang Defies Logic, Resists Destruction." *InSight Crime*, 2018. https://insightcrime.org/wp-content/uploads/2018/02/MS13-in-the-Americas-InSight-Crime-English-3.pdf.
Duggan, Lisa. *The Twilight of Equality? Neoliberalism, Cultural Politics, and the Attack on Democracy*. Boston: Beacon Press, 2003.
Durán, Miguel. *Don't Spit on My Corner*. Houston: Arte Público Press, 1992.

Durán, Robert J. "The Core Ideals of the Mexican American Gang: Living the Presentation of Defiance." *Aztlán: A Journal of Chicano Studies* 34, no. 2 (2009): 99–134.
Ebert, Roger. "American Me." *RogerEbert.com*, March 13, 1992. https://www.rogerebert.com/reviews/american-me-1992.
Edelman, Lee. *No Future: Queer Theory and the Death Drive*. Durham: Duke University Press, 2004.
Ellison, Ralph. *Invisible Man*. 2nd Vintage International ed. New York: Vintage Books, 1995.
Escobar, Martha D. *Captivity Beyond Prisons*. Austin: University of Texas Press, 2016.
Estill, Adriana. "In Father's Footsteps: Bad Girls in Ana Castillo's and Sandra Cisneros's Poetry." *Confluencia* 16, no. 2 (2001): 46–60.
Fanon, Frantz. *Black Skin, White Masks*. New York: Grove Press, 1952.
Fanon, Frantz. *The Wretched of the Earth*. New York: Grove Press, 1963.
Farfán-Santos, Elizabeth. "The Politics of Resilience and Resistance: Health Care Access and Undocumented Mexican Motherhood in the United States." *Latino Studies* 17, no. 1 (2019): 67–85.
Ferber, Abby L. "The Construction of Black Masculinity: White Supremacy Now and Then." *Journal of Sport & Social Issues* 31, no. 1 (2007): 11–24.
Flynn, Jimmy. "First Annual Queer Film Festival Premieres." *The Santa Clara*, May 14, 2015. https://www.thesantaclara.org/blog/first-annual-queer-film-festival-premieres.
Foucault, Michel. *Discipline and Punish: The Birth of the Prison*. Translated by Alan Sheridan. 2nd ed. New York: Vintage Books, 1995.
Foucault, Michel. *Society Must Be Defended: Lectures at the College de France 1975–1976*. Translated by David Macey. New York: Picador, 1997.
Franco, Jean. "Beyond Ethnocentrism: Gender, Power, and the Third-World Intelligentsia." *Marxism and the Interpretation of Culture*, edited by Cary Nelson and Lawrence Grossberg, 503–515. Champaign: University of Illinois Press, 1988.
Franklin, Bruce H. *Prison Literature in America: The Victim as Criminal and Artist*. New York: Oxford University Press, 1989.
Fraser, Nancy. "Rethinking the Public Sphere: A Contribution to the Critique of Actually Existing Democracy." *Social Text* 25–26 (1990): 56–80.
Freeman, Wayne. "'Noizy Minorityz': White Republicans Trapped in the Cypher." In *Decolonizing Latinx Masculinities*, edited by Arturo J. Aldama and Frederick Luis Aldama, 51–64. Tucson: University of Arizona Press, 2020.
Fregoso, Rosa Linda. *The Bronze Screen: Chicana and Chicano Film Culture*. Minneapolis: University of Minnesota Press, 1993.
Fregoso, Rosa Linda. "Re-Imagining Chicana Urban Identities in the Public Sphere, Cool Chuca Style." In *Between Woman and Nation: Nationalisms,*

Transnational Feminisms, and the State, edited by Caren Kaplan, Norma Alarcón, and Minoo Moallem, 72–91. Durham: Duke University Press, 1999.

Freud, Sigmund. "Repression." In *General Psychological Theory: Papers on Metapsychology*, 95–107. New York: Touchstone, 2008.

Galarte, Francisco J. *Brown Trans Figurations: Rethinking Race, Gender, and Sexuality in Chicanx/Latinx Studies*. Austin: University of Texas Press, 2021.

Galván, Lorena. "The Chola Loca in Landscapes of Struggle: Breaking Silence in the Works of Helena María Viramontes and Yxta Maya Murray." PhD diss., University of New Mexico, 2015.

García, Alma. "Studying Chicanas: Bringing Women into the Frame of Chicano Studies." In *Chicana Voices: Intersections of Class, Race, and Gender*, edited by Teresa Córdova, Norma Cantú, Gilberto Cardenas, Juan García, and Christine M. Sierra, 19–29. Houston: National Association for Chicano Studies, 1990.

García, Frank. "*Entre Maricones y Locos*: Disidentifications, Counterpublics, and Dino Dinco's *Homeboy*." *MELUS: Multi-Ethnic Literature of the United States* 44, no. 1 (2019): 132–159.

García, Frank. "Queer Whiteness, the Chicana/o/x Family, and *El* Malinche in *Quinceañera*." *Journal of Popular Culture* 56, no. 1 (2023): 150–169.

García, Frank. "Queering the Racial Contract: The Exiled Homeboy and Geographic Orientation in *La Mission*." *Quarterly Review of Film and Video* 39, no. 5 (2022): 1158–1181.

Gardiner, Judith Kegan. "Masculinity, the Teening of America, and Emphatic Targeting." *Signs: A Journal of Women in Culture and Society* 25, no. 4 (2000): 1257–1261.

Gaspar de Alba, Alicia. "Poor Brown Female: The Miller's Compensations for 'Free' Trade." In *Making a Killing: Femicide, Free Trade, and La Frontera*, edited by Alicia Gaspar de Alba and Georgina Guzmán, 63–93. Austin: University of Texas Press, 2010.

Gerber, Marisa. "With Gentrification, Echo Park Gang Members Move Outside their Turf." *Los Angeles Times*, February 3, 2014. https://www.latimes.com/local/la-xpm-2014-feb-03-la-me-echo-park-gang-20140126-story.html.

Gifford, Justin. *Pimping Fictions: African American Crime Literature and the Untold Story of Black Pulp Publishing*. Philadelphia: Temple University Press, 2013.

González, Bill Johnson. "The Limits of Desire: *On the Downlow* and Queer Chicago Film." *GLQ: A Journal of Lesbian and Gay Studies* 20, nos. 1–2 (2014): 13–39.

González, Gilbert G. "A Critique of the Internal Colony Model." *Latin American Perspectives* 1, no. 1 (1974): 154–161.

"Greaser Gangs: The Start of Old School White Gangs." *Kulture Vulturez*. https://www.kulturevulturez.com/old-school-white-greaser-gangs.

Gross, Terry. "Trump Uses MS-13 To 'Sell Draconian Overhauls Of Border Issues.'" *National Public Radio*, February 15, 2018. https://www.npr.org/2018/02/15/585937834/trump-uses-ms-13-to-sell-draconian-overhauls-of-border-issues-journalist-says.

Guerrero, Ed. *Framing Blackness: The African American Image in Film*. Philadelphia: Temple University Press, 1993.

Guidotti-Hernández, Nicole M. *Archiving Mexican Masculinities in Diaspora*. Durham: Duke University Press, 2021.

Gunckel, Colin. "'Gangs Gone Wild': Low-Budget Gang Documentaries and the Aesthetics of Exploitation." *The Velvet Light Trap* 60 (2007): 37–46.

Gunderson, Erica. "Sweaters and Other Strange Ephemera of Chicago's 1970s Street Gangs." *Window to the World*, May 18, 2017. https://news.wttw.com/2017/05/18/sweaters-and-other-strange-ephemera-chicago-s-1970s-street-gangs.

Hagedorn, John M. *People and Folks: Gangs, Crime, and the Underclass in a Rustbelt City*. Chicago: Lake View Press, 1988.

Hagedorn, John M. *The World of Gangs: Armed Young Men and Gangsta Culture*. Minneapolis: University of Minnesota Press, 2008.

Halberstam, Jack. *The Queer Art of Failure*. Durham: Duke University Press, 2011.

Halberstam, Judith [Jack]. *Female Masculinity*. Durham: Duke University Press, 1998.

Hall, Stuart. "Absolute Beginnings: Reflections on the Secondary Modern Generation." In *Stuart Hall: Selected Writings on Race and Difference*, edited by Paul Gilroy and Ruth Wilson Gilmore, 23–41. Durham: Duke University Press, 2021.

Hall, Stuart. "Black Crime, Black Proletariat." In *Stuart Hall: Selected Writings on Marxism*, edited by Gregor McLennan, 199–226. Durham: Duke University Press, 2021.

Hall, Stuart. "Black Men, White Media." In *Stuart Hall: Selected Writings on Race and Difference*, edited by Paul Gilroy and Ruth Wilson Gilmore, 51–55. Durham: Duke University Press, 2021.

Hames-García, Michael. *Fugitive Thought: Prison Movements, Race, and the Meaning of Justice*. Minneapolis: University of Minnesota Press, 2004.

Harrington, Carol. "What Is 'Toxic Masculinity' and Why Does it Matter?" *Men and Masculinities* 24, no. 2 (2021): 345–352.

Hebdige, Dick. *Subculture: The Meaning of Style*. New York: Routledge, 1979.

Hernández, Ellie. "*Fea, Firme y Formal*: Decolonizing Latinx Female Masculinity." In *Decolonizing Latinx Masculinities*, edited by Arturo J. Aldama and Frederick Luis Aldama, 168–184. Tucson: University of Arizona Press, 2020.

Hernández, Jillian. *Aesthetics of Excess: The Art and Politics of Black and Latina Embodiment*. Durham: Duke University Press, 2020.

Ibarraran-Bigalondo, Amaia. "Chicano Gangs/Chicana Girls: Surviving the 'Wild Barrio.'" *Miscelánea: A Journal of English and American Studies* 48 (2013): 45–59.

Ibarraran-Bigalondo, Amaia. "Wolves, Sheep, and *Vatos Locos*: Reflections of Gang Activity in Chicano Literature." *Journal of English Studies* 4 (2003–2004): 107–113.

Isaac, Tim. "Homeboy Trailer—Being Gay Inside a Latino Gang." *Big Gay Picture Show*, September 18, 2012. https://www.biggaypictureshow.com/bgps/2012/09/homeboy-trailer-being-gay-inside-a-latino-gang.

Johnson, Dominique. "Taking Over the School: Student Gangs as a Strategy for Dealing with Homophobic Bullying in an Urban Public School District." *Journal of Gay & Lesbian Social Services* 9, nos. 3–4 (2007): 87–104.

Jones, Zach. "1964." *Chicago Gang History*. https://www.chicagoganghistory.com/history/1964.

Kass, John. "Gangs that Came to Rule in Seats of Power." *Chicago Tribune*, June 22, 2012. https://www.chicagotribune.com/news/ct-xpm-2012-06-22-ct-met-kass-0622-20120622-story.html.

Kelley, Robin D. G. Introduction to *Discourse on Colonialism*, 7–28. New York: Monthly Review Press, 2000.

Klein, Malcolm. *The American Street Gang: Its Nature, Prevalence, and Control*. New York: Oxford University Press, 1995.

Klein, Malcolm. *Street Gangs and Street Workers*. Englewood Cliffs: Prentice-Hall, 1971.

Larson, Thomas. "The Adult Boys of Rancho Peñasquitos." *ThomasLarson.com*, December 7, 2000. https://www.thomaslarson.com/publications/san-diego-reader/129-adult-boys.html.

"The Latin Kings." *The United States Department of Justice*. https://www.justice.gov/entity-popup/file/432481#:~:text=Latin%20Kings%20associating%20with%20the,to%20be%2020%2C000%20to%2035%2C000.

"Latin Kings Manifesto." *Internet Archive*, June 19, 2008. http://archive.org/details/LatinKingsManifesto/page/n1/mode/2up.

Lawrence, Novotny. *Blaxploitation Films of the 1970s: Blackness and Genre*. New York: Routledge, 2008.

Lawrence III, Charles R. "If He Hollers Let Him Go: Regulating Racist Speech on Campus." In *Words That Wound: Critical Race Theory, Assaultive Speech, and the First Amendment*, edited by Mari Matsuda, Charles R. Lawrence III, Richard Delgado, and Kimberlé Williams Crenshaw, 53–88. New York: Routledge, 2018.

Lipsitz, George. "Con Safos: Can Cultural Studies Read the Writing on the Wall?" In *The Chicana/o Cultural Studies Reader*, edited by Angie Chabram-Dernersesian, 47–60. New York: Routledge, 2006.

Logan, Samuel. *This Is for the Mara Salvatrucha: Inside MS-13, America's Most Violent Gang*. Westport: Hyperion, 2009.

Lugones, María. "The Coloniality of Gender." *Worlds & Knowledges Otherwise* 2, no. 2 (2008): 1–17.
Lugones, María. "Toward a Decolonial Feminism." *Hypatia* 25, no. 4 (2010): 742–759.
Luibhéid, Eithne, and Lionel Cantú Jr. *Queer Migrations: Sexuality, U.S. Citizenship, and Border Crossings.* Minneapolis: University of Minnesota Press, 2005.
Maldonado-Torres, Nelson. "On the Coloniality of Being: Contributions to the Development of a Concept." *Cultural Studies* 21, nos. 2–3 (2007): 240–270.
Martinez, Danny. "Homeboy." *Homeboyfilms.* http://www.homeboyfilms.com.
Martínez, Ernesto Javier. "Shifting the Site of Queer Enunciation: Manuel Muñoz and the Politics of Form." In *Gay Latino Studies: A Critical Reader,* edited by Michael Hames-García and Ernesto Javier Martínez, 226–249. Durham: Duke University Press, 2011.
Martínez, Óscar. *The Beast: Riding the Rails and Dodging Narcos on the Migrant Trail.* New York: Verso, 2014.
Martínez D'Aubuisson, Juan José. "Así viven y mueren las mujeres pandilleras en El Salvador." *Revista Factum,* March 11, 2016. https://www.revistafactum.com/asi-viven-y-mueren-las-mujeres-pandilleras-en-el-salvador.
Martínez D'Aubuisson, Juan José. *A Year Inside MS-13: See, Hear, and Shut Up.* Translated by Natascha Uhlmann. New York: OR Books, 2019.
Maxson, Cheryl L., Arlen Egley Jr., Jody Miller, and Malcolm W. Klein. *The Modern Gang Reader.* 4th ed. New York: Oxford University Press, 2013.
May, Vivian M. *Pursuing Intersectionality, Unsettling Dominant Imaginaries.* New York: Routledge, 2015.
McFarland, Pancho. "Urban AlterNative Masculinity: Men, Land, and Re-Indigenization in Black Chicago's Food Autonomy Movement." In *Decolonizing Latinx Masculinities,* edited by Arturo J. Aldama and Frederick Luis Aldama, 80–93. Tucson: University of Arizona Press, 2020.
Méndez, Xhercis. "Decolonial Feminist *Movidas*: A Caribeña (Re)thinks 'Privilege,' the Wages of Gender, and Building Complex Coalitions." In *Theories of the Flesh,* edited by Andrea J. Pitts, Mariana Ortega, and José Medina, 74–93. New York: Oxford University Press, 2020.
Mendoza-Denton, Norma. *Homegirls: Language and Cultural Practice among Latina Youth Gangs.* Malden: Blackwell Publishing, 2008.
Metcalf, Josephine. *The Culture and Politics of Contemporary Street Gang Memoirs.* Jackson: University Press of Mississippi, 2012.
Mignolo, Walter D. *The Darker Side of Western Modernity: Global Futures, Decolonial Options.* Durham: Duke University Press, 2011.
Mignolo, Walter D., and Catherine E. Walsh. *On Decoloniality: Concepts, Analytics, Praxis.* Durham: Duke University Press, 2018.
Miller, Warren. *The Cool World.* Boston: Little Brown, 1967.
Mills, Charles. *The Racial Contract.* Ithaca: Cornell University Press, 1997.

Miranda, Marie "Keta." *Homegirls in the Public Sphere*. Austin: University of Texas Press, 2003.

Mirandé, Alfredo. *Gringo Justice*. South Bend: University of Notre Dame Press, 1987.

Mirandé, Alfredo. *Hombres y Machos: Masculinity and Latino Culture*. Boulder: Westview Press, 1977.

Moore, Joan W. *Going Down to the Barrio: Homeboys and Homegirls in Change*. Philadelphia: Temple University Press, 1991.

Moore, Joan W., and John Hagedorn. "Female Gangs: A Focus on Research." *Office of Juvenile Justice and Delinquency Prevention* (2001): 1–11.

Mora, Richard. "Abjection and the Cinematic Cholo: The Chicano Gang Stereotype in Sociohistoric Context." *THYMOS: Journal of Boyhood Studies* 5, no. 2 (2011): 124–137.

Moraga, Cherríe. *Loving in the War Years: Lo que nunca pasó por sus labios*. Boston: South End Press, 1983.

Mournian, Tomas. "HOMEBOY: Immigrants, Prisoners, and Gay Gangbangers at Outfest 2012." *Huffington Post*, July 7, 2012. https://www.huffpost.com/entry/homeboys-hot-gay-gang-ban_b_1658080?utm_hp_ref=moviefone&ir=Moviefone.

Muñiz, Ana. *Police, Power, and the Production of Racial Boundaries*. New Brunswick: Rutgers University Press, 2015.

Muñoz, José Esteban. *Cruising Utopia: The Then and There of Queer Futurity*. New York: New York University Press, 2009.

Muñoz, José Esteban. *Disidentifications: Queers of Color and the Performance of Politics*. Minneapolis: University of Minnesota Press, 1999.

Murray, Yxta Maya. *Locas*. New York: Grove Press, 1998.

Navarro, José Alfredo. "Machos y Malinchistas: Chicano/Latino Gang Narratives, Masculinity, & Affect." PhD diss., University of Southern California, 2012.

Navarro, José Alfredo. "Revisiting the Boulevard: The Gender & Sexual Politics of Michael Pressman's *Boulevard Nights*." *Journal of Popular Culture* 50, no. 4 (2017): 761–777.

Newman, Kathleen. "Reterritorialization in Recent Chicano Cinema: Edward James Olmos's *American Me* (1992)." In *The Ethnic Eye: Latino Media Arts*, edited by Chon A. Noriega and Ana M. López, 95–106. Minneapolis: University of Minnesota Press, 1996.

Nixon, Rob. *Slow Violence and the Environmentalism of the Poor*. Cambridge: Harvard University Press, 2011.

Ocampo, Anthony C. "Making Masculinity: Negotiations of Gender Presentation Among Latino Gay Men." *Latino Studies* 10, no. 4 (2012): 448–72.

O'Connor, Anne-Marie, and Tina Daunt. "The Secret Society Among Lawmen." *Los Angeles Times*, March 24, 1992. https://www.latimes.com/archives/la-xpm-1999-mar-24-mn-20461-story.html.

O'Connor, James, and Damen Corrado. *Compliments of Chicagohoodz: Chicago Street Gang Art & Culture*. Port Townsend: Feral House, 2019.
Olguín, B. V. *La Pinta: Chicana/o Prisoner Literature, Culture, and Politics*. Austin: University of Texas Press, 2010.
Omi, Michael, and Howard Winant. *Racial Formation in the United States*. 3rd ed. New York: Routledge, 2015.
Ortega, Mariana. "Decolonial Woes and Practices of Un-Knowing." *Journal of Speculative Philosophy* 31, no. 3 (2017): 504–516.
Oyěwùmí, Oyèrónké. *The Invention of Women: Making an African Sense of Western Gender Discourses*. Minneapolis: University of Minnesota Press, 1997.
Pacyga, Dominic A. "Bridgeport." *Encyclopedia of Chicago*. 2005. http://encyclopedia.chicagohistory.org/pages/165.html.
Padilla, Felix M. *The Gang as an American Enterprise*. New Brunswick: Rutgers University Press, 1992.
Panfil, Vanessa R. *The Gang's All Queer: The Lives of Gay Gang Members*. New York: New York University Press, 2017.
Paredes, Américo. *With His Pistol in His Hand: A Border Ballad and Its Hero*. Austin: University of Texas Press, 1958.
Paredes, Raymund A. "The Evolution of Daughter-Father Relationships in Mexican-American Culture." In *Daughters and Fathers*, edited by Lynda E. Boose and Betty S. Flowers, 136–156. Baltimore: John Hopkins University Press, 1989.
Patterson, Orlando. *Slavery and Social Death: A Comparative Study*. Cambridge: Harvard University Press, 2018.
Paz, Octavio. *The Labyrinth of Solitude: Life and Thought in Mexico*. Translated by Lysander Kemp. New York: Grove Press, 1961.
Pérez, Daniel Enrique. *Rethinking Chicana/o and Latina/o Popular Culture*. New York: Palgrave Macmillan, 2009.
Pérez, Emma. *The Decolonial Imaginary: Writing Chicanas into History*. Bloomington: Indiana University Press, 1999.
Pérez, Emma. "Sexuality and Discourse: Notes from a Chicana Survivor." In *Chicana Lesbians: The Girls Our Mothers Warned Us About*, edited by Carla Trujillo, 159–184. Berkeley: Third Woman Press, 1991.
Pérez-Torres, Rafael. *Movements in Chicano Poetry*. New York: Cambridge University Press, 1995.
Peterson, Dana. "Girlfriends, Gun-Holders, and Ghetto-Rats? Moving Beyond Narrow Views of Girls in Gangs." In *Delinquent Girls: Contexts, Relationships, and Adaptation*, edited by Shari Miller, Leslie D. Leve, and Patricia K. Kerig, 71–84. New York: Springer, 2012.
Pinderhughes, Charles. "Toward a New Theory of Internal Colonialism." *Socialism and Democracy* 25, no. 1 (2011): 235–56.
"The Q-Sides." *Galería de la Raza*. http://www.galeriadelaraza.org/eng/news/index.php?op=read&id=826&type=3.

Quijano, Aníbal. "Colonialidad, modernidad/racialidad." *Peru Indígena* 13, no. 29 (1991): 11–29.
Quiñonez, Ernesto. *Bodega Dreams*. New York: Vintage Books, 2000.
Rabinowitz, Paula. *They Must Be Represented: The Politics of Documentary*. New York: Verso, 1994.
Ramírez, Catherine S. *The Woman in the Zoot Suit: Gender, Nationalism, and the Cultural Politics of Memory*. Durham: Duke University Press, 2009.
Raymundo, Oscar. "SF Latino Film Festival Features Gays Cholos, Soldier Lovers and Lesbian Foodies." *Queerty*, September 14, 2012. https://www.queerty.com/sf-latino-film-fest-features-gays-cholos-soldier-lovers-and-lesbian-foodies-20120914.
Reddy, Chandan C. "*Home, Houses, Nonidentity*: Paris Is Burning." In *Burning Down the House: Recycling Domesticity*, edited by Rosemary Marangoly George, 355–379. Boulder: Westview Press, 1998.
Rincón, Bernice. "La Chicana: Her Role in the Past and Her Search for a New Role in the Future." *Regeneración* 1, no. 10 (1971): 15–18.
Riofrio, John D. *Continental Shifts: Migration, Representation, and the Struggle for Justice in Latin(o) America*. Austin: University of Texas Press, 2015.
Rivera Fellah, Nadiah. "Graciela Iturbide's Cholos/as Series: Images of Cross-Border Identities." *History of Photography* 43, no. 3 (2019): 308–330.
Rodríguez, Dylan. *Forced Passages: Imprisoned Radical Intellectuals and the U.S. Prison Regime*. Minneapolis: University of Minnesota Press, 2005.
Rodriguez, Luis J. *Always Running: La Vida Loca: Gang Days in L.A*. New York: Touchstone, 1993.
Rodríguez, Richard T. "The Architectures of Latino Sexuality." *Social Text* 33, no. 2 (2015): 83–98.
Rodríguez, Richard T. *Next of Kin*. Durham: Duke University Press, 2009.
Rodríguez, Richard T. "Queering the Homeboy Aesthetic." *Aztlán: A Journal of Chicano Studies* 31, no. 2 (2006): 127–137.
Rodríguez, Richard T. "X Marks the Spot." *Cultural Dynamics* 29, no. 3 (2017): 202–213.
Rodriguez, Sonia, and Reymundo Sanchez. *Lady Q: The Rise and Fall of a Latin Queen*. Chicago: Chicago Review Press, 2008.
Rosario, Vernon. "When Is a Gang Not a 'Gang'?" *Gay & Lesbian Review Worldwide* 25, no. 4 (2018): 33–34.
Rosas, Gilberto. *Barrio Libre: Criminalizing States and Delinquent Refusals of the New Frontier*. Durham: Duke University Press, 2012.
Rubio, Mauricio. "Elite Membership and Sexualized Violence Among Central American Gangs." Translated by Michael Solis. In *Maras: Gang Violence and Security in Central America*, edited by Thomas C. Bruneau, Lucía Dammert, and Elizabeth Skinner, 159–180. Austin: University of Texas Press, 2011.
Ruiz, Mona. *Two Badges: The Two Lives of Mona Ruiz*. Houston: Arte Público Press, 1997.

Salas, Elizabeth. *Soldaderas in the Mexican Military: Myth and History.* Austin: University of Texas Press, 1990.

Saldaña-Portillo, Maria Josefina. "The Violence of Citizenship in the Making of Refugees: The United States and Central America." *Social Text* 37, no. 4 (2019): 1–21.

Samora, Julian, Joe Bernal, and Albert Peña. *Gunpowder Justice: A Reassessment of the Texas Rangers.* South Bend: University of Notre Dame Press, 1979.

Sanchez, Reymundo. *My Bloody Life: The Making of a Latin King.* Chicago: Chicago Review Press, 2000.

Sanchez, Reymundo. *Once a King, Always a King.* Chicago: Chicago Review Press, 2004.

Sánchez-Jankowski, Martín. *Islands in the Streets: Gangs and American Urban Society.* Berkeley: University of California Press, 1991.

Savenije, Wim. *Maras y barras: Pandillas y violencia juvenil en los barrios marginales de Centroamérica.* El Salvador: FLACSO, 2009.

"Screening of *Homeboy.*" *Echo Park Now*, February 15, 2013. https://www.echoparknow.com/2013/02/15/screening-of-homeboy-film.

Sedgwick, Eve Kosofsky. *Between Men: English Literature and Male Homosocial Desire.* New York: Columbia University Press, 1985.

Shakur, Sanyika. *Monster: The Autobiography of an L.A. Gang Member.* New York: Grove Press, 1993.

Short, James F., and Fred L. Strodtbeck. *Group Process and Gang Delinquency.* Chicago: University of Chicago Press, 1965.

Shulman, Irving. *The Amboy Dukes.* Yorkshire: Critics Choice Paperbacks, 1986.

Silva, Gina. "LASD Whistleblower Claims Deputy Who Shot Andres Guardado Wanted to Join Alleged Law Enforcement Gang." *Fox11 Los Angeles*, September 1, 2020. https://www.foxla.com/news/lasd-whistleblower-claims-deputy-who-shot-andres-guardado-wanted-to-join-alleged-law-enforcement-gang.

Sitz, Teresa. "Free Movie Screening and Reception: HOMEBOY." *Silver Lake Star*, February 2, 2013. http://silverlakestar.com/events/free-movie-screening-and-reception-homeboy.

Souljah, Sister. *The Coldest Winter Ever.* New York: Pocket Star, 2006.

Stallings, L. H. *Funk the Erotic: Transaesthetics and Black Sexual Cultures.* Champaign: University of Illinois Press, 2015.

Stringer, Vickie. *Dirty Red.* New York: Pocket Star, 2009.

Sullivan, Rob. *Street Level: Los Angeles in the Twenty-First Century.* New York: Routledge, 2016.

Swart, William J. "Female Gang Delinquency: A Search for Acceptably Deviant Behavior." *Mid-American Review of Sociology* 15, no. 1 (1991): 43–52.

Tafolla, Carmen. *Sonnets to Human Beings and Other Selected Works.* Santa Monica: Lalo Press, 1992.

Tapia, Micael. "Machismo, Class, and National Oppression." *Brother* 14–15 (1976): 20.

Thiong'o, Ngũgĩ Wa. *Decolonising the Mind: The Politics of Language in African Literature*. Nairobi: East African Educational Publishers, 1986.

Thomas, Piri. *Down These Means Streets*. Thirtieth-Anniversary ed. New York: Vintage Books, 1997.

Thrasher, Frederick M. *The Gang: A Study of 1,313 Gangs in Chicago*. Chicago: University of Chicago Press, 1927.

Tobar, Héctor. *The Tattooed Soldier*. New York: Picador, 1998.

TomTom. Comment on "New Documentary 'Homeboy' Explores Gay Gang Members." *Streetgangs.com*. September 16, 2013. https://www.streetgangs.com/billboard/viewtopic.php?t=55386.

Totten, Mark D. *Guys, Gangs, and Girlfriend Abuse*. Peterborough: Broadview Press, 2000.

Tuck, Eve, and K. Wayne Yang. "Decolonization Is Not a Metaphor." *Decolonization: Indigeneity, Education & Society* 1, no. 1 (2012): 1–40.

Turner, Nikki. *A Hustler's Wife*. New York: One World, 2007.

Valdez, Al. "The Origins of Southern California Latino Gangs." In *Maras: Gang Violence and Security in Central America*, edited by Thomas C. Bruneau, Lucía Dammert, and Elizabeth Skinner, 23–42. Austin: University of Texas Press, 2011.

Valdez, Luis. *Zoot Suit and Other Plays*. Houston: Arte Público Press, 1992.

Valenzuela, Beatriz E. "Documentary 'Homeboy' Explores Gay Gang Members; Film to Show Sunday at 2013 QFilm Festival in Long Beach." *Press Telegram*, September 4, 2013. https://www.presstelegram.com/2013/09/04/documentary-homeboy-explores-gay-gang-members-film-to-show-sunday-at-2013-qfilm-festival-in-long-beach.

Venkatesh, Sudhir. *Gang Leader for a Day: A Rogue Sociologist Takes to the Streets*. New York: Penguin Books, 2008.

Vigil, James Diego. *Barrio Gangs: Street Life and Identity in Southern California*. Austin: University of Texas Press, 1988.

Vigil, James Diego. *Multiple Marginality and Gangs: Through a Prism Darkly*. Lanham: Lexington Books, 2020.

Vigil, James Diego. *A Rainbow of Gangs: Street Cultures in the Mega-City*. Austin: University of Texas Press, 2002.

Vigil, James Diego. "Streets and Schools: How Educators Can Help Chicano Marginalized Gang Youth." *Harvard Educational Review* 69, no. 3 (1999): 270–289.

Vigil, James Diego. "Urban Violence and Street Gangs." *Annual Review of Anthropology* 32 (2003): 225–242.

Wacquant, Loïc. *Urban Outcasts: A Comparative Sociology of Advanced Marginality*. Cambridge: Polity Press, 2008.

Ward, Jesmyn. *Men We Reaped*. New York: Bloomsbury, 2013.

Ward, T. W. *Gangsters without Borders: An Ethnography of a Salvadoran Street Gang*. New York: Oxford University Press, 2013.
Watson, Mark. *Romantic Violence in R-World*. Whiteout Press, 2013.
Weber, Max. *Basic Concepts in Sociology*. Translated by H. P. Secher. New York: Citadel Press, 1972.
Wheeler, William. *State of War: MS-13 and El Salvador's World of Violence*. New York: Columbia Global Reports, 2020.
White, Shane, and Graham White. *Stylin': African-American Expressive Culture, from Its Beginnings to the Zoot Suit*. Ithaca: Cornell University Press, 1999.
Wolf, Sonja. *Mano Dura: The Politics of Gang Control in El Salvador*. Austin: University of Texas Press, 2017.
Wolf, Sonja. "Mara Salvatrucha: The Most Dangerous Street Gang in the Americas?" *Latin American Politics and Society* 54, no. 1 (2012): 65–99.
Woods, Teri. *True to the Game*. Teri Woods Publishing, 1999.
Zamora, Javier. *Unaccompanied*. Port Townsend: Copper Canyon Press, 2017.

INDEX

Photos and illustrations are indicated by italicized page numbers.

absent father, 60–64, 68–70, 211n65
absent mother, 63–64
"Absolute Beginnings" (Hall), 11
Abuelo, El, 146, 199
activo/pasivo sexual system, 39–41
African Americans, street fiction by, 97, 214n24
Aldama, Arturo J., 4, 24
Aldama, Frederick Luis, 4, 24, 40, 41
Always Running (Rodriguez, L.), 33, 47, 138, 211n65
American hegemonic masculinity, 133–138
American Me, 39–40, 41, 128, 131–132, 152, 153, 199
Amezcua, Mike, 55
Anders, Allison, *Mi Vida Loca*, 35, 71, 199, 213n7
Angle, Sharron, 201n3
Anthony, Adelina, *Bruising for Besos*, 25, 94, 199
anti-assimilationist ideologies, 29, 43, 45, 48, 83–84, 87
Anzaldúa, Gloria, 3, 20, 67, 86, 180
Apodaca, Larry, 127, 142–143, 145, *145*, 146, 151
Arbery, Ahmaud Marquez, 11–12

Avila, Richard, 127, 146, 147, 152
Ayer, David, *End of Watch*, 131, 199
Aztecs, 70

Baca, Jimmy Santiago, 185–186
Ballad of Gregorio Cortez, The, 199, 206n110
Better Life, A, 185, 199
Bhabha, Homi, 71
black gangs, Chicago, 209n15
black men, cultural portrayals of violent, 11–12
"Black Men, White Media" (Hall), 11
black peoples, Chicago, 55, 209n15
blaxploitation films, 129–130, 131
Bogle, Donald, 130
Boulevard Nights, 66, 199
Bound by Honor, 199
Boyz n the Hood, 131, 199
Bratt, Peter, *La Mission*, 25, 146, 147, 153, 199, 220n1
Brown, Monica, 11, 32, 35–36, 41, 42, 108
Bruising for Besos, 25, 94, 199
Bruneau, Thomas, 8, 9, 13
butches, 93
Butler, Judith, 134–136, 144

Cacho, Lisa Marie, 46, 121, 185
California gangs, 31, 36
Caló (pachuco slang), 103, 104
Cantú, Lionel, Jr., 3, 4, 68, 136
capitalism, 31, 32, 68, 179
Cardoso, Patricia, *Real Women Have Curves*, 200
Casas, Bartolomé de las, 57
Castillo, Ana: "Daddy with Chesterfields in a Rolled Up Sleeve," 72, 73, 76–87; "Dirty Mexican," 71–72, 73–76, 83–84; "Electra Currents," 60–62, 211n48; *My Father Was a Toltec*, 43, 47–49, 53–56, 58–68, 70–87, 186, 196, 210n44, 211n63, 211n65; "Red Wagons," 62–63; "Saturdays," 54, 58–59, 62, 64, 67; "The Suede Coat," 71–73; "The Toltec," 54–56, 59–61, 67, 72, 84, 210n44
Catholic church, 69–70, 169
Chicago: black peoples in, 55, 209n15; Irish in, 49–51, 53, 55, 56, 209n15; Italians in, 49–51, 53, 74, 209n15; Mexican Americans in, 50–53, 74, 209n16; racism in, 50, 53, 55, 56, 74, 209n15–16
Chicago gangs: black, 209n15; compliment cards of, 209n14; Irish, 49, 50, 53, 55, 56, 209n15; Italian, 49, 50, 53, 209n15; Mexican American, 53, 74; overview, 49; sweaters of, 50, 51, 52
Chicana daughters, 62–63; Chicana mothers and, 76–80; Chicano fathers' violence against, 76–78; domestic labor of, 65–67; as female gang members, 74; sexuality of, 72–73, 79

Chicana gang members, 152; as anti-assimilationist, 29, 43, 83–84, 87; Chicana/o/x heteropatriarchy and, 76, 80–82; Chicano patriarchy and, 76, 80–83, 87; creation of new woman, 79; (de)colonial gang life of, 79–80; (de)colonial projects of, 71, 73, 76, 79–84, 87; female socialities of, 82; Italian women attacked by, 74–76, 80; makeup of, 29; private sphere and, 71, 72, 73, 79, 82, 83; public sphere and, 71, 72, 79, 82, 83; queer homoeroticism of, 79–82; rejection of "proper" gender decorum by, 35
Chicana girl gangs, 29, 35
"Chicana, La" (Rincón), 95
Chicana mothers, 65–67, 76–80
Chicana/o/x family, 68, 76–79, 81, 82
Chicana/o/x gangs, gender dynamics of, 37
Chicana/o/x heteropatriarchy, 35, 67, 76, 80–82
Chicana/o/xs: in *American Me*, 131–132; culture, 34–35, 59, 68; language, 86; pachuco and culture of, 34–35
Chicanas, 43, 58, 67, 77–78, 118
Chicano criminality, 32, 206n110
Chicano fathers: (de)colonial projects of, 48, 55, 61, 65, 66, 69; reading as white, 84–86; violence against Chicana/o/x family, 76–78; womanizing of, 58, 76
Chicano patriarchy, 35, 65–71, 73, 78–82, 87
child as the future, 161–163
cholas: aberrant femininity of, 28, 29, 97, 103, 109; aesthetic/style

of, 28–29, 102–104, 111, 114, 214n43; as challenging Chicana/o/x heteropatriarchy, 35; queering gender and, 38; racialized female masculinity of, 102–109, 111, 114, 115
cholo aesthetics, 146, 147, 192, 220n1
citizenship in gangs, 5, 42, 202n15
citizen-subjects in gangs, 34, 87, 105–109, 111, 114, 115, 117, 202n15
Clarke, John, 14, 25
class inequalities, 14, 15
clicas, 26, 27. *See also* gangs
colonial imaginary, 3
colonialism: coloniality compared to, 18; European, 19–23, 118; hierarchies, oppressions of Latina/o/x gang members and, 14; imposition of subordination of women by, 20; internal, 18–19, 203n51; land appropriation and, 22; material and immaterial in, 16; organization of life by, 18; racialized sexualized violence of, 57–58; toxified masculinity in Latino men and, 3–4, 202n11
coloniality, 1, 2, 3, 201n1; colonialism compared to, 18; decolonization and, 22, 23; families of gang members and, 138, 139; gangs and, 18, 27; gang violence and, 131, 133, 136, 137; gay gang members and, 179–180; gender, sexuality, race, class and, 196; homophobia and, 133, 136, 137; internal colonialism and, 18–19, 203n51; Latin American and Latina/o/x tradition on, 23; Latina/o/x gang literature, film and, 196; Latino men and, 133, 136, 137; of people of color, 168; role in gang membership/violence and gang-exploitation films, 131, 132; violence of heterosexuality in, 181; working-class/low-income Latino men and, 133, 134, 135, 137
coloniality of gender, 19, 20, 196; (de)colonial projects and, 57–58, 70; delinking from, 24–25; female members of male-dominated gangs and, 91–92, 96, 104, 108, 109, 115, 117, 118; female members of male heterosexual gangs as challenging, 33–34; gay members of male heterosexual gangs and, 33–34, 143, 151, 152, 181; Latina/o/x gang members in literature, film and, 24, 25, 27; misogyny and, 152; toxified female masculinity and, 118, 122–124
"Coloniality of Gender, The" (Lugones), 19
colonial matrix of power, 18, 21, 23
colonial projects, 16, 148–149
colonization, 5, 15–17, 22, 95–96
colonized, 17–18, 71
colonized men, racialized sexualized violence against, 57
colonizer: European, 19–22, 118; hybridity of colonized relationship to, 71; white male colonizer father, 57, 58, 59, 76, 118, 133
Colors, 128, 199
Connell, Raewyn, 105
Corrado, Damen, 49, 208n9
Cortez, Gregorio, 32, 206n110
counternations, gangs as, 32

counterpublic, 150, 151, 153–157
Crenshaw, Kimberlé, 201n2
crime, organized, 26
Cuevas, T. Jackie, 4, 6, 7, 24–25, 94
cultural bomb, 17

"Daddy with Chesterfields in a Rolled Up Sleeve" (Castillo), 72, 73, 76–87
Davis, Angela, 202n7, 208n153
Dean, Tim, 6
death drive, 162–163, 173, 174, 177, 181
decolonial, 22–23, 202n4
(de)colonial: concept, 2, 3, 5; decolonial compared to, 22, 202n4; decoloniality and, 24, 25; decolonial projects and, 5–6; decolonization and, 24, 25; gang members as, 2, 3, 24, 27, 196; gang violence as, 31, 205n108; Latina/o/x gang members and, 184; Latina/o/x gang members in literature, film as, 24, 25–26, 196; Latina/o/x gang subcultures and, 46; working-class Latina/o/x gangs and, 27
(de)colonial gang life, 5, 49, 59, 64, 66, 79–80
(de)colonial performance, 4, 44, 92, 96
(de)colonial projects: coloniality of gender and, 57–58, 70; queer failure and, 160, 163, 177, 182
(de)colonial projects in gangs: clicas and, 26, 27; contradictions in, 2–3, 13–14, 202n7; female gang members enacting male gangs into, 44, 91, 160; gay gang members enacting heterosexual gangs into, 44, 45, 138, 160; gender, sexuality, race, class and, 43; harm of multiple marginalized persons and, 13, 27; heterosexual male-dominated gangs and, 160; heterosexual male-dominated gangs failure and, 161, 163, 182; in Latina/o/x gangs, 27; masculinity in, 3; violent hypermasculinity and, 160
(de)colonial projects of Chicana/o/xs: of Chicana gang members, 71, 73, 76, 79–84, 87; of Chicano fathers, 48, 55, 61, 65, 66, 69
(de)colonial subcultures, gangs as, 32
decolonial imaginary, 3
Decolonial Imaginary, The (Pérez, E.), 3, 9, 24
decoloniality, 23–25, 196, 202n4
decolonial/postcolonial theory, 2–3
decolonial projects, 5–6
decolonial woes, 2, 3
decolonization, 4, 22–25, 202n4, 204n72
decolonize, 202n4
decolonized masculinity, 4, 5
Decolonizing Latinx Masculinities (Aldama and Aldama), 24
Delgado, Richard, 12
Dinco, Dino: *El Abuelo*, 146, 199; *Homeboy*, 10, 44–45, 125, 127–129, 132, 133, 136–157, 160, 186, 192, 196, 199
"Dirty Mexican" (Castillo), 71–72, 73–76, 83–84
disidentification, 128, 129, 142–144, 150, 151, 155
documentaries, 148–149, 150, 153
domestic labor, Chicano patriarchy and, 65–67

domestic violence against Latinas, 91, 119–124, 212n89
Donis, Alex, 41, 146–147, 149, 151
Down These Mean Streets (Thomas), 39, 40–41; crossdressers and, 40–41
DTO. *See* Dykes Taking Over
Durán, Robert J., 32, 119, 141
Dykes Taking Over (DTO), 38

Echo Park, 156, 215n67
Echo Park Locos, 213n7
Edelman, Lee, 115, 161–163, 182
"Electra Currents" (Castillo), 60–62, 211n48
El Salvador, 187–188, 190, 193–195
End of Watch, 131, 199
Escobar, Martha D., 184, 186, 187
Estill, Adriana, 60, 84–86
European colonialism, 19–23, 118
Executioners, 27

failed gay gang members, 160; utopian futurity of, 45, 161, 175–182. *See also* queer failure
families of gang members, 43; causing youth to join gangs, 47, 138, 139; coloniality and, 138, 139; gay men in gangs and, 139; homophobia of, 140
Fanon, Frantz, 15–17, 24, 56
female gang members: Chicana daughters as, 74; as citizen-subjects, 34, 87, 105–109, 111, 114, 115, 117; empowerment of, 36–37; enactment of (de)colonial projects in and through male gangs by, 44, 91, 160; enactment of (de)colonial projects into male gangs by, 44, 91, 160; exploitational stereotypes of, 115, 124; femininity of, 97–98, 109–115; gang narratives and, 5, 152; gang studies of, 34, 36; machismo of, 96; of male-dominated gangs, 37, 91–92, 96, 104, 108, 109, 115, 117, 118; male gang members treatment of, 90–91; of male heterosexual gangs, 1, 32–36; pregnancy and, 100, 103, 115, 116, 117; racialized female masculinity and, 43, 44, 92, 94, 96; racialized gang masculinity of, 4–5; as sexual objects for male gang members, 90, 110–112, 114–115, 116; as sheep, 100–112, 114, 116, 117, 121–124; subordination of, 34, 100–102, 104–105, 115, 116, 117; toxified female masculinity of, 4, 92, 95, 109, 111, 116, 118, 124; violence of, 36. *See also specific topics*
female masculinity, 44, 92–93; intersection with race and class, 95; Latina, 4, 94; subaltern, 94, 210n39. *See also* racialized female masculinity
Female Masculinity (Halberstam), 92
female socialities, 87; of Chicana gang members, 82; (de)colonial gang life and, 49, 59, 64, 66; of male gang members, 48, 59, 63, 66
feminine: gay men as, 152; male gang members perception of feminine women, 111–115; private sphere as, 105; sexualized feminine aesthetic, 110–115

femininity: cholas' aberrant, 28, 29, 97, 103, 109; conventional, 111–115; of female gang members, 97–98, 109–115; gay gang members and, 152; heterosexual masculinity and conventional, 111–115, 124; hypermasculine, male-dominated gangs and, 44, 92, 96–97, 109; in Latina/o/x gang literature, 97; male, 216n71; masculinity as repudiation of, 134, 135; of pachuca, 97

feminism: Latina, 83; white, 68

Fernandez, Antonio "King Tone," 165–166

"Fighting the Good Fight" (Cuevas), 24

Fire Girls, 91, 107, 108, 114, 121–122; attacks on working-class Latinas by, 116–117, 123–124, 140; Lobos and, 115–118; as queer girl gang, 115–116

Foucault, Michel, 173, 205n108

Foxy Brown, 130, 199

Fraser, Nancy, 64, 65

Freeman, Wayne, 4

Fregoso, Rosa Linda, 34–35, 36, 61, 64, 68, 71, 132, 152

Freud, Sigmund, 123, 134

Fukunaga, Cary Joji, *Sin Nombre*, 183, 185, 200

Fuqua, Antoine, *Training Day*, 11, 200

future: child as the, 161–163; futurity compared to, 221n15; queer persons and, 163

futurism, reproductive, 161–162

futurity: future compared to, 221n15; queerness and, 163. *See also* utopian futurity

Galarte, Francisco J., 95, 207n145

Galván, Lorena, 38

gang counterpublic, 151, 153–157

gang culture, homophobia and, 207n145

gang-exploitation films, 11, 130; *Homeboy* and conventions of, 128, 129, 132, 137, 150, 152–153; studies of, 129, 131–132

gang girls: queering gender and, 38. *See also* cholas; la pachuca

gang injunction, 156, 220n79

gang life: (de)colonial, 5, 49, 59, 64, 66, 79–80; at intersection of gender, sexuality, race, class, 124; Latina/o/x gang literature and film on reasons for, 3; shared experience of, 47, 60, 87

gang literature and film, 10; causes of gang membership, violence and crime in, 6; gang members involved in, 9, 203n26; gang subcultures and, 11; reformation of dominant perceptions and, 12

gang masculinities, alternate, 25

gang members: as (de)colonial, 2, 3, 24, 27, 196; decolonized masculinity for, 5; gang-exploitation films and coloniality's role in, 131, 132; gang literature and film involving, 9, 203n26; gang studies and direct engagement with, 8–9; gay sexuality and, 39–41, 181; in literature and film, 2

gang narratives: absent father in, 60–64, 211n65; female gang members and, 5, 152; gay gang members and, 5, 39–40; gay sexuality and, 41–42;

homophobia and, 41, 169–170; normative, 5; shared experience of gang life in, 47, 60; violence against female members of male heterosexual gangs in, 33, 36; violence against gay members of male heterosexual gangs in, 33
Gang Nation (Brown), 11, 32, 35–36
Gang Related, 11, 199
gang resistance: class inequalities and, 14; harm to working-class communities of color and, 2, 6; style as, 29–30
gangs: binary discussions of, 1–2; clicas and, 26; youth joining gangs due to families, 47, 138, 139. *See also specific topics*
Gang's All Queer, The (Panfil), 41–42, 128
gang studies: critical, 10, 32; direct engagement with gang members and, 8–9; of female gang members, 34, 36; of gang violence, 139–140; of gay gang members, 39, 41, 128; of gay men in gangs, 39, 41–42; gender and sexuality in, 197; humanities and, 7, 9–11, 13, 36; literature/film about women/ gay gang members and, 10–12; need for multidisciplinary approach, 13; police and, 8; researcher fears of gangs and, 8; social sciences and, 7–10, 13, 36
gang style/aesthetics: chola aesthetic, 28–29, 102–104, 111, 114, 214n43; cholo aesthetic, 146, 147, 192, 220n1; as gang resistance, 29–30; homeboy aesthetic, 147; Toltec, 54, 56, 63, 66–67, 72
gang subcultures: (de)colonial, 32; of female members of male heterosexual gangs, 1; in fiction, 11; in gang literature and film, 11; of gay members of male heterosexual gangs, 1; heterosexual male subcultures, 5; Latina/o/x, 45, 46, 48, 83–84; as resistance to class inequalities, 14; youth, 14, 25
gang violence, 27; capitalism and, 31, 32; causes in gang literature and film, 6; coloniality and, 131, 133, 136, 137; as (de)colonial, 31, 205n108; of female gang members, 36; fratricidal, 2, 205n108; gang-exploitation films and coloniality's role in, 131, 132; gang studies of, 139–140; of gay gang members, 139–140, 141–142; group cohesion built through, 140; immigrant/gang member trope and, 184; Mara Salvatrucha and, 183; member initiations through, 30; overview, 30–31; sensationalization of, 2, 201n3
García, Alma, 68
Garcia, Phillip, 127–128, 136, 138, 139, 142, 146
García, Tadeo, *On the Downlow*, 45, 128, 146, 153, 159–161, 163–182, 186, 196, 200, 220n1, 221n15
Gaspar de Alba, Alicia, 202n7
gay: queer and, 6; toxified masculinity and gay people, 4. *See also* homosexuality
gay gang members: coloniality and, 179–180; enactment of (de) colonial projects into heterosexual gangs by, 44, 45, 138, 160; gang narratives and, 5, 39–40; gang studies of, 39, 41, 128; gang violence of,

248 | Index

gay gang members (*continued*) 139–140, 141–142; homophobia and, 140–141, 169–171, 180, 181; hypermasculine, 128, 142, 144, 145, 147, 151, 160; misogyny and, 152; queering gender and, 37–40; racialized gang masculinity of, 4–5; survival strategy of, 142, 143; toxified masculinity of, 4; violent hypermasculinity and, 142, 145, 147, 151, 160, 170, 173–179; in white space, 178–181. *See also specific topics*

gay gang members, in film, 128, 222n40. *See also Homeboy*

gay gangs, 42, 128, 218n2

gay Latino men in gangs, 10, 44, 127, 142, 163. *See also Homeboy*

gay locos, 125, 147

Gaylords, 49, 50, 52, 53

gay members of male heterosexual gangs, 128; citizenship attained by, 42; as closeted, 127, 139, 141; coloniality of gender and, 33–34, 143, 151, 152, 181; disidentification of, 129, 142–143, 151, 155; gang subcultures of, 1; homophobia and, 127, 129, 136, 143; marginalization of, 1, 32; passing as straight, 143–144; violence against, 32, 33, 137

gay men: counterpublic, 153, 155–157; feminine, 152; homophobia and, 170–171, 180, 181; major architecture and, 173–174, *174*

gay men in gangs: citizenship and power attained by, 42; cultural representations of, 39; families of gang members and, 139; femininity and, 152; gang studies of, 39, 41–42; in heterosexual, homophobic gangs, 127, 128, 138, 143; in heterosexual male-dominated gangs, 136, 160, 182; Latina gang members and, 152; socialities of, 208n3

gay sexuality: barrio and, 172; Catholicism and, 169; gang members and, 39–41, 181; gang narratives and, 41–42; minor architecture and, 172–173, *173*; prison and, 155; violent hypermasculinity and, 160

gender and sexuality: gang studies on, 197; in Latina/o/x gang literature and film, 197; low socioeconomic status and performance of, 136

gender and sexuality in gangs: Chicana gang members rejection of "proper" gender decorum, 35; (de)colonial, masculinity, race, class and, 5; male heterosexual gangs and non-normativity of, 42

gender identity, 136

gender, sexuality, race, class: coloniality and, 196; (de)colonial projects in gangs and, 43; gang life at intersection of, 124; male heterosexual gangs and, 1

gender/sexual system: activo/pasivo, 39–40; European colonizers imposition of, 19–22

gender system: cis-gender, 215n47; of Native Americans, 19–20; racialization of, 20

Gender Trouble (Butler), 144

Gifford, Justin, 97

girl gangs: California, 36; as challenging heteropatriarchy, 35, 36; queer, 115–116; resistance of, 36. *See also specific topics*
Glatzer, Richard, *Quinceañera*, 128, 146, 153, 200, 220n1
Going Down to the Barrio (Moore), 37, 139
González, Bill Johnson, 167–168
Gray, F. Gary, *Set It Off*, 94, 200
greaser gangs, 49–50
greasers, 49, 50
Greencard Warriors, 185, 199
Gringo Justice (Mirandé), 32
Guidotti-Hernández, Nicole M., 176, 192
Gunckel, Colin, 131
Gunderson, Erica, 50
Gutmann, Matthew, 136

Habermas, Jürgen, 64, 65
Hackford, Taylor, *Bound by Honor*, 199
Halberstam Jack, 92–93, 161, 163, 164, 210n39
Hall, Stuart, 11, 14, 31
Hamburg Club, 55
Havoc, 89–90, 115, 199
Hebidge, Dick, 28–29
la Heredera (heiress), 73
Hernández, Ellie D., 4, 94
Hernández, Jillian, 29
heteronormativity: queer failure and, 161–162; utopian futurity and, 164; women and, 163
heteropatriarchy: Chicana/o/x, 35, 67, 76, 80–82; girl gangs as challenging, 35, 36; literature/film about Latina/o/x families and, 211n63
heterosexual gangs: gay gang members enacting (de)colonial projects into, 44, 45, 138, 160; gay men in homophobic, 127, 128, 138, 143
heterosexuality: coloniality and violence of, 181; European colonizers imposition of, 20; homosexuality rejection and, 134–135; hypermasculine, 45
heterosexual male-dominated gangs: (de)colonial projects and failure of, 161, 163, 182; (de)colonial projects of, 160; gay men in, 136, 160, 182; hypermasculine, 125, 138; queer failure in, 161; violent hypermasculinity and, 160
heterosexual masculinity: conventional femininity and, 111–115, 124; hypermasculine, 45; violent, 159
heterosexual men: gangs as heterosexual male subcultures, 5; homophobia of, 170–171
Hewlett, Sylvia Ann, 162
Hill, Jack, *Foxy Brown*, 130, 199
Homeboy, 10, 44–45, 125, 127, 133, 136, 138–147, 149, 151, 160, 186, 192, 196, 199; documentary form of, 148, 150, 153; exhibition of, 154–156; gang counterpublic of, 153–157; gang-exploitation film conventions and, 128, 129, 132, 137, 150, 152–153; gang viewership and engagement with, 156; reception of, 154–155
homeboy aesthetic, 147, 220n1. *See also* cholo aesthetics
homegirls. *See* cholas
Homegirls in the Public Sphere (Miranda), 36, 71, 82
homonormative tolerance of white LGBTQ+ people, 135

homophobia: American hegemonic masculinity and, 134; barrio and, 173, 180, 181; coloniality and, 133, 136, 137; of families of gang members, 140; gang culture and, 207n145; gang narratives and, 41, 169–170; gangs and, 38, 41, 127, 128, 137, 141, 181; gay gang members and, 140–141, 169–171, 180, 181; gay members of male heterosexual gangs and, 127, 129, 136, 143; gay men and, 170–171, 180, 181; of heterosexual men, 170–171; Latina/o/x culture and, 137; Mexican American culture, 207n145; use of violent hypermasculinity to fight, 170–171; violent, 127; of white people, 170–172; of working-class/low-income Latino men, 135–138

homosexuality: activo/pasivo sexual system and, 39–41; heterosexuality and rejection of, 134–135; indigenous nations recognition of, 20

Hondagneu-Sotelo, Pierrette, 136

Hopper, Dennis, *Colors*, 128, 199

Hoyo Maravilla, El, 37, 90

Hughes Brothers, *Menace II Society*, 131, 199

humanities, gang studies and, 7, 9–11, 13, 36

hypermasculine gay gang members, 128, 144; violence of, 142, 145, 147, 151, 160, 170, 173–176

hypermasculine, male-dominated gangs: femininity in, 44, 92, 96–97, 109; heterosexual, 125, 138; male femininity in, 216n71

hypermasculinity of gangs, 33, 40, 41, 43, 45

hypermasculinity of Latino men, 133; violent homophobic, 136–137; of working-class/low-income Latino men, 136, 137, 138

Ibarraran-Bigalondo, Amaia, 117

identity: gender, 136; performance of, 144–145

immigrant/gang member binary, 46, 193

immigrant/gang member trope: anti-immigrant legislation and, 184, 190; exploitable immigrant labor and, 184; gang violence and, 184; Latin American immigrants and, 45–46, 184–186; Latina/o/x literature, film and, 46, 185–187, 191, 195, 196; Latina/o/xs and, 45; Mara Salvatrucha and, 45–46, 183, 184, 186, 187, 190, 191

immigrants: Mara Salvatrucha and, 183; undocumented, 118–120, 184, 217n107

indigenous nations, 20

inequality: class, 14, 15; gang subcultures as resistance to, 14; racist portrayals of people of color and systemic, 12

internal colonialism, 18–19, 203n51

intersectionality, 201n2

Irish in Chicago, 51; Irish gangs, 49, 50, 53, 55, 56, 209n15

Italians in Chicago, 51; Italian gangs, 49, 50, 53, 74, 209n15

Italian women, Chicana gang members attacking, 74–76, 80

Iturbide, Graciela, 38, 97

Jefferson, Tony, 14

Jenkins, Barry, *Moonlight*, 146, 199, 220n1

Johnson, Dominique, 38
Jones, Zach, 50

Kelley, Robin D. G., 18
Kopple, Barbara, *Havoc*, 89–90, 115, 199
Kouf, Jim, *Gang Related*, 11, 199
Kruishoop, Miriam, *Greencard Warriors*, 185, 199

LA 92, 131, 199
Lady Q (Sanchez and Rodriguez, S.), 203n26
land repatriation, decolonization and, 22, 204n72
Lane, Christopher, 6
Latina gang members: gay men in gangs and, 152; private sphere, 104–105; public sphere, 104–105; racialized female masculinity and, 98, 102–105
Latin America: patriarchal culture of, 68; tradition, 22–23
Latin American immigrants: immigrant/gang member trope and, 45–46, 184–186; state criminalization of, 183–185; as violent animals, 184
Latin American immigration: Latin American gangs and, 45–46; Latina/o/x literature and film and gang stigma of, 46
Latina/o, 7
Latina/o/x culture: homophobia and, 137; as patriarchal, 68; racialized female masculinity in, 94
Latina/o/x gang literature and film, 125, 186–187; coloniality and, 196; decoloniality and, 196; femininity in, 97; gender and sexuality in, 197; reasons for gang life in, 3. *See also specific topics*

Latina/o/x gang members: colonialism and hierarchies, oppressions of, 14; (de)colonial and, 184; in literature and film, 24–27, 196; women and gay gang members, 14
Latina/o/x gangs: language of, 28; styles, 28–30; subaltern status of, 30, 32; subcultures, 45, 46, 48, 83–84
Latina/o/x literature and film: gang stigma on Latin American immigration and, 46; heteropatriarchal mothers and daughters in, 211n63; immigrant/gang member binary in, 46, 193; immigrant/gang member trope in, 46, 185–187, 191, 195, 196; Latina/o/x women and gay gang members, 14
Latina/o/xs, 7; capitalism and, 179; colonization of, 5, 15; immigrant/gang member trope and, 45; language of, 28, 86; racism against, 179; tradition of, 22–23
Latina/o/x studies: on decoloniality, 24; of gang-exploitation films, 129, 131–132
Latinas: domestic violence against, 91, 119–124, 212n89; female masculinity of, 4, 94; feminism of, 83
Latin Kings, 45, 159, 160, 164–167, 174, 178, 181, 203n26, 222n33
Latino men: coloniality and, 133, 136, 137. *See also specific topics*
Latinx, 6; queer and, 7
Lawrence, Novotny, 130
lesbian gang members, 38, 39
lesbians of color, 93

LGBTQ+ people, homonormative tolerance of white, 135
Lindsay, Daniel, *LA 92*, 131, 199
literary and film studies, deconstructive methodology, 13
literature and film about women and gay gang members: effect on gangs and gang cultures of, 12; gang studies and, 10–12; normative gang narratives and, 5. *See also specific topics*
Lobos, 92, 106–114, 140, 213n7; domestic violence and, 91, 119–120; Fire Girls and, 115–118; subaltern masculinity of, 98–102; subordination of female gang members in, 100–102, 104–105
Locas (Murray), 36, 38, 43–44, 87, 91, 93, 96–125, 140, 186, 196, 213n7, 215n67
locos, 145, 219n51; gay, 125, 147. *See also* violent hypermasculine gang members
Lugones, Maria, 2, 4, 19–21, 23, 181, 196
Lynwood Vikings, 27, 205n90

machismo: characteristics, 95; female gang members and, 96; racialized female masculinity and, 96, 116; racializing sexism and, 68; studies of, 133; as subaltern masculinity, 15, 95–96, 99
macho, queer, 151
major architecture, gay men and, 173–174, *174*
Maldonado-Torres, Nelson, 18, 23, 57
male-dominated gangs: female members of, 37, 91–92, 96, 104, 108, 109, 115, 117, 118. *See also* heterosexual male-dominated gangs; hypermasculine, male-dominated gangs
male femininity, 216n71
male gang members: (de)colonial gang life of, 59; female gang members as sexual objects for, 90, 110–112, 114–115, 116; female socialities and, 48, 59, 63, 66; perception of feminine women, 111–115; sexualized feminine aesthetic and, 110–115; treatment of female gang members by, 90–91. *See also specific topics*
male gangs: female gang members enacting (de)colonial projects into, 44, 91, 160; pregnancy and, 100. *See also specific topics*
male heterosexual gangs: female members of, 1, 32–36; gender and sexual non-normativity in, 42; gender, sexuality, race, class and, 1. *See also specific topics*
Mano Dura (Iron Fist), 194–195
Mara Salvatrucha (MS), 188, 223n23; El Salvador and, 190; immigrant/gang member trope and, 45–46, 183, 184, 186, 187, 190, 191; Salvadoran immigrants and, 189–190; *Unaccompanied* and, 191–193
Mara Salvatrucha Stoners (MSS), 189
marginalization of gang members, 1, 32, 35–36
marianismo, 15, 71, 73
Martínez D'Aubuisson, Juan José, 47, 190
Martínez, Ernesto Javier, 48
Martin, T. J., *LA 92*, 131, 199
masculine, public sphere as, 105
masculinity: as cultural performance, 4, 92, 210n39;

(de)colonial, gangs, gender,
  sexuality, race, class and, 5;
  (de)colonial projects in gangs
  and, 3; delinking from violence,
  25; dominant, 92–93; as
  independent cultural
  phenomenon, 210n39; as
  repudiation of femininity, 134,
  135; of young men of color, 134.
  See also specific masculinity topics
masculinity of Latino men:
  American hegemonic
  masculinity and, 133, 134;
  hypermasculine, 133, 136–138;
  subaltern, 133; theorization of,
  136; toxified, 3–4, 202n11.
  See also specific topics
May, Vivian M., 201n2
McFarland, Pancho, 4, 133
McMichael, Travis and Gregory,
  11–12
Menace II Society, 131, 199
Méndez, Xhercis, 18
Mendoza-Denton, Norma, 28, 29,
  103–104, 214n43
men of color, masculinity of young,
  134
Men We Reaped (Ward), 47, 68–69,
  211n65
Messner, Michael A., 136
Mexican Americans: Chicago and,
  50–53, 74, 209n16; gangs in
  Chicago, 53, 74; homophobia
  and culture of, 207n145;
  working-class/low-income,
  179; zoot suit and, 34
Mignolo, Walter, 2, 22, 23, 24, 25
Mills, Charles, 16, 171
minor architecture, gay sexuality
  and, 172–173, *173*
Miranda, Marie "Keta," 36, 71, 82
Mirandé, Alfredo, 3, 4, 32, 133
misogyny, 152

Mission, La, 25, 146, 147, 153, 199,
  220n1
Mi Vida Loca, 35, 71, 199, 213n7
Moonlight, 146, 199, 220n1
Moore, Joan W., 37, 90, 139
Mora, Richard, 133–134
Moynihan, Daniel Patrick, 211n65
MS. *See* Mara Salvatrucha
MSS. *See* Mara Salvatrucha Stoners
mujer mala, 67
multiple marginality, 201n2; harm
  of persons of, 13, 27
Muñoz, Carlos, 19, 142, 143, 150,
  157
Muñoz, José Esteban, 44, 128–129,
  161–164, 175, 181, 221n15
Murray, Yxta Maya, *Locas*, 36, 38,
  43–44, 87, 91, 93, 96–125, 140,
  186, 196, 213n7, 215n67
My Bloody Life (Sanchez), 203n26
My Father Was a Toltec (Castillo),
  43, 47–49, 53–56, 58–68,
  70–87, 186–196, 210n44,
  211n63, 211n65

Navarro, José, 66
Negro Family, The (Moynihan),
  211n65
Nixon, Rob, 205n108
No Future (Edelman), 161–163
non-normative gang members, 44

O'Connor, James, 49, 208n9
Oedipal-conquest-triangle, 57–58
official economy of paid
  employment, 61, 64, 65
Olguín, B. V., 129, 132
Olmos, Edward James, *American Me*,
  19, 39–40, 41, 128, 131–132,
  152, 153
On the Downlow, 45, 128, 146, 153,
  159–161, 163–182, 186, 196,
  200, 220n1, 221n15

organized crime, 26
Ortega, Mariana, 2, 3, 19

el pachuco, 34, 35
la pachuca, 34, 35
pachuca/os, 97; gangs, 34, 35; slang, 103, 104
Panfil, Vanessa R., 41–42, 128, 139–140
panopticism, 173–174
Paredes, Raymund A., 68
passing, 143–144
patriarchy: capitalism, subordination of women and, 68; Catholic church and Spanish, 69–70; Chicano, 35, 65–71, 73, 78–82, 87; collection of women, womanizing and subaltern masculinity of, 58; heteropatriarchy, 35, 36, 67, 76, 80–82, 211n63; of indigenous nations, 20; Latina/o/x culture of, 68
Patterson, Orlando, 12–13, 184
Paz, Brenda, 190, 223n23
Paz, Octavio, 69
people of color: coloniality of, 168; state violence and, 205n108; systemic inequality and racist portrayals of, 12
Pérez, Daniel Enrique, 39, 41, 90, 108, 147, 151
Pérez, Emma, 3, 9, 24, 57, 58, 77–78, 82–83, 117–118
Pérez-Torres, Rafael, 59
Peterson, Dana, 37
police, 8, 121
police gangs, 27, 205n90
Post-Borderlandia (Cuevas), 94
Poveda, Christian, La Vida Loca, 8, 199
practices of un-knowing, 2, 3

pregnancy: female gang members and, 100, 103, 115, 116, 117; male gangs and, 100, 116
Pressman, Michael, Boulevard Nights, 66, 199
prisons: El Salvador gangs in, 194–195; gay sexuality and, 155; prison gangs, 208n153, 222n40; prison writers, 208n153
private sphere, 61, 65; Chicana gang members and, 71, 72, 73, 79, 82, 83; as feminine, 105; Latina gang members and, 104–105; public sphere hybridization with, 72–73
public discourse, 64–65
public sphere, 61, 64–65; Chicana gang members and, 71, 72, 79, 82, 83; Latina gang members and, 104–105; as masculine, 105; private sphere hybridization with, 72–73
Puerto Rican gangs, 164–166

queer: gay and, 6; Latinx and, 7; queering homeboy/cholo aesthetic, 220n1; sociality of, 48
queer failure: (de)colonial projects and, 160, 163, 177, 182; heteronormativity and, 161–162; in heterosexual male-dominated gangs, 161; utopian futurity and, 161, 163, 164, 175–182. See also failed gay gang members
queer girl gang, 115–116
queer homoeroticism, of Chicana gang members, 79–82
queering gender: cholas and, 38; gang girls and, 38; gay gang

members and, 37–40; lesbian gang members and, 38
queer Latina/o/x films, 25, 39–40
queer masculinity, 25, 118
queerness, 161; death drive and, 162–163, 173, 174, 177, 181; futurity and, 163; reproductive futurism and, 162
queer persons: future and, 163; toxic, impoverished present for, 161; utopian futurity and, 164, 175–182
Quijano, Aníbal, 2, 19, 23, 24
Quinceañera, 128, 146, 153, 200, 220n1

Rabinowitz, Paula, 148–149
race and class: (de)colonial, gangs, masculinity, gender, sexuality and, 5; female masculinity intersection with, 95. *See also* gender, sexuality, race, class
racial contract, 171–172, 178, 222nn40–41
Racial Contract, The (Mills), 171
racial, gender, sexual hierarchies, decoloniality and, 23–24
racialization: of colonization, 15–17; of gang masculinity, 4–5; of gender system, 20; of sexism, 68, 70; of sexualized violence and colonialism, 57–58
racialized female masculinity: attacks on working-class Latinas and, 116–117, 123–124; of cholas, 102–109, 111, 114, 115; as (de)colonial performance, 44, 92, 96; female gang members and, 43, 44, 92, 94, 96; Latina gang members and, 98, 102–105; in Latina/o/x culture, 94; machismo and, 96, 116; subaltern masculinity as, 96; toxified, 4, 92, 95, 109, 116, 118, 121–124
racial Other, 205n108
racing, 171–172, 178, 222nn40–41
racism: Chicago and, 50, 53, 55, 56, 74, 209n15–16; Latina/o/xs and, 179; portrayals of black men as violent and racist vigilantism, 11–12; systemic inequality and racist portrayals of people of color, 12
Ragen's Colts, 55
Ramírez, Catherine S., 28, 35, 36, 97
Real Women Have Curves, 200
Real World, The, 150, 157, 219n63
"Red Wagons" (Castillo), 62–63
reproductive futurism, 161–162
resistance: Chicano criminality as, 32; gang, 2, 6, 14, 29–30; of girl gangs, 36; of subcultures, 29
Rincón, Bernice, 95, 96
Rios, Cisco, 127, 139, 140, 141–142, 148, *149*, 154
Rivera Fellah, Nadiah, 28, 38, 97
Roberts, Brian, 14
Rodriguez, Luis J., 33, 47, 138, 139, 211n65
Rodríguez, Richard T., 7, 28, 103, 118, 147, 172
Rodriguez, Sonia, 203n26
Romero, Sergio, 127, 140–141, *141*
Rosario, Vernon, 42
Ruiz, Mona, 36

Salvadoran immigrants, 188–190
"Salvador, El" (Zamora, J.), 193–194, 196
Sanchez, Reymundo, 203n26
Santos, Ramon "King Papo," 164
"Saturdays" (Castillo), 54, 58–59, 62, 64, 67

Scott, Kody, 156, 220n81
"Second Attempt Crossing" (Zamora, J.), 191–193, 196
Sedgwick, Eve, 41
Set It Off, 94, 200
sexism, racializing, 68, 70
sexuality: of Chicana daughters, 72–73, 79; gender identity and, 136; sexualized feminine aesthetic, 110–115. *See also specific sexuality topics*
shared experience of gang life, 47, 60, 87
Silva, Hector, 41, 146–147, 149, 151
Singleton, John, *Boyz n the Hood*, 131, 199
Sin Nombre, 183, 185, 200
slavery, 12, 13
socialities, 43; of gay men in gangs, 208n3; of queer, 48; shared experience of gang life between members and, 87. *See also* female socialities
social sciences: gang studies and, 7–10, 13, 36; humanities and, 13; police and, 8
spacing, 171–172, 178, 222nn40–41
Spanish colonialism, 69–71
Spanish patriarchy, Catholic church and, 69–70
style: subcultures and, 28–29; *Subculture: The Meaning of Style*, 28–29. *See also* gang style/aesthetics
subaltern masculinity: alternative, 118; collection of women, womanizing and patriarchal, 58; female, 94, 210n39; of Latino men, 133; Lobos and, 98–102; machismo as, 15, 95, 96, 99; racialized female masculinity as, 96; subaltern women performing and queering, 210n39; violence against women and, 99; womanizing and, 58
subaltern men, sexual relations with white women by, 58–59, 210n41
subaltern people: of colonized, 17–18; Latina/o/x gangs as, 30, 32; toxified masculinity at center of, 4
subaltern women, performing/queering subaltern masculinity by, 210n39
subcultures: resistance of, 29; style, 28–29; youth, 14, 25. *See also* gang subcultures
Subculture: The Meaning of Style (Hebidge), 28–29
subordination of female gang members, 34, 104–105; Lobos and, 100–102; resistance to, 115, 116, 117
subordination of women: Chicanas and gendered, 67, 77–78; colonialism's imposition of, 20; patriarchy, capitalism and, 68
"Suede Coat, The" (Castillo), 71–73
Sweet Sweetback's Baadasssss Song, 130, 200

Tapia, Micael, 95–96
Their Dogs Came with Them (Viramontes), 38
Thiong'o, Ngugu Wa, 17
Thomas, Piri, 39, 40–41
Toltecs, 48, 49, 55, 86–87; overview, 53–54; style of, 54, 56, 63, 66–67, 72. *See also* Chicana/o/xs; *My Father Was a Toltec*
"Toltec, The" (Castillo), 54–56, 59–61, 67, 72, 84, 210n44
toxified female masculinity: causes of, 122–124; coloniality of

gender and, 118, 122–124; of female gang members, 4, 92, 95, 109, 116, 118, 124; performing toughness and, 121; racialized, 109, 116, 118, 122, 124
toxified masculinity, 5; in Latina/o/xs, 4, 202n11; in Latino men, 3–4, 202n11
Training Day, 11, 200
Trump, Donald, 183
Tuck, Eve, 18–19, 22–23, 204n72
Two Badges (Ruiz), 36
Two Six, 45, 159–160, 164, 166–167, 169, 170, 172–178, 180–182, 208n9

Unaccompanied (Zamora, J.), 45–46, 187, 191–196
United States (US): colonial matrix of power of, 23; zoot suiters attacked by service members of, 34
US-European academy, on decolonial, 23
utopian futurity, 221n15; of failed gay gang members, 45, 161, 175–182; heteronormativity and, 164; queer failure and, 161, 163, 164, 175–182; queer persons and, 164, 175–182; in white space, 179–181

Valdez, Al, 37
Valdez, Luis, *Zoot Suit*, 32, 200
valuing, 46, 185, 186
Van Peebles, Melvin, *Sweet Sweetback's Baadasssss Song*, 130, 200
Vida Loca, La, 8, 199
Vigil, James Diego, 36, 201n2
violence: colonization use of material and cultural, 17, 22; against female members of male heterosexual gangs, 32, 33, 36; against gay members of male heterosexual gangs, 32, 33, 127; of heterosexuality in coloniality, 181; homophobia of Latino men and, 127, 136–137; Latin American immigrants as violent animals, 184; masculinity delinking from, 25; slow, 205n108; violent heterosexual masculinity, 159
violence against women: Mara Salvatrucha and, 189–190; racialized sexualized violence of colonialism, 56–57; subaltern masculinity and, 99
violent hypermasculine gang members, 139, 219n51; gay, 142, 145, 147, 151, 160, 170, 173–179
violent hypermasculinity: combatting homophobia with, 170; (de)colonial projects in gangs and, 160; gay gang members and, 142, 145, 147, 151, 160, 170, 173–179; gay sexuality and, 160; heterosexual male-dominated gangs, 160; Latino men's homophobic, 136–137
Viramontes, Helena Maria, 38

Wacquant, Loïc, 7, 19, 30, 31
Walsh, Catherine E., 22, 23, 25
Ward, Jesmyn, 47, 68–69, 211n65
Ward, T. W., 31, 90, 96–97, 100, 190
Watson, Mark, 50–53
Weber, Max, 15
Weitz, Chris, *Better Life, A*, 185, 199
West, Cornel, 162
Westmoreland, Wash, *Quinceañera*, 128, 146, 153, 200, 220n1
We the Animals, 25
When I Walk through That Door, I Am (Baca), 185–186

white: Chicano fathers reading as, 84–86; white feminism, 68
White Fence, 37, 90, 97
white people: homonormative tolerance of LGBTQ+, 135; homophobia of, 170–172; subaltern men's sexual relations with white women, 58–59, 210n41; working-class/low-income, 171–172
white space, 178–181
white supremacist gangs, 27
Wolf, Sonja, 8, 26, 30, 190, 195
Woman in the Zoot Suit, The, 35
womanizing, 58, 76
women: colonialism's imposition of subordination of, 20; heteronormativity and, 163; patriarchal subaltern masculinity, womanizing and collection of, 58; shared experience of gang life and, 47, 60; subaltern men's sexual relations with white, 58–59, 210n41; subordination of, 20, 67, 68, 77–78; toxified masculinity and, 4
women gang members. *See* female gang members
working-class communities of color: gang resistance and harm to, 2, 6; slang dialects in, 56
working-class Latina/o/x gangs, 25; (de)colonial and, 27
working-class Latinas: Fire Girls attacks on, 116–117, 123–124, 140; racialized female masculinity and attacks on, 116–117, 123–124
working-class/low-income Latino men: American hegemonic masculinity and, 133–138; coloniality and, 133, 134, 135, 137; homophobia of, 135–138; hypermasculinity of, 136, 137, 138
working-class/low-income Mexican Americans, 179
working-class/low-income white people, homophobia and, 171–172
Wretched of the Earth, The (Fanon), 15–16, 56

Yang, K. Wayne, 18–19, 22–23, 204n72
Young, Robert M., *Ballad of Gregorio Cortez, The*, 199, 206n110
youth: joining gangs due to their families, 47, 138, 139; subcultures of, 14, 25; working-class, 25, 26

Zamora, Javier: "El Salvador," 193–194, 196; "Second Attempt Crossing," 191–193, 196; *Unaccompanied*, 45–46, 187, 191–196
Zamora, Pedro, 150, 157, 219n63
Zapata, Angie, 207n145
zoot suit, 34
Zoot Suit, 32, 200